The Bonners

of

Chowan County, North Carolina:

A

Family History

The Bonners of Chowan County, North Carolina: A Family History

JOHN WESLEY CURRY

Forefathers Press

Publishing Genealogical Histories

3005 66th Street, Lubbock, TX 79413-5707

Email DuckworthP@aol.com

Curry, John Wesley
The Bonners of Chowan County, North Carolina: A Family History

Bibliograpy: y
No index.
1 Genealogy. 2. Title

Library of Congress Catalog Card No. 96-86417

ISBN 0-9653328-3-7

9 8 7 6 5 4 3 2 1

Printed in the United States of America

To Nannie Mae Mathis Curry
12 July 1910 - 3 February 1988
"Miss Nannie"

What a love story!

Semper Fi, Mom

JWC

The Bonners of Chowan County, North Carolina: A Family History

The Bonner Coat of Arms hereby illustrated is officially documented in Burke's General Armory. The original description of the arms (shield) is a follows:

"QUARTERLY, GU, AND SA, A CROSS PATTEE QUARTERLY, ERM, AND OR, ON A CHIEF OF THE LAST A DEMI ROSE, STREAMING RAYS, BETW. TWO PELICANS VULNING THEMSELVES OF THE FIRST."

When translated the blazon also describes the original colors of the Bonner arms as:

"QUARTERED RED AND BLACK; A CROSS PATTEE QUARTERED ERMINE AND GOLD; ON A GOLD UPPER THIRD A HALF ROSE STREAMING RAYS BETWEEN TWO RED PELICANS VULNING THEMSELVES."

Above the shield and helmet is the crest which is described as:

"A SILVER HUNTING DOG'S HEAD, COLLAR BLUE, STUDS, EDGES AND RINGS GOLD."

Table of Contents

Part One

PART TWO

PART THREE

FOREWORD

PART ONE of this work starts with Thomas Bonner (ca 1744 - 1804) and his ancestors when they lived in Chowan County, North Carolina, near the present town of Edenton and ends in Clarke County, Georgia. The Bonner plantation was just north of Edenton in a section of the county known as "Greenhall." On modern day maps "Green Hall Road" can still be found. Thomas emigrated with his wife, four small children and at least one Negro girl named Rose, to South Carolina about 1777. Exactly where he resided in South Carolina is not known but evidence suggests that it was in the area known as "Upper South Carolina" in what was then the Camden District. There he fought in the American Revolution with Colonel Roebuck's Regiment.

CHAPTER ONE of Part One is about Henry Bonner (1) (ca 1620 - 1689), a great-great-grandfather of the above Thomas Bonner. Henry Bonner arrived in Jamestown, Virginia prior to March 1664 with his wife and two children. From there, he made his way (probably by ship), prior to 1672, to what was known then as Shaftsbury Precinct of Albemarle County in the "North of Carolina." Shaftsbury Precinct was later renamed Chowan (after the Chowanoke Indians) Precinct and later Chowan County. Henry Bonner (I) was involved in the Culpepper Rebellion of 1677/79, a member of Parliament during the Rebellion, a member of the Chowan House of Burgesses, and was a Lord Proprietor Deputy when he died in July 1689.

CHAPTER TWO of Part One is about the son of the above Henry Bonner, Henry Bonner (2) (ca 1650 - ca 1725). This Henry Bonner was appointed a Lord Proprietor Deputy upon the death of his father in July 1689. He may be the father of (Sheriff) Thomas Bonner of Beaufort County, North Carolina. Although "exact" evidence does not support this premise, the names and ages of those found in the records who might be his siblings strongly suggest that this premise is true.

CHAPTER THREE of Part One is about Henry Bonner (3) (ca

1679 - September 1738), a son of the above Henry Bonner. He first shows up as a Captain in the early 1710's; as a Major in the miliatia in the 1720's and as a Colonel in the early 1730's, a rank he was holding at his death in 1738. The records show him as a practicing Attorney in the 1710's, and as a Member of the Lower House of Assembly in Edenton in 1725, 1726 and 1727 when Edenton was the Colonial Capital of North Carolina. He was involved in the affairs of the Episcopal Church in Edenton as a Church Warden.

CHAPTER FOUR of Part One is about Henry Bonner (4) (ca 1708- July 1766), a son of the above Henry Bonner. Henry held the rank of Captain in the Chowan Militia. He was appointed a Justice of the Peace in 1730. He also was involved in the affairs of the Episcopal Church in Edenton by serving as Secretary at the same time his father was serving as Church Warden.

CHAPTER FIVE of Part One is about Thomas Bonner (ca 1744 - 1804), a son of the above Henry Bonner. The chapter begins with his marriage in 1767 in Edenton and concludes with his death in Clarke County, Georgia on 30 December 1804. Upon the close examination of a Deed of Gift from his father dated 7 July 1766, it can be concluded that he was born between July 1745 and May 1746.

PART TWO of this work is a reproduction and updated version of the work of Dr. James C. Bonner, Ph.D., who wrote about Thomas Bonner (ca 1744 - 1804) and his descendants after their emigration to Georgia from South Carolina. Dr. Bonner's work was entitled, *Migration Pattern of the Descendants of Thomas Bonner - A Family History,* written in 1964.

PART THREE is about some allied families related to this Bonner Clan; the families of Applewhite, Barnes, Blanchard, McConniell and Tate.

The purpose of this work was to establish proof that Thomas Bonner of Chowan County, North Carolina was the same Thomas Bonner who died in Clarke County, Georgia in 1804 through the use of legal documents. It was also done to enlighten the descendants of Thomas Bonner about who he was and the historical significance of the roles that his ancestors played in the formation of the North Carolina colony. Also in an effort to assist a future researcher, source documents were referenced.

A section of this work also has been included to show the origin of the Bonner clan in England. This information is traditional and can be found in almost every work done about the Bonner family, regardless of the ancestry/descendant branch of the family. Especially of interest to a new reader of the Bonner family history is information about the infamous Reverend Edmund Bonner (ca 1499 - 1569) who was a Chaplain to King Henry VIII. It is written that when Reverend Bonner was defending King Henry's position about divorce to the Pope, Bonner so infuriated Pope Clement VII that the Pope threatened to boil Bonner in a cauldron of molten lead.

Much appreciation is extended to the efforts of Dr. James C. Bonner, Ph.D. (1904 - 1984) who spent much of his life researching the Bonner family in Georgia and other states. Without his effort much of what we know now would have been lost forever.

Semper fi, cousin.

John Wesley Curry
First Lieutenant
United States Marine Corps (Retired)
Greenville, North Carolina

(Permanent mailing address:
259 Sun Rise Lane
Sylacauga, Alabama 35150)

DEDICATION

This work is also dedicated to the memory of my mother, Nannie Mae Mathis Curry (1910 - 1988).

Mom was always interested in her family roots, especially those that came from her grandmother, Martha Caroline Bonner McConniell (1846-1933). Over the years Mom gathered photographs, and saved letters she had received from family members and passed them to her children. Those letters and the information she gathered was the basis of our Bonner family history. It was obvious from the letters of her grandmother Martha there was much mutual love between them.

On Christmas day in 1977, Mom and I went to her birth-site near Cooley Crossroads in Clay County, Alabama. It was her first visit there since she left in 1925. The area had changed because the old farm houses and barns had been torn down and trees and undergrowth had taken over. She hesitated only briefly as she directed me down a dirt road that lead to the place of her birth. We found it and she then directed me into a field and finally I yelled to her that all I could find was two piles of stones. She just yelled back, "That's it!" She made her way to me, took a deep breath and begin to describe the house, it being just a two room structure with a chimney at each end. The chimneys were constructed with flat stones that were stacked and sealed with mud. She described the barn locations and other outbuildings. She told me where the corn fields, cotton fields and where the orchard had been. Finally she looked to her left and said, "Over there down that valley was a spring of water that we used for everything." I made my way in the direction she pointed and after a distance of about three hundred feet I found a small stream of water and told her that I had found it. She made her way to me and confirmed that it was, in fact, the same stream of water. She made a sobbing sound and when I looked at her tears were rolling down her cheeks. She was deeply overcome with emotion as she remembered the days of her youth. I will remember that day as long as I live.

We also visited the old McConniell home site. As with the Mathis home site stones were on the ground where the chimneys had been. Grandma McConniell's rose bushes were still growing, but had turned wild.

We then went to the cemetery at Cragford (Cragford was once known as Wesobulga) where we visited the graves of Mom's maternal grandparents, James Allen and Martha Caroline Bonner McConniell. Also buried at Cragford are many of my cousins, great uncles and great aunts, many who had held me when I was a baby. It was truly a day to remember!

Lastly, this is dedicated to my children, grandchildren, brothers and sisters, nieces and nephews and to all my Bonner family kin. I truly hope they find lost ancestors and enjoy reading about who they were. A sad but very special dedication is to my distant cousin, Mr. Darrell Harrington who lived in Stonewall, Mississippi. He passed away in October 1994. Darrell was a descendant of Jordan Bonner. Before his death Darrell was instrumental in helping me to connect and correct information about Jordan Bonner and his rightful place in our Bonner history. Darrell also furnished the name of Thomas Bonner's daughter who was married to Richard Vanderford whose name was unknown to me until he made it available. She now has her rightful place in our history. Her name was Deborah and she had the name of her great-grandmother, Deborah Whedbee Bonner (1689 - ca 1728) and of her great-great grandmother, Deborah Astine-Sutton-Whedbee-McClendon (ca 1652- 1732). With the name "Deborah" being made available to me I was finally able to prove, through legal documents, that Thomas Bonner of Chowan County, North Carolina to be the same Thomas Bonner who died in Clarke County, Georgia.

THE LINEAL LIST

(Of the author)

1. **Henry Bonner (1) (ca 1620 - July 1689)**
   Wife: unknown
   Children: a. Henry Bonner (2) (ca 1650 - ca 1725)
   b. William Bonner
   c. May have been the father of Thomas Bonner who died in 1685 in Chowan.

2. **Henry Bonner (2) (ca 1650 - ca 1725)**
   Wife: unknown
   Children: a. Henry Bonner (3) (ca 1679 - September 1738)
   b. James Bonner (living in Chowan in 1703)
   c. William (Will) Bonner (living in Chowan County in the 1710's)
   d. Thomas Bonner (ca 1690 - April 1765 in Beaufort County, North Carolina)

3. **Henry Bonner (3) (ca 1679 - September 1738)**
   Wife: 1st unknown
   Children: a. Elizabeth Bonner (ca 1703 - ca 1742)
   Wife: 2nd: Deborah Whedbee (28 January 1689 - ca 1728)
   Children: b. Henry Bonner (4) (ca 1708 - July 1766)
   c. Deborah Bonner (ca 1724 - 1784)
   d. Mary Bonner (ca 1726 - 1759)
   e. Thomas Bonner (ca 1728 - 1784)

4. **Henry Bonner (4) (ca 1708 - July 1766)**
   Wife (1st): Sarah Luten (ca 1710 - ca 1750)
   Children: a. Thomas Bonner (ca 1744 - 1804)
   b. William Bonner (ca 1747 - 1781)
   c. Henry Bonner (5) (ca 1750 - 1797)
   Wife (2nd): Elizabeth Hardy (ca 1740 - about 1800
   Married 4 January 1759.
   Children: d. Richard Bonner (ca 1759 - 1781)

5. Thomas Bonner (ca 1744 - 30 December 1804)
Wife: Margaret Jones (ca 1750 - ca 1818)
Where: Edenton, North Carolina on 6 May 1767.
Children: a. Jordan Bonner (12 December 1767 - 8 May 1841)
b. Zadock Bonner (17 June 1769 - 1848)
c. Deborah (Nancy) Bonner (1772 - after 1860)
d. Whitmel Bonner (ca 1775 - 1819)
e. Thomas Bonner (1779 - 1860)
f. Mary Elizabeth Bonner (1779 - after 1865)
g. Allen Bonner (1781 - 1828)
h. Willis Bonner (ca 1785 - ?)
I. Josiah Bonner (5 May 1787 - 9 December 1851)
j. Daniel M. Bonner (ca 1789 - ?)

6. Thomas Bonner (1779 - August 1860)
Wife: Elizabeth Duke (1786 - after 1870)
Where: About 1802 in Clarke County or Greene County,Georgia
Children: a. William Bonner (13 September 1803 -
b. James Bonner (16 May 1806 - ca 1865)
c. Bidda Bonner (31 January 1808 -
d. Nancy Bonner (16 December 1809 -
e. Thomas Bonner (12 March 1812 -
f. Mary Bonner (4 February 1814 -
g. Elizabeth Bonner (9 November 1816 -
h. Allen Bonner (11 February 1818 -
I. Susan Bonner (9 November 1819 -
j. Josiah Bonner (24 February 1821 -
k. Sarah Ann Bonner (7 January 1823 - before 1860)
l. Bennett W. Bonner (16 November 1824 -
m. Caroline Bonner (28 July 1826 -

7. James Bonner (16 May 1806 - ca 1865)
Wife: Nancy Telitha Applewhite (1810 - after 1870)
Where: Morgan County, Georgia on 7 August 1828
Children: a. Josiah Bonner (Went to the Civil War and never came home)
b. Benjamin (Bennie) Bonner

c. Sarah Bonner
d. Mary Bonner
e. Harry Bonner
f. Susannah Bonner (7 January 1838 - 1 April 1923)
h. Martha Caroline Bonner (20 September 1846 - 19 January 1933)
I. Emily Bonner (The baby of the family)

8. **Martha Caroline Bonner (20 September 1846 - 19 January 1933)**
Husband: James Allen McConniell (12 November 1838 - 31 July 1917)
Where: Heard County, Georgia on 2 August 1866
Children: a. Julie Ann Frances McConniell (1867 - 25 December 1912)
b. Nancy Telitha McConniell (25 August 1869 - 22 December 1951)
c. John Melton McConniell (? - 9 July 1933)
d. Emma Ardamisa McConniell
e. Susannah Victoria McConniell (1876 - 19 April 1941).
f. Tullula Sadenia McConniell (14 April 1877 - 4 May 1971)
g. Josiah (Joseph) Franklin McConniell (7 January 1880 - 29 January 1957)
h. Lewis Monroe McConniell (1881 - 22 December 1884)
I. Lola Lee McConniell (31 January 1884 - 2 February 1884) Bled to death (Navel).
j. "Little Buddy" McConniell (Stillborn 1884). Never named.
k. James Asbury McConniell (27 April 1885 - 14 May 1954)
l. Mattie Eula McConniell (15 April 1888 - 21 October 1979)

9. **Mattie Eula McConniell (15 April 1888 - 21 October 1979)**
Husband: William Wesley Mathis (4 February 1845 - 4 January 1928)
Where: In Clay County, Alabama on 2 September 1909
Children: a. Nannie Mae Mathis (12 July 1910 - 3 February 1988)
b. Elsie Ava Lee Mathis (21 October 1916 - 27 November 1993)
c. John Allen Mathis (11 December 1922 - still living in June 1996).

10. Nannie Mae Mathis (12 July 1910 - 3 February 1988)
Husband: Leo Dewey Curry (11 December 1908 - 13 December 1993)
Where: In Talladega County, Alabama, 1 August 1931
Children: a. John Wesley Curry (2 June 1934 -
b. Loyace Dean Curry (14 March 1936 -
c. Nannie Sue Curry (31 July 1937 -
d. Charles Michael Curry (Stillborn March 1939)
e. Roderick Selton Curry (20 September 1940 -
f. Leo Wayne Curry (9 October 1942 -
g. Mary Louise Curry (8 May 1944 -
h. Robert Allen Curry (19 July 1945 - 25 November 1975)
I. Linda Dianne Curry (27 October 1947 -

10-1 John Wesley Curry (2 June 1934 -
Wife (1st): Rosa Katherine Hudson (16 September 1938 -
Where: In Dillon, Dillon County, South Carolina on 27 February 1955
Children: a. John Wesley Curry (30 September 1957 -
b. Dempsey Diane Curry (23 May 1959 -
c. Katherine Anne Curry (6 July 1960 -
d. Sandra Leigh Curry (10 August 1962 -
e. Tracy Denise Curry (9 November 1963 -
Wife (2nd): Rebecca Lynn Elvington (Divorced)

10-2 Loyace Dean Curry (14 March 1936 -
Husband: (1st): Bill Williams
Children: a. Michael Williams
b. Cynthia Gayle Williams (13 August 1959 -
c. Billy Lester Williams (7 July 1961 -
d. Lisa Dianne Williams (20 July 1961 -
Husband: (2nd): J. W. (Bob) Johnson
Children: e. Barbara Michelle (Shell) Johnson (16 December 1968 -

10-3 Nannie Sue Curry (31 July 1937 -
Husband: (1st): Robert Milton Barnette
Where: In Talladega County, Alabama on 9 April 1955
Child: Suszan Faye Barnette (26 June 1957 -
Husband: (2nd): Ray Sasser

10-4. Roderick Selton Curry (20 September 1940 -

Wife: Linda Ann Hudgins (5 August 1948 -
Where: In Newport News, Virginia on 27 August 1966 -
Children: a. Carolyn Ann Curry (27 July 1968 -
b. Roderick Selton Curry, Jr. (27 May 1971 - 20 April 1984)

10-5 Leo Wayne Curry (9 October 1942 -
Wife: Judith Ann Hines (10 February 1941 -
Where: In Wichita Falls, Texas on 11 September 1969
Child: Barbara Rene Curry (18 March 1975 - in Redding, Berkshire, England.

10-6 Mary Louise Curry (8 May 1944 -
Husband: John Marion Snyder (22 October 1944 -
Child: David Wayne Snyder (17 August 1965 -

10-7 Robert Allen Curry (19 July 1945 - 25 November 1975)
Wife: Susan Lynda Williamson
Where: England
Child: Jonathan Francis Allen Curry

10-8 Linda Dianne Curry (27 October 1947 -
Husband: Millard Mellon Haynes
Child: Richard Todd Hayes (7 March 1966 -

INTRODUCTION

The original purpose of this work was just to satisfy a curiosity after I learned of the existence of Thomas Bonner (ca 1744 - 1804), and that he was married in Edenton, North Carolina in 1767.

The year was 1991 and I was living in Greenville, North Carolina, just eighty miles from Edenton. So, I decided to see what I could find about the ancestors of Thomas. What I found was beyond my wildest expectations. The more I found, the more I wanted to find. So for the next four years, the Bonner family became my hobby. I subscribed to a genealogy magazine in Georgia and requested information from its readers and I received information from many unknown cousins, who also were interested in the history of our branch of the Bonner family. None of them knew for sure that Thomas had ever lived in North Carolina although some knew that he married in Edenton. Some thought that he was visiting from Virginia when he married Margaret Jones. (Remember that in those days a girl had to marry in the county of her residence). Some of them were able to fill in gaps about the Bonners of Clarke County, Georgia and that information is included here.

In my search I found that our ancestral grandmother, Deborah Astine-Sutton-Whedbee-McClendon was a mother-in-law to two direct descendants of George Durant who is recognized as being the co-founder of the first permanent white settlement that grew into what is now the great State of North Carolina. In fact, her sons had a very peculiar relationship to each other because of their marriage into the Durant family. To start with they were half-brothers, the oldest, Joseph Sutton married Parthenia Durant, a daughter of George and Ann Durant, and the other brother, Richard Whedbee, married Sarah Durant, daughter of John Durant, son of George and Ann.

I found that the great-great grandfather of Thomas Bonner was Henry Bonner who died in 1689. This Henry Bonner established a plantation on what was then Mattacomack Creek just north of present day Edenton in an area of the County they called GREEN HALL. For the next one hundred years the Bonner clan would call this area of Chowan County home. Thomas Bonner (died 1804) left

Chowan County about 1778 and emigrated to South Carolina, probably to the Upper Region near Indian territory. It was there he enlisted in the South Carolina Militia about 1780 and fought with Colonel Benjamin Roebuck's South Carolina Regiment during the American Revolution.

I read once that in genealogy "if there is wealth, there will be a paper trail," and the Bonners were in this category. They were wealthy and exerted great political influence during their lifetime. It appears that in most of the Bonner family lines their money and influence disappeared during and just after the American Civil War. Probably the only Bonners to survive the greatest financial harm were the Carroll County, Georgia, Bonners and maybe some of the families who went further west to Texas.

John Wesley Curry
P.O.Box 8301
Greenville, NC 27835-8301
(919) 758-8199

Part One

I

THE BONNERS IN ENGLAND AND THE NEW WORLD

Edmund Bonner, an English prelate, notorious for his persecution of the Protestants during the Reign of Queen Mary was born at Hanley in Worcestershire, about the end of the 15th century and was generally passed for the natural son of Georgia Savage, a priest who was the natural son of Sir John Savage, of Clifton in the same County. "Strype" in his memorials of Bishop (Thomas) Cramer, however, says he was positively assured that Bonner was the legitimate offspring of a poor man, who lived in a cottage long afterwards known as "Bonner's Place." About 1512, Edmund Bonner entered as a student of Broadgate Hall (now Pembroke College), Oxford; and in 1519, he was admitted as a student as Bachelor of the Canon and of Civil Law. Having been admitted into orders, he obtained some preferment in the diocese of Cardinal Wolsey. Bonner was with the Cardinal at Cawood when he was arrested on charges of high treason. After the death of Cardinal Wolsey, he adopted Lutheran sentiments and insinuated himself into the favor of King Henry VIII, who made him one of his Chaplains, and employed him in several embassies abroad. In 1532, he was sent to Rome with Sir Edward Carne to answer for the King who had been cited to appear in person or by proxy in regard to the divorce of Queen Catherine.

In 1533, being again dispatched to Pope Clement VII, then at Marseilles, to intimate Henry's appeal to a future general council from the sentence pronounced against his divorce, he (Bonner) threatened the Pope with so much resolution that His Holiness talked of having him burned alive or thrown into a cauldron of melted lead. Clement did not foresee that the man whom he had thus menaced with the flames was destined to burn heretics in England in support to the very faith which, under Henry, he had lent his aid to overthrow.

In 1538, being then Ambassador at the Court of France, he was nominated Bishop of Hereford; but before consecration, he was translated to the See of London and was enthroned in April 1540. When Henry VIII died in 1547, Bonner was Ambassador at the Court of the Emperor, Charles V. During Henry's reign he was constantly zealous in his opposition to the Pope, and favoured the Reformation in obedience to the King, who exacted rigid compliance with all his caprices. On the accession of King Edward [King Edward VI, {born 1537 - died 1553}, son of King Henry VIII and Jane Seymour] however, Bonner refused to take the oath of supremacy, and he was committed to the fleet where he remained until he promised obedience to the laws. After his release he assented to the Reformation, but with such manifest reluctance, that he was twice reprimanded by the Privy Council and in 1549, was after a long trial, committed to the Marshalsea, and deprived of his Bishopric, to which, however, he was restored on the accession of Queen Mary; [Queen Mary I (Mary Tudor born 1516 - died 1558), Queen of England from 1553 to 1558, daughter of King Henry VIII and Catherine of Aragon, wife of Philip II of Spain] and soon afterwards he was appointed, in place of Bishop Cramer, viceregent and President of the Convocation. From this he became the chief instrument of persecution and is said to have condemned no less than 200 Protestants to the flames in the space of three years. On the accession of Queen Elizabeth, he appeared with the rest of the Bishops at Highgate, to congratulate her, but the Queen refused to permit him to kiss her hand. Having, in the second year of her reign, refused to take the oath of supremacy, he was again committed to the Marshalsea, where he died on 5 September 1569, after a confinement of ten years. The character of Bonner was remarkable for obstinacy and inflexibility in everything save principle; yet even in this respect it exhibits some striking contrasts. In his early career he accommodated his principles to his convenience and ambition; after his return to Catholicism, he remained steadfast to the church, and when disgraced, bore his deprivation and imprisonment with apparent resignation. The charge of atheism brought against one so defiled with blood was superfluous. He was constitutionally merciless austere, fitted by nature for a persecutor, and equally capable of employing the same ardent zeal either against or in favor of any cause that he espoused. Among his works are, *Responsum et Exhortation in Lauden Sacredotiv*, a preface in Gardner's treatise, *De Vera Obedientia*, and several homilies.

From *Encyclopedia Britannica - Volume VIII*, page 338

The strictly religious changes began with the promulgation of a Book of Homilies in the first year of King Edward. It marks the state of things at the time that one of these homilies, which are still to this day set forth by authority to be read in Churches, was the work of Edmond Bonner. The position of the prelates who clave to the old system during King Edward's reign should be carefully noticed. They neither resigned their Sees nor refused obedience to the new law. It does not appear that any Bishop declined the use of the first prayerbook. Gardiner and Bonner were imprisoned and deprived of their Sees on various pretenses as were several Bishops later in the reign for refusal to comply with various orders, some of which certainly had no parliamentary authority.

From *Encyclopedia Britannica - Volume VIII,* page 340

In the year of Queen Mary's marriage, Cardinal Reginal Pole, came back to England as Legate, and the Lords and Commons of England, knelt to receive his absolution for the national schism. He confirmed by authority various acts done during the time of the separation, and it does not appear that the ordinations of Bishops and Priests which had been made during King Edward's reign were ever called in question. And, to quiet a doubt which made many minds uneasy, the actual owners of church lands were confirmed in their possession. An act of parliament followed by which the papal authority was restored as it had stood before the changes of King Henry. Gardiner and Bonner, the strenuous opponents of the Pope in King Henry's days, and Thirlby, who had gone a long way with the changes under Edward, were now Bishops of a church in full communion with Rome. In 1555, the persecution began and it lasted till the end of Queen Mary's reign....where King Henry's victims of either faith were comparatively few and were persons of some importance, Queen Mary's victims fell mainly on victims whom King Henry would have scorned to destroy; the poor, the halt, and the lame. In three years of the persecution of Queen Mary, more victims were burned than in all the reigns before or after. Five Bishops perished, of these were Ridley and Latimer - true martyrs on one side, as More (Thomas More) and Fisher on the other - Hooper, the professor of a straiter sect of Protestantism and the less famous Farrer of St. Davids. The Primate followed the next year. He had been lawfully condemned to death for his treason in the insuration of Jane [Note - Jane was made Queen upon the death of King Edward VI in the hope that Mary Tudor would not be made Queen. However, Mary had powerful allies and Jane was overthrown and executed (beheaded)] and his execution under that sentence, though it would have been a harsh measure, would have been a small matter compared with many an execution in the days of King Henry. He was spared, probably in mercy; but he was spared only to bring on Queen Mary and her government the deeper infamy of burning one who had recanted his heresies. The persecution was throughout more the work of the council, by whom Bonner was blamed for slackness, than of the Bishops.

(Author's note - Lady Jane Grey (October 1537 - 12 February 1554) for just nine days in July 1553 was Queen of England. She was born in Bradgate, Leicestershire and was a daughter of Henry Grey, Duke of Suffolk. She worked in the household of King Henry VIII when she was nine years old. When Jane was deposed she was placed in the Tower of London and after a failed uprising against Queen Mary, the Queen signed Jane's death warrant and she was executed by having her head chopped off.)

From *Cramer, Volume VI*, page 550

The course taken by Bishop Cramer in promoting the Reformtion exposed him to the bitter hostility on the reactionary party of, "men of the old learning," of whom Bishops Gardiner and Bonner were leaders, and on two occasions, in 1543 and 1545, conspiracies were formed in the council to effect his (Cramer's) overthrow. The King (Henry) however remained true to him, and both conspiracies signally failed.

(Author's note - The records show that Thomas Cramer (2 July 1489 - 21 March 1556) was the first Archbishop of Canterbury of the reformed Church of England. He assisted in finding a way for King Henry VIII to annul his marriage to Catherine of Aragon without having to consult and obtain permission from Pope Clement. Cramer supported the crowning of Lady Jane Grey as successor to King Edward VI who died of tuberculosis in 1553. However, the plot failed when Jane's supporters failed to gain public support for her to be Queen. She was denounced and removed from the throne and Mary I was installed as Queen. Cramer was eventually denounced by Queen Mary and tried for treason, convicted of heresy and burned at the stake in 1556.)

From *Queen Mary, Volume XV*, page 594

The cruel persecution of the Protestants which had cast so much infamy upon her reign, began about six months after her marriage (to Philip II of Spain); and it is not difficult to see that it was greatly due to the triumph of ideas imported from the land of Inquisition. Rogers, the first of the martyers, was burned on the 4th of February 1555. Hooper, Bishop of Gloucester, had been condemned six days before, and suffered the same fate on the 9th of February 1555. From this time, the persecution went on uninterrupted for more than three years, numbering among its victims; Bishops Ridley, Latimer, and Cramer. It seemed to be most severe in the eastern and southern parts of England, and the largest number of sufferers was naturally in the diocese of Bonner, Bishop of London. From the first to the last nearly 300 victims are computed to have perished at the stake.

From *Encyclopedia Britannica,* 1973 editon, page 916

The King (Henry) however, had been directed against the Bishop before there was any Marian persecution of Protestants, but the virulent pen of John Bale, Bishop of Ossory. Another contemporary, the Protestant martyrologist, John Foxe, continued this vituperation of Bishop Bonner, so effectively indeed that Bales denunciation of his as. *Bloody Bishop Bonner,* has persisted through the centuries and prejudiced most historians against him. Bonner was an outstanding Oxford lawyer who served King Henry VIII on various foreign embassies. He accepted from Henry, first, the Bishopric of Hereford, and later, Bishop of London, and promoted Henry's ecclesiastic adventures. He opposed, however, the advancing Protestantism of King Edward VI's reign and spent most of this period in prison, being deprived of his Bishopric. Restored to his See on Queen Mary's accession, he devoted himself to the affairs of his diocese, the importance of which made him an outstanding figure in that persecution of Protestants which marked Queen Mary's reign. Bonner's reluctance to intensify the persecution in London, however, brought him a rebuke from Queen Mary's government. Again deprived of his Bishopric on refusal to take the oath of supremacy at the beginning of the reign of Queen Elizabeth I [Queen Elizabeth I (born 1533 - died 1603) Queen from 1558 to 1603, daughter of King Henry VIII and Anne Boleyn] he spent the last ten years of his life a prisoner in the Marshalsea and died there on 5 September 1569.

(Ref. *My Lord of Canterbury* by Godfrey Turton, 1967, page 115 from selected paragraphs).

Dreams end in waking up. The repercussions provoked abroad by the coronation were more violent even than we feared. Far from acquiescing in the annulment and remarriage as an accomplished fact, the Pope - in the first shock of the news - was bitterly offended and pressed on with his own investigation in the Court of Rota. His temper was not improved when King Henry sent a **Chaplain, Edmund Bonner,** to explain our views. Later events have brought me so often into conflict with Bonner that my opinion of him possibly is warped; but even in those days I disliked his hectoring manner which despised conciliation as weakness, and I myself was inclined to despise him in turn for his likeness to a little strutting cock-pigeon, paunchy and pompous. He certainly made a deplorable impression on the Pope, who threatened to have him boiled in a tub of molten lead. On his return home, Bonner never tired of repeating the story, flinging up his hands to inveigh against Papal barbarity preening himself on the courage with which he defied it. I am afraid that I chuckled as I listened very sure that the lead would be stone-cold before Pope Clement made up his mind. [Pope Clement VII, born Giulio de' Medici in 1478 - died 1534. Was Pope from 1523 to 1534, excommunicated King Henry VIII.]

From Title Page - Chapter 12 of *My Lord of Canterbury*

Queen Anne hated bloodshed and had the courage to despise rather than to fear her enemies. Eyewitnesses told me (Cramer) that she showed more amusement than annoyance when the Holy Maid interrupted her at dinner with King Henry at Canterbury and chastised her in public with pious invective. The decision of the Papal Court was a much more serious rebuff however, and she deserves the more credit for preserving a sense of proportion, refusing to vent her disappointment on the helpless.

She was, in fact, bitterly disappointed, as we all were, and with better reason than at first appears. In spite of the Pope's outburst of anger, his threat to boil Bonner in molten lead, negotiations were in progress with him which encouraged great hopes.

At Marshalsea, where he (Bonner) attended the wedding of his niece, Catherine de Medici [(born 1519 - died 1589) was Queen of King Henry II of France 1547 - 1559.] to the young French Prince, he admitted in private to King Francis as plainly as he dared that King Henry's cause was just, and hinted that only a formal act of submission was needed to obtain a favorable judgement. King Francis [King Francis I, born 1494 - died 1547, King of France from 1515 to 1547] reported the hint to us at once through his Ambassador......

From page 258 of *My Lord of Canterbury*

My advice would have carried more weight perhaps if I had not been put to shame by an incident arising in my own department, the affairs of the church. Bonner, the ill-mannered priest whom Pope Clement threatened to stew in molten lead, and who had risen in the course of the years to become Bishop of London, was ordered to preach a sermon at the Paul's Cross reaffirming the Royal supremacy, to banish any doubt of its validity during the King's minority. He failed to obey, and as he persisted in his defiance a commission was appointed over which I presided to decide whether to expel him from his See. The examination to which we summoned him at Lambeth is an occasion painful to recall, so ill was I able to cope with him. He relied for defence on the loudness of his voice, the insolence of his bluster, digressing from the simple issue of loyalty to the Crown into the field of controversial doctrine, and shouting me down when I tried to keep him to the point. He behaved indeed as if he were the judge, I the defender.

At the next sitting, I swallowed my pride and asked Sir Thomas Smith, my fellow commissioner, Secretary to the Council, and a friend of Somerset's to preside in my place. He repaid Bonner in his own coin, replied to rude insult with fiercer reprimand and threat, and when the argument dragged on, he ordered him to be arrested for contempt, and committed to the Marshalsea prison. I pronounced judgement depriving Bonner of his See, and soon afterwards Nicholas Ridley was moved from Rochester and installed in London to succeed him. The outcome was satisfactory, but it was a humbling experience. [Reverend Edmund Bonner died in Marshalsea Prison on 5 September 1569. The Marshalsea Prison was a British court of Justice, abolished in 1849, under the Marshall of the Royal household].

AN INQUIRY INTO THE ORIGIN AND ARMORAL BEARING

of

BONNER

Bonner of Oxfordshire, Leicestershire, and the Virginia Colony
Noticing the Royal Descent of Bonner Distinguished Families
with
Whom this House is Matrimonially Allied
and
Some Account of their History
Complied by:
Jerome A. Ringrose, Ph.D.
(Author of, *Ringrose's Heraldry, Scottish Notes,* etc.

Lineage - The family of Riddell is Norman. The surname is one of the earliest personal in Scotland. Gervase Riddell who had a chapter of Whitunes, Lillieclive, etc., in Roxburghshire, from David

I for Knightly service, was succeeded by his brother Assketia Riddell the harmony of Zourche remained in abeyance and William (the conqueror?) Had presented a petition resumption of the earle? But it was given Sir Cecil Bishop Barnette who presented another heiress.

There is an altar tomb with canopy surmounted by crest, on the south side of the Chancel at Hardingstone to the memory of the late Sir William Tate who left 50 ponds for that purpose. The arms are shown as Bonner's, as follows:

> Paly of six or and gules on a chief azure, three lions rampart or.
> Crest: A talbots head argents collared azure studded edge and ringed or.
> Motto: Semper Fidelis (Always Faithful)

This being the Bonner Family Coat-of-Arms.

The name of Bishop Edmund Bonner is inscribed upon a bronze plaque with other Bishops of London at St. Paul's Cathedral. The original Saint Paul's Cathedral was totally destroyed in the Great Fire of London.

In Relation to Bishop Bonner
(From the Golden Sayings of Epictertus)

Kings and tyrants have armed guards wherewith to chastise certain persons, though they be themselves evil. But to the cynic conscience gives this power not arms and guards. When he knows that he hath watched and labored on behalf of mankind that sleep hath found him pure, and left him purer still that his thoughts have been the thoughts of a Friend of the Gods - Of a servant, yet of one that hath a part in the government of the Supreme God; that the words are ever on his lips, "*Lead me, O God, and thou, O Density! If this be God's will so let it be.*"

Remember that thou art an actor in a play,
and of sort as the Author chooses,
whether long or short.
If it be his good pleasure to assign thee to the part of a beggar,
a ruler, or a simple citizen, thine is to play it fitly.
For thy business is to act the part assigned thee, well:
To choose it, is another's.

In 1533, Bishop Bonner was deputed to appear before the Pope, at Marseille, to appeal for the excommunicated monarch to a general council. In 1540, he was made Bishop of London. His cousin, William Bonner, Clerk of the Holy Order, and his brother, Reverend Anthony Bonner, were also active in the Reformation.

Following the death of King Henry VIII, Bishop Bonner's Protestant zeal cooled, and when Queen Mary came to the throne, she restored Bonner to office. As viceregent and President of the Concave, he became an agent against the Reformers. Following the death of Queen Mary, and the accession of Queen Elizabeth, Bonner refused to take the Oath of Supremacy and was imprisoned in the Marshalsea, where he died in 1569. Immediately following his death, his cousin William Bonner, Clerk of the Holy Order, was fighting at the Courts in London for his interest in divers estates, some of which were by purchase from the Bishop. William Bonner was married to Alice Gorham, of Glapthorne in 1568 and resided chiefly at *Elmsmere*, a splendid mansion in the Parish of the Blessed Mary of Bow in Cheapward, London. This property had formerly belonged to the Monastery of Newark in Surrey, and had been purchased by Bishop Bonner, however, it became cause of considerable litigation at Guild Hall, London. However, William Bonner came off victorious at the Lord Mayor's Courts. He held this splendid fabric, as the youngest son of an illustrious family until his death, when it passed to George Leonard of St. Stratfield Say in Hampshire, by marriage.

John Bonner, born in 1607, son of William and Alice Gorham resided at Hinckley in Leicestershire. He married Mary Walker of the same place. They had six sons and four daughters. On 2 November 1636, John Bonner was on the passenger list, sailing "from ye port of London," after having been examined by the ministers of the Town of Gravesend, vouching his conformity to the order of discipline of the Church of England, he was on Hotten's list of passengers embarked in the "Expedition" by Peter Blackler, which passed from "ye port of London" to the Barbados, going later to Jamestown, Virginia.

His cousin, Richard Bonner, born in 1619 at Quinton, Gloucestershire, England, son of Reverend Anthony Bonner sailed for America on the "Friendship" from "ye port of London," arriving at James City, Virginia in March 1636. He was a staunch patriot serving the Colony from 1636 to 1643.

BONNER FAMILY IN ENGLAND, VIRGINIA AND MARYLAND

Some Colonial and Revolutionary Families or North Carolina, Compiled by: Marilu Burch Smallwood, 1964, as furnished by the late Robert T. Bonner of Aurora, North Carolina. (Author's Note - Mr. Robert T. Bonner passed away in 1959). Information here also comes from, *Dictionary of Family Names of the United Kingdom,* by Mary Anthony Lower, pages 30 and 33:

BONAR: A village of Sutherlandshire and a feudal barony of which the family was passed tempore (in the time of) William the Lion before the year 1200 A.D.

BONNER COAT-OF-ARMS

by

James A. Ringrose

Oxfordshire, 1574, As certified by Sir Richard Lee

ARMS: Paly of Six Or and Gules, on a Chief Azure Three Lions Rampart, Or.

CREST: A Talbot's Head Argent, Collared Azure, Studded Edged and Ringed Or

MOTTO: Semper Fidelis (Always Faithful).

(Author's Note - There are many variations in the descriptions of the Bonner Coat-of-Arms because each descending generation added their own little variation to it; as with other family coat-of-arms. Ringrose's description of the Bonner coat-of-arms is different than Burke's for that reason).

BONNER

The Bonner coat-of-arms is officially documented in, *Burke's General Armory*. The original description of the arms (shield) is as follows:

Quarterly, Gu. And Sa. A Cross Pattee Quarterly, Erm. And Or. On a Chief of the Last a Demi Rose, Streaming Rays between two Pelicans Vulning themselves of the first.

When translated the blazon also describes the original colors of the Bonner arms as follows: Quartered Red and Black; A cross Pattee quartered ermine and gold; On a Gold upper third a half Robe streaming rays between two red pelicans vulning themselves. Above the shield and helmet is the crest which is described as : A silver hunting dog's head, collar blue, studs, edges and rings, gold.

The most remote ancestor of the Bonner family, Quentin de

Riddell, ancestor of the Noble House of Buchanan-Riddell bore the Ensign of Bonner as above described, and from whom descended the notorious Bishop Edmund Bonner. The ancestry of the Bishop is well established as from the Norman House of Riddell, commencing with Francoise Bonnaire (Francis Bonner) Edward Riddell, who flourished at Banbury the Oxfordshire stronghold of Riddell or Bonner. Here on many local monuments was blazoned Bonner, *Paly of Six Or and Gules,* in which from, and without the lions in chief the ancient house always displayed it.

To Andrew Bonner, Gentleman, of this county, is attributed the first escutcheon displaying the entire arms (i.e., paly Or gules, on a chief azure, three lions rampart Or) and such was duly assigned by two learned officials of the Herald's College. (Sir Richard Lee, Porticullis and Robert Cook, Clarenceus King of Arms in the Visitation of Oxfordshire in 1574.)

It is of some importance, bearing as it does the original of the surname, *Bonner,* that these Heralds note the emblem to both Bonner and Riddell, Bishop Bonner, signed *Paly of six Or and gules,* being the identical emblem of the ancient House of Bonner or Riddell, from which circumstances it is assured that the surname, *Bonner* had its origin from the French "Boner" (meaning gracious and kind). As such it became the fixed cognoment of the younger House of Riddell and there are several charters in the records of the House of Riddell, wherein the persons are called Riddell in the body, and Bonner (Bonnaire) in the margin, dated in Reign of King Henry VIII (King Henry Vii, born 1491 - died 1547, was King of England from 1509 to 1547. He broke with the Papacy in 1534 and established the Church of England) and in the absence of other light on the subject there is ample evidence to establish the origin of Bonner as from Riddell, it being accepted fact that Bonner is not an ancient appellation, nor one transplanted in England from France. The learned antiquary Camden also tells us that "where two families bear the same arms, the younger, in all probability, will be found to descend from the elder." Horace Smith's dictum that "all surnames ever go contraried" is excellently illustrated by the Bishop (Bonner), who was disgracefully notorious for his atrocious persecution of the Protestants during the cruel Reign Queen Mary. He (Bonner) had a withal a long and happy career, amassing a great fortune which little availed him on the accession of Queen Elizabeth when refusing to take the oath of supremacy and was sentenced to the prison at Marshalsea and died there on 5 September 1569 after an imprisonment of ten years.

Immediately after his death we find his cousin, William Bonner, of Banbury, Oxfordshire, Clerk in Holy Orders, fighting at the courts in London for his interest in divers estates, some of which were had bu purchase from the Bishop. This William Bonner married Alice Gorham of Glapthrone in 1568 and was raised chiefly at "Elmshere," a splendid mansion if the parish of the Blessed Mary of Bow, in Cheapeward, London. This property had formerly belonged to the Monastery of Newark, in Surry and had probably been mulched from the Monks by the Bishop (Bonner) or his predecessor.

Certainly it was the cause of considerable litigation at Guild Hall, London, before both Lord Mayor Osborne in April 1584 and Lord Mayor Harte in May 1590. William Bonner came off victorious at the Lord Mayor's Courts and held this splendid fabric at a time when he was the younger son of an illustrious but impoverished family and it eventually passed to George Lennard, Stratsfield Say in Hampshire, by marriage.

Reverend Anthony Bonner (brother of William Bonner) had a son, Anthony, whose son, Anthony, was born at Quinton in Gloucestershire having married Marion Vaughan of the Vaughan of Gloucestershire, a family of good note and had issue: (1) Richard Born at Quinton in 1615; (2) Thomas born at Quinton in 1617; (3) Ellen born at Quinton in 1624. As appears by the will of Thomas Coomb of Stratford, Warwickshire (proved 14 July 1657). Thomas apparently had no issue. Ellen married a member of the Wells family, the Honorable Edward Wells and Richard Bonner had gone abroad (to Virginia.)

In the absence of other evidence it is an excellent document upon which to establish the standard of the ancestor of the Virginia house of that period. By this time most of the Bonners had embraced the Protestant faith and Thomas Coomb was a most devoted apostle of the church. He left 50 pounds to Anthony Bonner, Gloucestershire, Gentleman (and to have been "Gentleman" in those days signifies an ownership of house property.)

Richard Bonner, the elder, born at Quinton in 1615, had long been absent from the Gloucestershire home of the Bonners at the demise of his wealthy cousin, Thomas Coomb, for his sailing from the Port of London and taking the oath of allegiance is duly of record. For some cause he left his home when but twenty years of age, sailing in the "Friendshippe" and arriving at James City, Virginia in March 1636. He married and had considerable issue, none of which held any office as a civic character whatsoever at the Virginia Colony. They were withal staunch patriots who served the Colony (as did their father, Richard Bonner, from 1636 to 1643) in the ranks and privates against the common foe.

It was about this period that the Bonners took lands under the Act of 17, Charles I, Chapter 33, A.C. 1642 in Ireland, the pioneer being Thomas Bonner, who acquired a considerable estate by royal grant in Ulster. He was the forerunner, though not the founder of a very considerable tribe in the kingdom, men who the Irish listed as, "Adventurers for lands in Ireland," and whom they opposed with every means within their power.

Returning to William Bonner of Elmsmere; he had a son, John Bonner, who resided at his father's death at Hinckley, in Leicestershire and who was the founder of that branch of the Bonner family. He married (at the Parish Church in Hinckley in 1607.) Mary Walker of the same place and had issue. His brother, Thomas, also married at the same church to Anne Botfishe of Sheasby and had considerable issue. This John Bonner left issue: six sons and four daughters, of whom no notice of birth and marriage appear in nearby churches, except that at Howby in the same county notice of the marriages of these six sons appear, viz: The marriage of Michael Bonner, son of John, to Alice Wilson, at the Parish Church of Howby in 1629. He probably had been away from Hinckley for some years, as the records obtainable advises us of the marriage at Hinckley of his son, Joseph Bonner, with one of the McDonalds in that Parish, and is followed by records of the marriage in the same church of four of his daughters and two sons. One son, John, (the successor of his father, Joseph) Mary Burton at the same church in 1699 and had issue: twelve sons and several daughters. Of this family, one son, Richard Bonner of Hinckley, Gentleman, married in 1719, Ann Taylor, at the nearby Church of All Saints, Leicestershire, and the father of Captain John Bonner of the "Pink Elizabeth." Captain John Bonner went to Boston in 1678 and later settled at Cambridge about 1697. He was born ca 1642, the son of John Bonner of London. Captain John married Mary Clark (his second marriage) who died in 1697. In 1705, he sold his house in Cambridge and moved back to Boston where he died on 30 January 1725 at the age of 83 years. He is buried in the Old Granary Burying ground in Boston and the Bonner coat-of-arms is on his tomb. The obituary of John Bonner, written a the time of death, depicts his as, "A gentleman very skillful and ingenious in many arts and sciences, especially in navigation, drawing, molding of ships, etc., one of the best acquainted of coasts of North America of any of his time, of great knowledge and judgement of marine affairs, was very much consulted, relied upon by the government as principal pilot of our marine expeditions and with diligent care and faithfulness discharged his trust."

By his second wife, who was a daughter of the famous Elder Clark of Cambridge, he had several children, but only a son and a daughter survived him. His children were: Jane who died in 1686; Jonah who died in 1687; Mary who was born in 1686 and died in 1699; and Jane, who apparently was named for her elder sister who died. The second Jane was born on 2 May 1691 and later went to London. Other children were: John; Sarah, born 6 December 1693 and died 2 December 1721. She was baptized in Boston and also went to London. Thomas who was born in Cambridge on 6 January 1695 and moved to South Carolina where he died on 3 June 1719, at age 24.

Returning to the main stem of this family, we find Anthony Bonner, the elder (before recited as a brother of William Bonner), who formed a most illustrious alliance with the Tates of de la Pre Abbey, he having married Elizabeth Tate, (daughter of William Tate) who was born in 1671 at the historic North Hamptonshire mansion. She was the co-heiress and direct lineal descendant of the noble House of Tate, all of which is duly recorded in a pedigree complied from a manuscript volume begun by Mawson, Portcullis and continued by Warburton, Somerset Herald, which pedigree commences with John Tate of Conventry, who held lands in Whitley during the reign of King Richard II (King Richard, born 1637 and died in 1400. He was King of England from 1377 to 1399 and was the last Plantagenet King; deposed; son of Edward the Black Prince.) Previous to this the Tates are recorded as having founded Tate's Chantry in the Church of St. Michael, during the reign of King Henry III (King Henry III, born 1207 and died in 1272, King from 1216 to 1272.) The pedigree is interesting to the Bonners for it shows the high honors which one maternal side of the Bonner House have possessed, viz: Sir Robert Tait (Tate), Sheriff of London and Lord Mayor in 1481; Sir John Tait, Sheriff of London in 1435 and Lord Mayor of London in 1496.

Sir Bartholomew Tate who received the honor of Knighthood from King Henry VIII. His grandson, Sir William Tate of de la Pre Abbey, married in 1597, Elizabeth, the oldest daughter and heir of Edward, the eleventh and last Baron Zouche, of Haryngworth, and by her had considerable issue. The Zouche family was descended in line from the Sovereign Kings of Brittany (Brittany and the Bay of Biscay, French name - Bretagne), a fact which gives the American House of Bonner a Royal Descent. (Author's note - It is this Tate family that is believed to be the ancestors of William Tate of South Carolina. See the Tate family in part three of this work.)

II

HENRY BONNER (1)

(ca 1620 - 1689)

IT is this Henry Bonner who is believed to be the progenitor of the Chowan County Bonner clan. He arrived in the New World prior to March 1664 according to a request for a headright in his name in March 1664. He could have been in the country from 5 to 10 years prior to 1664 since claims for headrights did not have to be filed in a timely manner. He was probably born in the period of 1620 to 1635 with about 1620 being the best target date. He came to America with his wife (unnamed) and two children (also unnamed). Other children were probably born after his arrival in Virginia and North Carolina. An interesting fact that can be derived from the Legal records for the period is the that no Bonner was residing in what in now Chowan County, North Carolina until this Henry Bonner arrived in the New World.

The man who received a headright in Bonner's name was Thomas Davyies. This fact is a manner of record: *Cavaliers and Pioneers, Abstracts of Virginia Land Pantents and Grants, 1623 - 1666,* by Nell Marion Nugent, page 451, can be found the following:

"*Thomas Davyes, 400 acres Upper Parish Nansemond County, 11 March 1664, page 179 (68). Beginning by the Southern Branch adjoining land of Richard Harmon. (For) transportation of 8 persons:* ***HENRY BONNER, TWICE; HIS WIFE, ONCE; 2 CHILDREN;*** *Edward Joyner; Maid Servant; Thomas White.*"

The above Henry Bonner may be the same Henry Bonner named in the Last Will and Testament named in the below excerpt:

"Brandon Wetherill. Published 1642, probated 29 October 1659....my friends Mr. Charles Harris; Mr. Henry Bonner, Thomas Coghill, Overseers." (Ref: *Virginia Settlers & English Adventurers,* by Noel Currer-Briggs, 1969, page 384.)

If we assume that they are the same Henry Bonner and that he was at least 21 years of age when the above Will was published , then we can establish that Bonner was born about 1620.

It is believed that the two children mentioned with Henry Bonner in 1664 were probably between the ages of 5 to 15 years. Henry Bonner is the only Bonner mentioned in the legal records of the Colony until the 1680's when William Bonner and Henry Bonner are noted as witnesses to the last will and testament of a Thomas Bonner. Thomas Bonner published his will in Chowan in March 1685 and it was probated in November 1685. The will is extremely hard to read because of old age combined with the unusual style of handwriting. It can be read that Thomas left a wife, named Mary, a young son, named Thomas, and his wife was pregnant. His plantation was left to his son, Thomas, through his wife. The will was witnessed by: Henry Bonner, William Bonner and Samuel Warren. Although it cannot be proven, it is felt that the above Thomas, Henry and William were sons of Henry Bonner (1). Legal records show that in July 1689, there was an adult Henry Bonner (2) in Chowan County, so the above assumption is not without foundation.

It appears that Henry Bonner (1) , who arrived prior to 1664, was wealthy and well-connected politically before and after his arrival in Chowan. From the beginning of the records of the era, he is mentioned in a prominent way with the movers and shakers of the colony. Bonner was in Chowan prior to 1672, for the diary of Revered George Fox, mentions a Bonner on Mattacomack Creek in the fall of 1672. And the legal records strongly suggest that it had to be this Henry Bonner and coupled with the fact that in later years all the Bonners lived on the Mattacomack Creek tends to prove this point. As previously stated, in the fall of 1672, George Fox visited a Bonner who was living on Mattacomack Creek. Bonner had been there long enough to build a house, necessary outbuilding, and had an area fenced to keep horses. He also had to have land cleared for crops in order to survive. All of this before the fall of 1672.

Reading the diary of Reverend George Fox, it can be surmised that Henry Bonner was a tolerant man and respected a religious view different of his own. He accepted Fox into his home, kept his horses for him and gave him a boat; knowing that Fox was of the Quaker religion. Being a Quaker in those days did create ill-feeling among some members of the Colonies.

The following can be found in, *The Colonial Records of North Carolina, Volume I, 1662-1712*, pages 216, 217 and 218, as it was extracted and reprinted from pages 458 and 459 of the edition published at Friends Store, Philadelphia.

"EXTRACT FROM THE JOURNAL OF GEORGE FOX FOR THE YEAR 1672"

"After this, eighth day of the ninth month (8 November 1672) our way to Carolina grew worse, being much of it splashy and pretty full of great bogs and swamps; so that we were commonly wet to the knees and abroad a-nights in the woods by a fire; saving one of the nights we got to a poor house at Sommertown (Author's note - Sommertown is near the present Virginia/North Carolina state lines, in Virginia, just north of Gates County, North Carolina) and lay by the fire. The woman of the house had a sense of God upon her. The report of our travel had reached thither and drawn some that lived beyond Sommertown to that house in expectation to have been and heard us but they missed us.

"Next day the twenty-first day of the ninth month (21 November 1672) having traveled hard through the woods and over many bogs and swamps, **we reached Bonner's Creek**; there we lay that night by the fireside, the woman lending us a mat to lie on.

"This was the first house we came to in Carolina; *(underlined by author)* here we left our horses, over-wearied with travel. From hence we went down the Creek to Mattacomack River (actually Mattacomack Creek) and came to Hugh Smith's where people of other professions came to see us, 'no friends inhabiting that part of the country' and many of them received us gladly. Among others came Nathaniel Batts who had been Governor of Roan-Oak. He went by the name of Captain Batts and had been a rude, desperate man. He asked me about a woman in Cumberland, who, he said, he was told, had been healed by our prayers and laying on of hands after she had been long sick and given over by the physicians; he desired to know the certainty of it. I told him as did not glory in such things but many such things had been done by the power of God.

"Not far from hence we had a meeting among the people and they were taken with the Truth; Blessed be the Lord! Then passing down the River Maratick (now the Roanoke River) in a canoe we went down the Bay Connie-Oak to a Captain's who was loving to us and lent us his boat for we were much weted in the canoe, the water flashing in upon us. With this boat we went to the Governor's but the water in some places was so shallow that the boat being loaden could not swim: so that we put off our shoes and stockings and waded through the water a pretty way. The Governor, with his wife, received us lovingly; but a doctor there would need dispute with us. And truly his opposing us was of good service giving occasion to the opening of many things to the people concerning the Light and Spirit of God which he denied to be in every one; and affirmed it was not in the Indians. Whereupon I called an Indian to us and asked him, 'Whether or no, when he did lie or do wrong to anyone there was not something in him that did reprove him for it' He said, 'There was such a thing in him that so reprove him; and he was ashamed when he had done wrong or spoken wrong.' So we shamed the doctor before the Governor and people; insomuch that the poor man ran out far at length he would not own the Scriptures. We tarried at the Governor's that night; and the next morning he very courteously walked with us himself about two miles through the woods to a place whither he had sent our boat about to meet us. Taking leave of him we entered our boat and went about thirty miles to Joseph Scott's, one of the representatives of the country. There we had a sound precious meeting; the people were tender and much desired after the meeting. Wherefore at a house about four miles further we had another meeting; to which the Governor's secretary came who was Chief Secretary of the Province and had been formerly convinced.

"I went from this place among the Indians and spoke to them by an interpreter, shewing them, 'That God made all things in six days and made but one woman for one man; and God did drown the world because of their wickedness. Afterwards, I spoke to them concerning Christ, shewing them, that He died for all men, for their sins, as well as for others; and had enlightened them as well as others; and that if they did that which was evil he would burn them; but if they did well they should not be burned.' There was among them their young King and others of their chief men who seemed to receive kindly what I said to them.

"Having visited the North part of Carolina and made a little entrance for the truth among the people there we began to return again towards Virginia having several meetings in our way wherein we had good service for the Lord, the people being generally tender and open; Blessed be the Lord! We lay one night at the Secretary's to which we had much ado to get; for the water being shallow we could not bring our boat to shore. But the Secretary's wife seeing our strait came herself in a canoe her husband being from home and brought us to land. By next morning our boat was sunk and full of water; but we got her up and mended her, and went away in her that day about twenty-four miles, the water being rough and the winds high; but the great power of God was seen in carrying us safe in that rotten boat. In our return we had a very precious meeting at Hugh Smiths, Praised be the Lord forever! The people were very tender and very good service amongst them. There was at this meeting an Indian Captain who was very loving; and acknowledged it to be truth that was spoke. There was also one of the Indian Priests, whom they called Pauwaw who sat soberly among the people. The ninth of the tenth month (9 December 1672) we got back to Bonner's Creek (underlined by author) where we had left our horses; having spent about eighteen days in North of Carolina."

It must be remembered that Reverend George Foxe was a Quaker and was using the Quaker calendar (old style calendar) where March is the first month and February the last. This would explain why Reverend Foxe slept beside a fireplace; it was cold in North Carolina in November. Also if one counts the calendar days that he spent in Carolina it would appear that he spent more than eighteen days on his Carolina trip. However, Foxe was counting the days from his arrival at Bonner's Creek to the day he arrived back to Bonner's Creek since as he put it, "Bonner's place was the first house we arrived at in the North of Carolina." Of equal interest is his description of his departure from the Bonner plantation. He left the Bonner place in a canoe and went down a creek to the Mattacomack River. It can be surmised that Bonner lived on a branch of the main body of water, in this case, it was called the Mattacomack River, when actually it was the Mattacomack Creek. In those days the Mattacomack was probably a wide and deep body of water like a river to an outsider. Foxe's journal places the Bonner clan on the Mattacomack where the main body of the family would live for the next 100 years. On modern day maps the Mattacomack Creek no longer exists. The area where the creek was is now known as "Pollack Swamp." (When this writer rode through the area in 1994, on Green Hall Road, there was not enough water in the creek to draw attention to it. It was rich farm land with very healthy soy beans growing. Also remember that the Army Corps of Engineers has drained many swamps over the past years (the Mattacomack was one of them). However, Pollack Swamp does seem to follow the old creek stream of water, (when compared to old maps) it begins north of Edenton, snaking southwest and empties into the Pembroke Creek which flows into Edenton Bay and Albemarle Sound.

There were others living on or near the Mattacomack and some properties that the Bonner's owned fit the description of patents issued to the following people:

Anthony Slocumb, 600 acres on North Side of Mattacomack

and Mirey Swamp. Land granted in 1684.

Joseph Slocumb, 200 acres on North West side Mattacomack a the north of Mirey Swamp. Land granted in 1684.

John Slocumb, 400 acres on the North side of the Mattacomack called Poplar. Land granted 1684, adjoining Joseph Slocumb.

In the very beginning of the North Carolina Colony, present day Chowan County was known as, "Shaftsbury Precinct of Albamarle County of Carolina," In 1685 Shaftsbury was changed to "Chowan Precinct" (probably in honor of the Chowan Indians). About 1732, Chowan Precinct was changed to "Chowan County." It appears that Albemarle County was just a name and not a seat of government.

During the period from 1677 to 1679, there was a rebellion in the North Carolina Colony. It involved tariffs imposed by the King that did not set too well with the colonists. The center of the revolt was situated in Chowan and Prequimans precincts. The main participates are described in, *The North Carolina Colonial Records, 'Volume I, 1662 - 1712,* pages 255 to 261, as follows:

PRESENTATION TO THE LORDS PROPRIETORS OF CAROLINA CONCERNING THE REBELLION IN THAT COUNTRY, TO BE MADE USE OF IN FURTHER EXAMINATIONS

It is humbly tendered to be the considerations of the Most Illustrious and Right Honorable the Lords Proprietors of the Province of Carolina. That the Rebellion of the Inhabitants of the County of Albemarle was not accidentall or casually arose from any present or sudden provocation given, but rather the effect of a more mature or deliberate contrivance, which I humbly conceive will so appear to your Lordships by the ensuring particulars as here circumstanced, the mane substance whereof can be clearly proved by the evidence of divers credible witnesses upon oath before any person or persons, your Honors shall think fit to empower to take cognizance of the premises.

That the principalls and heads of this rebellion were not only prompted thereunto by ambition and envy or the private pekes and particular disgusts they had to those gentlemen yours thought fit to entrust with the government, but also more especially those personall and particular crimes they knew themselves guilty of and accountable for whenever a Governor should come.

That this was a deliberate design of no sudden growth may be proved by their generall charge wherein all their former actions seem to have a naturall tendency to this their last and horrid end. At first their severall times disturbing the courts, subverting the Government, dissolving Parliaments, their industrious labor to be poplar and continued making of factions and parties.

Their poysoning the peoples eares, unsetling and disquieting their minds, by diffusing and dropping abroad, by their agents false and dangerous reports tending much to the indignity of your Honors and reproach of your Government, and among divers, that your Honors intended to raise the pence and from two pence to six pence per acre. Now what they have done since is so notorious and obvious to every eye, as the imprisoning your Lordship's Deputies, putting the President who was likewise His Majesty's Collector into Irons, their general arming on the first appearance of Gilham's shipp in Pascontanke River, their seizing and carrying away the records, lastly their arrogating and assuming to themselves the supreme and sovereign power, by first dissolving then erecting Courts of Judicature, convening Parliaments without Writs, and as if they had the sovereign and absolute power they put out new officers, not only in courts and other publick services of ther country, but even where the King is more immediately concerned, turning out His Majesty's Collector, putting in others, clearing and discharging ships, but last of all their most horrid treasonable and tyrannicall acting in erecting a court for tryall of life and death without the Lords Deputies or Commission of Oyer and Terminer or any other colour or pretence of Authority, either from His Sacred Majesty or Your Lordships, and particularly in the cases of Mr. Thomas Miller and Mr. Timothy Biggs.

But their speciall, particular and respective crimes are here annexed to their severall names here in the margin in the order following (viz):

CAPTAIN VALENTINE BIRD. He being by the Country to be Collector of His Majesty's Duty of the penny per pound, for all tobacco not exported for England, did without power from or the privity of consent of either my Lord High Treasurer or His Majesty's Commissioners of the Customs suffer the New England traders to load and carry away the tobacco of the country without paying the said duties, by which meanes they are now in arreares to His Majesty one hundred and fifty thousand weight of tobacco, and finding the hazard he had run in case another Collector should be sent he with above one hundred more, most whereof were Pastotankians (residents of Pasquotank Precinct), which after led other precincts into Rebellion there, with him subscribing a paper against the payment of the said duty, but after hearing by the report of Crawford (Captain William Crawford) and that Mr. Eastchurch was coming Governor and Mr. (Thomas) Miller, Collector. (Valentine) Bird and the rest of the subscribers were the first that took armes and opposed Miller at his first landing fearing they should be questioned for what they had done, as soone as ever Gilham arrived they again take armes and by their agents invite the other precincts to joyne with them, and till the generall elaps of the country they were only in this defection and Bird was their leader and drew the first sword, encouraged hereunto by Captain Zackery Gilham who supplied them with many fire armes and other weapons of war, came with some of his seamen armed to Captain Crawford's house, where the President and two of the Deputies were taken prisoners.

"**George Durant**, hath several times before not only contemned but opposed the authority established by your Honors, and in the head of a rebell rout by force subverted the government turning out and placing in whom he and they thought fit at pleasure, and openly threatening that, if Mr. Thomas Eastchurch came in as Governor, he would turn Rebell. And as if these were too small crimes, he hath viciated a Record of Court by adding, razing and other wayes altering the verdict of a jury, and as foreman giving it in contrary to what the whole jury had returned upon oath, particularly in case of Mr. Thomas Miller. And in fact hath all along when at home beene one of the most violent, active and the most outrageous of all the Conspirators and Insurrectors.

"**Captain William Crawford**, hath formerly as well as now industriously made it his business to be popular, make factions, and then head them and very subtilty through clandestinely and underhand, will be found one of the chief contrivers as well as acters in this rebellion, but his particular crime, in the imbezling and taking of the file of the records, a gratious grant of your Lordships to the country. And having formerly got the records into his custody, divers of them are since not to be found; and this he did, as may be judged; (since he could make no private advantages thereby) purposely to keep the people ignorant of your Honors goods intentions to this country and might find fitter occasions thereby to insence them against your Lordships and the Government.

"**Captain John Willoughby.** He is a person that runs himself into many errors and premuniries through his extra-judicial and arbituary proceedings in the Courts of Judicature, and for instance in the case of Mr. Thomas Eastchurch, who by reason of their tyranny and injustice to himwards would have appealed to your Lordships, but was thus answered by Willoughby that they were the Court of Court and Jury of Juries. He is a person that through a naturall habit of pride or ambition hath been alwaies imperious amongst his equals, courteous to his inferious, because factions and would be popular; stubborne and disobedient to superiors, evidenced by his scornful and preemptory refusing obedience to the summons of the Palatine's Court and his beating the sworn officer that served the same; and for this and other scornes and contempts put upon the Court, and continuing still abstinate, he was outlawed: The next Parliament approving of the proceedings aginst him, set a fine on his head for his said contempt. And hereupon he disavowes your Government by addressing his complaints to the Governor and Councill of Virginia, yet he returns not homewards till he heard the country was up in armes.

"**Captain Thomas Cullum,** frequently sells powder, shot, and fire-armes, as well to those Indian Nations that are not as those that are in amity with the English, expressly contrary to the Laws of all the English Province which make it death to sell either to our enemies. And on notice given to the Magistrates of Virginia. Warrants were there issued out for apprehending him, and if he had been there taken (although in another Government) he must have stood tryall for his life for the same of like fact there committed.

"**Lieutenant Colonel John Jenkins,** being some time made Governor by the appointment of Cartwright was after for severall misdemeanours displaced and imprisoned; yet although never legally discharged, raiseth a party of riotous persons in armes, and these with some others voted him Generalissimo, neither he or they pretending to any right or authority than what he derived from this Rebell Rout, and these turne out the Palatines Court, dissolve the assembly, place and displace whom he any they pleased by an arbitrary power and force. But yet although Jenkins had the title yet in fact Durant governed and used Jenkins but as his property, for of all the factious persons in the country he was the most active and uncontrollable.

"**John Culpepper,** a person never is in his element but whilst fishing in troubled waters, he was forced to fly (flee) from Ashley River for his turbulent and factious carriage there. He both here and in New England with some of the discontented traders plotted there and underhand here incouraged the hot-headed people to this rash and ill-advised rebellion. Culpepper being their Secretary or Register and one of their Caball or Grand Councill in matter of advise, this being the second disturbance he hath made here besides what he hath done in Ashley River, New England, and Virginia and therefore a man they much hearken to for his experience sake.

"**Patrick White**, is one that with Willoughby applyed himself to the Governor of Virginia, that beate Mr. Miller when he landed, and an active man in this Rebellion, and hath formerly been a disturber of the Government.

"**Captain James Blount**, although one of the Great Councill or Assistant to the Deputies is one of the chief persons amongst the insurrectors, and although I wrote him, the Speaker and the rest of the Burgesses of Chowan Precinct, yet when the Sheriffe or Chief Martiall came with my letter and endeavoured to raise Possee Comitatis for keeping the peace and securing of that your Lordships country, he the said Blount with one **Captain John Verham** took the Martiall and his men prisoners and raised forces against the Government.

"**(Henry) Bonner and (Anthony) Slocum, two other of the Burgesses joyne with (Thomas) Cullen, (James) Blount and (John) Verham, so that all five Burgesses of Chowan**, although to their Oaths of Allegiance and Obedience, and to their preceedings in Parliament, are in this defection and by their sad example have drawn in the country people. There are besides these about eighty or an hundred which may be ranked in a second class differing no more from the former than second rates from first. And all of most of these have been guilty of former insurrections with some of their leaders above named, especially such as live in Pascotanke (Precinct), viz: Lieutenant Wells; Seares; Jennings; Ellis; Bonesby and his two sons; Cotes with divers others of the Precinct. Now the rest of the people may rather be reputed newtrall, for if they have complyed (as many of them have done) it is only through want of courage that they have sacrificed their faith to their fears, and for the same reason will on the first appearance of a party from your Honors although but 60 or 70 men on pardon published and exemplary justice done the Ring-leaders who do overawe them, they will then gladly returne to their duties, their necessities also constreighning them, for they cannot subsist without planting of Corne and Tobacco, well knowing that without these two (having made them their sole dependency) they must perish by hunger or want of cloathing, unless the Chief Leaders build Capers and imploy them to rob the merchants to supply their wants as they come into the Capes of Virginia which is not above 20 or 30 leagues from this inlet; and they are apt enough to tell them, that in respect of the openess of the road, shallowness of the Inlet, fastness of the country, and by reasons of the woods, swamps, rivers, creeks, and runs, this country being no waies accessible by land but to the northward from Virginia, and that but by three passes or avenues, by which meanes they may possible be persuaded they may be safe from His Majesty's Frigates as if they were in sally. I mention this not to discourage Your Honors , but do likewise assure you that they are as inconsiderable, as rash and disobedient; the whole number I do not say of men but Tythables that is of working hands consist of about 1400 persons, a third part whereof at least being Indians, Negros, and women, will the rest once being declared Rebells, quickly desert them and come in hope either of liberty or better usuage. So that in time I can no way bring the number of Rebells that may be expected in armes to amount to 100 men, and these by reason of the several rivers and creeks which run north and south, and divide the severall precincts, so that they cannot suddenly joyne. If therefore a ship from England with goods and servants which I am confident would answer the charge, two or three Sloopes prest from Virginia, all man'd with 60 or 70 men divided into two parties, one whereof might run up to Chowan up the Sound in a-night, and there I am sure they would meet with many Loyall and Lusty young men, who would immediately joyne with them and on notice divers who fled to Virginia would return for Pasquimans (Perquimans), there were but 3 or 4 noted Rebells as: Jenkins; Durant; Sherrell; Greene; Pricklove, and Lininton (Lillington), most of the rest being Quakers, who stand firme in their obedience although they will fight, the archest Rebells and greatest number being in Paccotanke. And although it is easy to reduce then either by the way above proposed or by those soldiers as are yet behind in Virginia or by volunteers from thence, near two hundred having promised Mr. Eastchurch to march in with him as soone as he should obteine License from the Governor there, but his death prevented his designe, the Governor assuring him by his messingers that nothing should be wanting on his part wherein he might serve him, they there and also in Maryland being exceeding sensible of the suddenly subdued hundreds of idle debters, theeves, Negros, Indians and English servants will fly into them & from thence inroads and dayly incursions, whence great mischief may be better be forseene and prevented than after remedied, for considering the vast coast and wild woods of the backside of Virginia they may come from Maryland & the wilderness between Virginia and Albemarle extending one hundred miles without one inhabitant they may and some already do go into them in defiance of all the care the Governor and Magistrates there take for prevention."

The below document also contains details of the Culpepper Rebellion. It can be found in, *The Colonial Records of North Carolina, Volume I, 1662-1712*, pages 272, 273 & 274. The document is dated 31 January 1679 but there is ample evidence that it should be dated 31 January 1680.

".....these instructions being given the said Foster with his Burgesses carryed this desponant a prisson along with them to one **George Durant's** house which was ye appointed place for all yer meetings and where aforesaid Mr. Miller and ye Lord Deputyes and other Officers were prissoners and where they kept this desponant under a guard of thre files of soldiers takeing violently from this desponant all the King's bond accounts and consarnes whatsoever from him and after delivered them to John Culpepper thier Collector where ye aforesaid Gillam (note - this man was called "Gilham" in the precious document) was and countenancing them with his presence & furnishing them with drink nor would be open store untill he see what would be done about ye Governor and also when they created a Parliament consisting of: Thomas Cullen, Speaker; James Blount; Anthony Slocum; John Verham; **Henry Bonner**; John Jenkins; Samuel Pricklove; William Terrill; Caleb Calloway; Alexander Lillington; William Crawford; Valentine Bird (since dead); William Jennings; Thomas Jarvies; Enoch Billing; Richard Sanders; Patrick White & William Sears who was their Drummer in all 18 of them this parliament separated five of yer members, viz; John Jenkins; William Crawford; James Blount; Patrick White and Valentine Bird to joyne with one Mr. Richard Foster their Cheef Judge to make a court of and then this court impanelled a Grand Jury out of ye Soldiers and Confused Rable, the foreman whereof was one Mordecay Bowden, a New England Traider, and one much indebted to ye King which foreman consulting with one John Culpepper (thier Collector aforesaid and Cheef Scribe and Counsellor) how he should bring in ye Inditement aginst ye said Miller the said Culpepper told him he must Indosse Billa versa...."

The above affidavit was made by one Henry Hudson, aged about 54 years "or thereabouts" concerning his observation of the Culpepper Rebellion. This affidavit also places Henry Bonner in Chowan Precinct and as a participant in the Rebellion by sworn testimony.

"Att the courte for ye precinct of Shaftsbury, the first day of Aprill 1680. Att Edward Smithwick's house, Present: Mr. Thomas Cullen, Judge; Mr. Joseph Chew; Mr. Josiah Gilbert; Mr. Henry Bonner and Mr. Joseph Gilbert, Commissioners." (Ref: Hathaway,

Volume 1, Number 4, page 613.)

This Henry Bonner (1) died in 1689, as noted below. He lived at an interesting but harsh time in the Colony of North Carolina. He left a secure environment in England to pursue his future and fortune in an unknown land with an element of danger far beyond any he could imagine. But he forged his way and established a foothold for his descendants that is well documented in the Colonial Records of North Carolina.

The following document is the only known record that makes note of Henry Bonner's death in the Summer of 1689. It does document that he left a son, Henry Bonner (2).

From, *The Governor's Papers, 1684-1685, 1689-1690,* page 385: found in *The Colonial Records of Norh Carolina* is the following:

(CCR)

Council Order and Writ of Election
1689 July

Att the house of Thomas (torn)rne(tt), Seth Sothell, Esquire, Governor; William Wilkerson, Esquire; Thomas Jarves; Thomas Miller; John Hunt, Lord Deputies.

Ordered that Writte be issued forth to the inhabitants of Chowan Precinct to Chose three substantial Freeholders our of the said precinct for to meet on Tuesday next at the house of Fra. Hartley there to meet the rest of the Burgess for to act and mak such Lawes as shalbe for the peace of the County.

A true Copp per Henderson Walker, Clerk.

ALBEMARLE

Whereas William Wilkinson, Esquire is chosen out of the Burgess of Chowan to fill up the Vagancy of the Proprietors Deputies and **Mr. Henry Bonner** and Mr. Robert West **being dead** and there being occasion for filling up the assembly.

There are therefore in (torn) Lord Proprietors to require to Summon (torn) of the said Precinct to the usual place the (torn) choise of three of them in the roome of the aforesaid William Wilkerson. William Wilkerson, **Henry Bonner,** and Robert West and **send them to the house of Francis Hartley** on Tuesday next being the 16th Instant July there to meet the rest of the Burgesses and you are to make Returne of this to Henderson Walker.

Given under our Hands the (blotted) July 1689.
To: William Woollard, Sheriff.

(Signed) Seth Sothell, Thomas Jarvis,
William Wilkerson,
Thomas Miller
John Hunt.

As noted above, both Henry Bonner (Jr) and Robert West (Jr) were summoned to the home of Francis Hartley to take the oath of office for the House of Burgesses. The Last Will & Testament of Henry Bonner (1) has not been located but the Will of Robert West (Sr) has been found and it is published to show the validity of the above order of the Governor's Council.

"Robert West, Chowan. Published 28 March 1689. Probated at Court 4 June 1689. Sons: Robert; Thomas; John; Richard. Brothers: John and Benjamin. Brother-in-law: Thomas Simons. Wife: Martha, exrs. Test: James Dammerell, James Farley, Benjamin Messler." (Ref: Hathaway, Volume 1, Number 4, page 500.)

III

HENRY BONNER (2)

(ca 1650 - ca 1725)

Family Data:
Henry Bonner (2): (ca 1650 - ca 1725)
Wife: Unknown
Children: 1. Henry Bonner (3): (ca 1679 - 1738)
May be the father of the following:
2. William "Will" Bonner (Living in Chowan in 1705)
3. James Bonner (Living in Chowan in 1703)
4. Thomas Bonner (ca 1690 - 7 April 1765). Lived and died in Beaufort County, North Carolina.

It was this Henry Bonner who was mentioned in the previous chapter's Governor's papers in July 1689. He was hard to document because of the scarcity of legal documents for Chowan County for the period of the 1690's but beginning in the 1700's he is mentioned many times.

The wife of this Henry Bonner is not known. There are hints but no sound proof. For instance, there was a Henry Bonner who married a Mrs. Elizabeth Taylor, widow of John Taylor on 1 September 1674 in Maryland. And Elizabeth is a favorite name for the known Bonner girls. In 1711, in Chowan County, Henry Bonner (2) was named as a brother-in-law to James Welsh in the latter's Last Will & Testament.

There may be more to the history of this man than the records show. For instance, in one version of the recorded history of Washington, North Carolina, it is stated that three Bonner brothers, James, William and Thomas came to North Carolina from Maryland and that William went to a nearby county, probably Chowan, that James founded the City of Washington, North Carolina and Thomas served in the capacity of Sheriff in Beaufort County among other public duties. The actual facts do not support this thesis.

First, there was a William Bonner living in Chowan in 1705,

but the above James Bonner did not establish the City of Washington, North Carolina but a Thomas Bonner did become Sheriff. The historical legal documents of the period show that James Bonner, the son of Sheriff Thomas Bonner laid out the streets for the town in the 1750's and the town was chartered about 1785. It is felt that the above mentioned, James, William and Thomas probably were the sons of Henry Bonner (2) and if they came from Maryland it was only after they had left Chowan County to go to Maryland. (Remember that a Henry Bonner married Elizabeth Taylor in Maryland in 1674.) The legal records of Chowan County show that a James Bonner was in Chowan in 1703, a William Bonner was in Chowan, as noted previously. (Sheriff) Thomas Bonner was in Hyde County as a Freeholder in 1715, and soon thereafter he removed to a plantation at the end of Tar River as it enters the Pamplico River where the City of Washington would be laid out on part of his plantation. However, it goes without saying that all of the Bonners of Beaufort and Chowan are kin but the records are silent as to how.

For instance, a Thomas Bonner moved to Chowan from Nansemond County, Virginia in the 1710's. He used Captain Henry Bonner (3) as an attorney to dispose of land just before he moved into the County. There is no mention of the kin of the two.

As previously stated, there was a James Bonner in Chowan in 1703.

"Matthew Adams, Chowan. Will published 9 August 1703. Probated 26 November 1708. Son: Matthew. Daughter: Ellinor. Wife, Sarah named exrs. Test: Thomas Blount, **James Bonner**." (Ref: Hathaway, Volume 1, Number 2, page 1.)

The evidence of "Will" Bonner being in Chowan is in the following:

Bonner to Blount

A DEED OF SALE passed from Henry Bonner to James Blount and ordered to be registered 3d April 1705.

Chowan Precinct in ye province of North Carolina, To All Xtain people to whom these presents shall come Henry Bonner for divers good causes and consideration me moving thereunto but now more especially for ye consideration of eighteen pounds Sterling to me in hand paid or secured to be paid by Mr. James Blount, Senior of the precinct aforesaid wherewith I do by these presents acknowledge myself to be freely and fully satisfied contended and paid have therefore Bargained and Sold and do by these presents Bargain Sell Enseal and make over and forever confirm unto ye aforesaid Mr. James Blount, Senior all yet my Plantation and track of land situate lying and being on ye Southwest Side of Mattacomack Creek bounded by ye said Creek on ye North and North side and on ye North west and West side by ye land of **Will Bonner** and on the South east side and south side and south west by the Great Swamp and Pecosun ye tract of land and Plantation together with all Housing, Orchards, Gardens, Fruit trees, Timber and Timber trees thereon standing laying or being with all _?_ and easements profits and commodities waters and water courses....

IN WITNESS whereof I have hereunto Sett my Hand and Fixt my Seal this 18th day June 1704/05 in Ye Fourth Year of Ye Reign of Our Sovereign Lady Anne, Queen of England, Scotland, France, and Ireland, Defender of Ye Faith.

Sealed and Delivered
in presence of: Henry Bonner (Seal)
Will Windley
Nathaniel Chevin

In 1705, a Katherine Bonner filed a law suit with the Clerk of Court, Nathaniel Chevin. There is no hint of whom Katherine was, no mention of her before or after 1705.

The Bonners of Chowan are listed in many records as witnesses to legal documents:

"John Wheatley, Chowan, December 1706. Daughters: Elizabeth and Martha Plantation given to me by Cotton Robinson, deceased, to Mary, eldest daughter of Susannah Williams, formerly Skittlethorpe. My five daughters. Samuel Patchett and wife, exrs. Test: Thomas Luten, **Henry Bonner**, Nathaniel Chevin." (Ref: Hathaway, Volume 1, Number 4, page 509.) Note: Thomas Luten died on 6 November 1709 while living in Rockyhock Swamp north of Edenton, N. C.

A family that was very close to the Bonner family for more than 70 years was the Benbury family. Although not recorded, it goes without saying that surely there was intermarriage between the two families.

"William Benbury, 13 July 1709. (No precinct listed but is

Chowan by fact.) Son-in-law, James Watch (Welch); wife, Jane. Son, William. Daughter, Martha and Hannah.... Witnesses: **Henry Bonner**, Edward Mosely, Ann Mosely." (Ref: Hathaway, Volume 1, Number 1, page 34.) Note - Ann Mosely, above, was a relict of the late Governor of the Colony, Henderson Walker, who died in 1704.

As noted above, James Welch was a son-in-law to William Benbury. The name of James's wife is never listed. James may have resided at Welch's Creek at the mouth of the Roanoke River in what was then, the South Shore of Chowan Precinct. Today the location of Welch's Creek would be in the Northern part or Washington County.

"James Welch of Bath to James Long of Chowan. 500 acres on Welch's Creek and Morattack (now Roanoke) River. 13 December 1701. Test: John Lillington, Humphrey Legg." (Ref: Hathaway, Volume 1, Number 1, page 119.)

James Welch died in 1711. The item that makes his death notice interesting is his kinship to Henry Bonner. The Henry Bonner he made note of has to be Henry Bonner (2). The records show that in 1711, there are three Henry Bonners in Chowan. Henry Bonner (2) (born about 1650), Henry Bonner (3) (born about 1679 - who was newly married to Deborah Whedbee) and Henry Bonner (4) born about 1708. By process of elimination, Henry Bonner (2) is the subject of James Welch.

"James Welch. 11 November 1711. Daughter, Mary. Child-in-esse **Brother-in-law, Henry Bonner**, named executor." (Ref: Hathaway, Volume 1, Number 1, page 84.)

"North Carolina - §. At a court for the precinct of Chowan at the house of William Branch, the third Tuesday in April Anno Domo, 1711. Ordered overseers appointed for the Highways for the ensuring year. Mr. Henry Bonner from Terrapin Hill to James Welch's; Thomas Hoskins from Welch's to the Lower part of the usual limits." (Ref: Hathaway, Volume 3, Number 3, page 441.)

Question - Was Henry Bonner married to a sister of James Welch, or was Henry and James married to Benbury sisters? Note the Will of William Benbury on the previous page.

"William Benbury's Last Will and Testament was proved by Henry Bonner. Robert Buckner, Clerk of Court in 1712." (Ref: Hathaway, Volume 1. Number 1, page 119.)

As suggested earlier, it was hard to separate the Henry

Bonners of Chowan County. The records show that every Bonner generation had a son named Henry Bonner. In a few places, senior or junior was used.

The colonist had to "donate" part of their crops to the community for the common good as noted in the following:

"Received of the following, corn for public use: **Henry Bonner, 3 bushels; Captain (Henry) Bonner, 3 bushels;** John Yelverton, 6 bushels; Captain Nicholas Crisp, 6; Edwin Standing, 6; Thomas Hoskins, 6; Joseph Gilbert, 3; William Charlton, 6; Samuel Patchett (Padgett), 12; John Jones (Junior), 3; Richard Lewis, 3; Francis Branch, 9; Jeremiah Vail, 12; William Haughton, 6; James Benbury, 3; John Jones, 6; Edward Mosely, 18; Thomas Peterson, 9; William Yeates, 3; William Fallaugh (Fallow), 3; John Blount, 18; Captain Fred Jones, 9; Charles Wilkins, 3; John Goreham, 3; Nicholas Blackman, 3; William Tanner, 3; Smithwick Warburton, 3; William Davis, 3; John Porter, 18; John Taylor, 3; Argyle Simmons, 3; Thomas Houth, 3; George Moye, 3; John Watkins, 3; T. Johnson, 3; Conrad Eichorn, 3; Thomas Jones, 3; John Bently, 3; William Sadler, 3; William Jones, 3; Thomas Williams, 3; John Lillington, 6; Thomas Edge, 3; John Marks, 3; John Stevens, 3; Robert Warburton, 3.

A TRUE ACCOUNT of corn received by Edward Mosely for the Publick Account. Attested: 29th December 1712. Signed by: Edward Mosely." (Ref: Hathaway, Volume 1, Number 3, page 489.)

The above is a good roster of the Planters of Chowan in 1712. It is the first roster showing that Henry Bonner (3) was an officer in the Militia.

Sometime after about 1715, Henry Bonner's (2) health began to decline. He was approximately 65 years of age and that was considered an old man in his society. By 1718, he was unable to attend to his affairs and asked assistance from the court.

"At a Court held for Chowan Precinct 15 April 1718.

Present: James Beasley; William Charlton; Thomas Luten, Junior, Esquires, JUSTICES.

Henry Bonner prays to choose his guardian. Ordered that John King be appointed his guardian, take into his custody his estate." (Ref: Hathaway, Volume 1, Number 1, page 153.) Note - John King was a physician.

It appears that in spite of poor health, Henry Bonner continued to cultivate or supervise the operation of his plantation at least until 1721. He acquired land in 1721 but he failed to cultivate the land as required by law, that being that the land must be cultivated within three years or convert back to the "government." By 1724, at the approximate age of 74 years, Henry Bonner (2) is near the end of his life.

The following can be found in, *The North Carolina Colonial Records, Volume II,* pages 522 and 523:

North Carolina - §

At a Council held at Edenton April the 9th Anno Dom 1724.
Present: The Honorable George Burrington, Esquire, Governor.

Christopher Gale	John Blount
J. Lovick	Thomas Pollock
Edward Mosely	Thomas Harvey
Francis Foster	Arthur Gosse, Esquires - Members of Council

Read the petition of **Henry Bonner, Junior**, shewing that in the year 1720 **Henry Bonner, Senior**, obtained a patent for 340 acres of land which is not cultivated as the Law prescribes and therefore prays for a lapse Patent for the said land &c.

Ordered that a Patent Issue as prayed for.

From the above, it is obvious that Henry Bonner (Sr) is still alive since he is not listed as being "deceased." After the above document was published only two Henry Bonners are shown in the records, Henry Bonner born about 1679, also shown in the records as: Captain, Major and Colonel and his son, Henry Bonner born about 1708.

It was mentioned earlier that Sheriff Thomas Bonner lived in present Beaufort County, North Carolina during most of his adult life. The kinship between him and the Chowan County Bonners is unknown but the most likely theory is that Thomas was a son of Henry Bonner (2). To skip ahead to make a point. When Thomas Bonner, son of Henry Bonner (4) emigrated to South Carolina about 1778 he went to that part of the state known as "Upper South Carolina" which is up near the mountains, probably in present day Cherokee County, near present city of Gaffney, S. C. Where did he live? Whom did he live with, if anyone? It is of record that a grandson of Sheriff Thomas Bonner, Benjamin Bonner, lived on a plantation in Upper South Carolina near the present town of Gaffney, South Carolina, where he raised a family and was buried on his plantation. Did Thomas Bonner, son of Henry Bonner (4) live with Benjamin? Did Thomas go to that part of South Carolina because he knew Benjamin?

Thomas Bonner, son of Henry (4) was allotted bounty land for his service to the American Revolution and that land was located just north of Gaffney in Cherokee County. To add more suspense to the story, it is of record that Jordan Bonner, the eldest son of Thomas Bonner, son of Henry Bonner (4) moved to present day Toxey, Choctaw County, Alabama and died there in 1841. It is also a manner of record that a grandson of Benjamin Bonner of South Carolina also lived near Toxey at the town of Gilbertown, (about three miles from Toxey) at the same time that Jordan was a resident of Choctaw County. Were all of these events just accidents or were they planned so they could be near family that they knew? The records are silent!!!

IV

Section One

HENRY BONNER (3)

(ca 1679 - 1738)

Family data: Henry Bonner (ca 1679 - 1738)
Wife: 1st: Unknown
Married: About 1700
Children: 1. Elizabeth Bonner (ca 1703 - ca 1742)
Wife:2nd: Deborah Whedbee (28 January 1689 - ca 1728)
Children: 2. Henry Bonner (ca 1708 - July 1766)
3. Deborah Bonner (ca 1724 - 1784)
4. Mary Bonner (ca 1725 - 1759)
5. Thomas Bonner (ca 1727 - 1785?)

The name of the first wife of this Henry Bonner is unknown but it is believed that she was the mother of Elizabeth Bonner, born about 1703. Henry's first wife probably died in childbirth. About 1 April 1705, Henry Bonner married Deborah Whedbee, the daughter of John and Deborah Astine-Sutton-Whedbee in Perquimans County, North Carolina.

In the absence of conflicting evidence, it is believed that Deborah was the mother of Henry's four youngest children. However, there is no explanation as to why there is such an age gap between Henry Bonner (4), born about 1708, and the remaining children. There is a possibility that, if there were children between his birth about 1708 and about 1724, they died very young and before September 1738 when Colonel Henry Bonner published his will. It is of note that the name, Deborah, does not show up in the Bonner family line until after Deborah Whedbee married into the Bonner family in 1705.

Colonel Henry Bonner was a man of prestige and wealth. He was a leader in the Colony as evidenced by the fact that he served in the Lower House of Assembly at Edenton (when Edenton was the Colonial Capitol of North Carolina). At his death in 1738, he left many plantations and slaves to his next of kin. It appears that his wealth, and that of his Chowan County Bonner Clan, was at its zenith at his death for soon afterwards the records show that most of his property was put up for sale.

The census of 1800 shows that no Bonners were living in Chowan County as head of household.

In order to set the stage for this Henry Bonner, his last will and testament has been placed at the beginning of this chapter where it can be used as a reference.

THE LAST WILL AND TESTAMENT OF HENRY BONNER

IN THE NAME OF GOD, AMEN! I, Henry Bonner of Chowan Precinct in the Province of North Carolina, PLANTER, calling to mind the uncertainty of this Life, do make and ordain this instrument of writing to be and purport my Last Will and Testament and as to what estate if hath pleased God to bless me with here, I give and Bequeath in the manner and form following, to wit:

I give to and bequeath **to my son, Henry Bonner,** all that my plantation, tract, or seat of land lying in the precinct aforesaid and where I now live with the appurtenances to him and his heirs forever. I give and bequeath all that my plantation, tract or seat of land lying in **Green Hall** in the precinct aforesaid and the appurtenances to my son, Henry Bonner and his heirs forever.

I give and bequeath **to my son, Thomas Bonner**, all these my three plantations, tracts or seats of land lying in the precinct aforesaid, commonly called and known by the names of: Brinn's, Hole's and Jones' plantations, with their appurtenances to him and his heirs forever.

I give and bequeath all that my plantation tract or seat of land lying in the precinct aforesaid commonly called by the name of Baye's plantation, **to my grandson, Richard Lewis** and his heirs forever.

I give and bequeath unto my son, Henry Bonner, all the stock of what kind soever that is now on and belonging to the aforesaid plantation in Green Hall and six Negroes called, to wit: Sam, James, Maria, Priss, Kate, and Bob. One new feather bed and furniture, one oval table, one brass kettle, six new peuter dishes, four peuter basons, six peuter sup plates, six peuter flat plates.

I give unto my son Thomas Bonner all and every of the stock that is now on and belonging to the aforesaid two plantations called Brinn's and Hole's and five Negroe slaves called, to wit: Cush, Sue, Tom, Boy, and Doll. One new feather bed and furniture, one oval table, six new pewter dishes, four pewter basons, six sup plates, six flat plates, and one mare.

I give and bequeath **to my daughter, Elizabeth Lewis**. One Negro woman slave called Grace, one new feather bed and furniture.

I give and bequeath to my grandson, Richard Lewis, a Negro girl slave called Nan.

I give and bequeath **to my daughter, Deborah Bonner**, one new feather bed and furniture and three Negroe slaves called: Minge, Simon, and Phebe.

I give and bequeath **to my daughter, Mary Bonner**, one new feather bed and furniture and three Negroe slaves called: Daniel, Dinah, and Jane.

I give and bequeath unto **my grand-daughter, Sarah Lewis**, one Negroe slave called Joan.

I give and bequeath unto **my grand-daughter, Deborah Lewis**, one Negroe slave called Moll.

I give and bequeath all the rest and residue of my personal estate **unto my said children: Henry; Thomas; Elizabeth; Deborah and Mary**, to be equally divided amongst them.

All the rest and residue of my Real Estate I order and direct my executor hereafter mentioned to dispose of and the moneys arising therefrom to be laid out for the educating and maintaining **my two daughters, Deborah and Mary in their minority** and that they live with my daughter, Elizabeth, and that she have the care and management of them.

And further it is my will and pleasure that my son Henry before the Negroes are divided between him and his brother Thomas do make or cause to be made upon one of the plantations herein bequeathed unto the said Thomas which he the said Thomas shall direct sixty thousand bricks for building a house thereon.

It is my will and pleasure **that my son, Thomas, do live with my son, Henry, during his minority** and I appoint my friend John Benbury to take care the estate herein bequeathed to the said Thomas by not in the meantime be embeziled or wasted.

And I do hereby appoint my said **son Henry Bonner to be**

executor of this my Last Will and Testament revoking and annulling all former Wills by me heretofore made and pronouncing, publishing and declaring this to be my Last Will and Testament.

In testimony whereof I have hereunto set my Hand and Seal at Chowan Precinct aforesaid the **Twenty-First day of September 1738**.

Sealed, Pronounced, Published	His
and declared in the presence of:	Henry B Bonner
Joseph Anderson	Mark
Abraham Blackall	
James Potter	
October ye 7th, 1738.	

Came before me, Dr. Abraham Blackall & James Potter & made oath that they saw Col. Henry Bonner sign seal & publish ye within as his Last Will and Testament that he was of sound & disposing mind and memory & that Mr. Joseph Anderson subscribed as a witness thereto. At the same time Mr. Henry Bonner took ye oath appointed by law to be taken by executors.

W. Smith, Clerk.

The above document is on file at the State Archives in Raleigh, North Carolina. The death of Colonel Bonner occurred between 21 September 1738, when he published his will, and before 7 October 1738 when it was probated. His illness was sudden and deadly.

The marriage of Henry Bonner (3) and Deborah Bonner took place on or about 1 April 1705 in Perquimans County, North Carolina, and the marriage is affirmed in the following court order. (Ref: *The Colonial Records of North Carolina, Volume I, 1662 - 1712,* pages 619, 620, and 621.)

"At a Court (in Perquimans Precinct) held att the House of Mr. Dennis Macclendon the 10th of Aprill 1705.

Present: The Worpll - Francis Foster; Captain James Coles; William Barcliffe; John Stepney; Dennis Macclendon, Esquires, Justices.

A new commission being published the above members take & subscribe to the Oaths appointed by Law. Thomas Snoden, Clerk of this Court takes and subscribes to the Oath appointed by Law.

Conditional bond from John Norcum & Elizabeth his wife acknowledged to Henry Warren & ordered to be recorded.

.......The Marshall was comanded to cause to come twelve true

& lawfull men &c to whom &c who neither &c by whom the matter may be found and there came: Mr. Archibald Holmes; Mr. Francis Beasley; Mr. Henry Warren; Mr. Edward Wilson; Mr. Joseph Sutton, Senior; Mr. Lawrence Megue; Mr. Henry Bonner; Mr. Joseph Sutton, Junior; Mr. Andrew Reed; Mr. Richard Burtenshall; Mr. John Falconer & Mr. Robert Hosea who impannelled & sworn say Wee of the Jury find noe case of accon. Ordered that the accon be dismist & plantiff pay costs als exo.

.....and the Marshall was comanded to cause twelve true and lawful men &c to whom &c who neither &c by whom the matter may be found and there came: Mr. Archibald Holmes; Mr. Francis Beasley; Mr. Henry Warren; Mr. Edward Wilson; Mr. Joseph Sutton, Senior; Mr. Lawrence Megue; Mr. Henry Bonner; Mr. Joseph Sutton, Junior; Mr. Andrew Reed; Mr. Richard Burtenshall; Mr. John Falconer & Mr. Robert Hoses who Impannelled & sworn say wee of the find for the plantiffe.

Upon peticon of **Henry Bonner praying the estate of Deborah Whitby his now wife** out of the hands of Dennis Macclendon, Guardian of the said Deborah.

Ordered Dennis Macclendon deliver unto the peticon all the estate of Deborah the peticon now wife into the hands & custody of the peticon."

In Chapter IV, the reader will find that the above Dennis MacClendon was the step-father to Deborah Whedbee. After Deborah's father, John Whedbee, died in 1700, Deborah's mother, Deborah Sutton Whedbee, married Dennis McClendon in 1702. As noted above, Deborah Whedbee is the "now" wife of Henry Bonner. This was the court's way of stating that Henry had been married before. Much thought has been given about which children Deborah gave birth to. The records suggest that Elizabeth Bonner was probably the oldest child, and was born to Henry's first wife. Henry (4) was next in line. Elizabeth is considered the oldest because of the way her father's Will was written. It should be noted that Elizabeth's brother, Thomas, was a minor and his inheritance was left in the hands of a trustee until he became of age. It also should be noted that Elizabeth's son, Richard Lewis, was also left a plantation but a trustee was not named and that suggests that Richard Lewis was of age which places his birth year on or before 1717 which suggests that he was the oldest of his siblings and his mother was probably born before 1701, about the time that it is estimated that Henry Bonner (3), the father, would have been about 21 years of age.

A clue to the age of Deborah Bonner, the daughter of Colonel Henry Bonner is contained in the following: "Henry Bonner had daughters. Mary and Deborah Bonner. Deborah married James Thompson, petitioned of William Lewis and wife Elizabeth - 1739." (Ref: Hathaway, Volume 2, Number 3, page 469.) By law Deborah could not marry before the age of 13 and did not need permission at age 16, which was used as the age of majority for such decisions in those days for women. This fact places Deborah's birth year between 1724 to 1726.

As noted earlier, the name "Deborah" was new to the Bonner family line and was not used as a name for the Bonner women until Henry married Deborah Whedbee in 1705. The name "Deborah" was not in any other Bonner line during this period. As the reader progresses through this family history the name "Deborah" will be noticed in many family lines that the "original" Deborah originated, she being Deborah Astine (Austin) who was born about 1652.

This Henry Bonner (3) was a Militia officer in Chowan. He was a Captain before 1712, a Major before 1725 and was promoted to Colonel about 1730.

"John Baye to Henry Bonner, 150 acres adjoining John Slocumb's line. 21 April 1713. Test: William Crawford & Ephraim Lewerton." (Ref: Hathaway, Volume 1, Number 1, page 101.)

In 1738, in his Will, Colonel Henry Bonner would leave this plantation to his grandson, Richard Lewis.

The following can be found in *Deed Book B-1,* pages 56 & 57 at the Register of Deeds Office, Chowan County Court House in Edenton, N. C:

John Slocumb
to — A Conveyance
Henry Bonner

TO ALL XTAIN people to whom these presents shall come I John Slocumb of ye County of Bath, Planter, send Greeting:

KNOW YE YET I YE said John Slocum for & in consideration of ye sum of fifty pounds current money to me in hand paid by Henry Bonner of ye Precinct of Chowan the receipt whereof I do by these presents acknowledge myself to be fully satisfied and do by these presents make bargain sell & assign forever all yet plantation or tract of lands conveying two hundred acres lying situate & being on the Northern branch of Mattacomack Creek as appear by a Pattent bearing ye (____?____).

IN WITNESS whereof I have hereunto sett my Hand and Seal this 5th day of March 1714.

Signed, Sealed & Delivered in presence of us;
Robert Heick (Hicks)
Charles Wilkins

John Slocumb

Another Bonner family whose kinship is not known to the Chowan County Bonners (by this writer) is the Bonners of Bertie County. The progenitor of that Clan was William Thomas Bonner who arrived from Nansemond County, Virginia about 1714.

The following document can be found in Book B-1, page 59 in Edenton, as noted in the location above:

Thomas Bonner to Henry Bonner - Lre of Attorney,

Know all men by these presents yt I Thomas Bonner & Elizabeth my wife of Virginia, Government in Nansemond County, doth constitute & appoint my trusty & loyall friend **Captain Henry Bonner** of Chowan Precinct in ye government of North Carolina to be there to acknowledge a Deed of Sale for fifty acres of land which bears date with aforesaid Lre of Attorney.

Witness our Hands and Seal this 18th day of October 1714.

Test: Thomas Gates
John Nairne

Thomas (TB) Bonner
Elizabeth (E) Bonner

The following is from *Deed Book B-1*, pages 57 and 58 in Edenton, NC.

Thomas Bonner
to
Samuel Pattachat (Padgett)

A Conveyance

TO ALL XTAIN people to whom these presents shall come greetings. Know ye yt I Thomas Bonner of ye government of Virginia & in ye County of Nansemond, Cordwinder (note - a Cordwinder was a shoemaker) with ye advice & consent of Elizabeth, my now wife, for & in consideration of ye sum of four pounds in hand .... unto ye said Mr. Sam'll Pattachat ...forever one mesuage & tract of land situate lying & being on ye West side of

Mattacomack Creek and containing fifty acres more or less known and call'd by the name of Thomas Bonner's Tract butted & bounds with ye Creek aforesaid surveyed in all rented with ye lands of ye said Mr. Sam'll Pattachat.

Seal'd Delivered in
presence of us, Thos TB Bonner
his Elizabeth E Bonner
Thos X Gates
Mark
John Nairne

The below document is from *Deed Book F-1*, pages 175 to 180 in Edenton.

Thomas Bonner & Wife Elizabeth Bonner
to & Power of Attorney
(To) John Homes

Know all men by these presents I Thomas Bonner of the County of Albemarle in the Precinct of Chowan in the Government of North Carolina due authorize ordain & impower John Homes my lawfull Attorney to acknowledge in Court held at Queene Anne's Town (old name for Edenton) for the said precinct one parcell of land to Leonard Langston containing one hundred acres of land and to acknowledge two acres of land to Mullford Langston...likewise Elizabeth Bonner the wife of Thomas Bonner... doth authorize John Homes to acknowledge all rights of dower....

So witness our Hands & Seals this the 14th day of July 1721.

Signed, Sealed, & Delivered
in the presence of us: Thomas Bonner
Josiah Bridges Elizabeth Bonner
William Moore

At a court held for Chowan Precinct at the court aforesaid in Edenton in Queen Anne's Creek the 18th July 1721 - The Power of Attorney from **William Bonner and Elizabeth** his wife to John Homes & is ordered to be recorded & is recorded.

Test: Thomas ___?___, Clerk of Court.

Thomas Bonner & wife Elizabeth Bonner
to DEED
Mullford Langston

TO ALL PEOPLE to whom these presents shall come

greetings and know ye that I Thomas Bonner of the County of Albemarle in the Precinct of Chowan in the Government of North Carolina on the one part & Mullford Langston of the County and Government aforesaid ...... for the sum of twenty-five pounds current money.... convey to Mullford Langston one parcell of land lying and being on the North side of Dotacofir Creek by estimation two hundred acres upon Dotacofir Creek on the South side of a branch commonly called the Spring Branch....a branch commonly called Reedy Branch to a White Oak..being a part of a tract that Thomas Bonner hath a Pattent for in his own name dated the March 9th 1718.

To have and to hold ...Elizabeth Bonner of the wife of me the said Thomas Bonner doth by these presents freely give all her rights of Dowry..

In witness whereof we have Sett our Hands and Fixed our Seals this fourteenth day of July & in the Seventh Year of the Reign of Our Sovereign Lord George of Great Britain France & Ireland, King, & in the Year of Our Lord One Thousand Seven Hundred and Twenty-one - 1721.

Signed, Sealed & Delivered in the presence of us,
Josiah Bridge
William Moore

Thomas Bonner (Seal)
Her
Elizabeth X Bonner
Mark

Test: John ___?___.

Thomas Bonner & Elizabeth Bonner
to DEED
Leonard Langston

To all to whom these presents shall come greetings & know ye that I **William Thomas Bonner** of the County of Albemarle in the Precinct of Chowan in the Government of North Carolina of the one part & Leonard Langston of the other part..for in consideration of the sum of twenty pounds...one parcell of land lying and being in the North side of the Patacisic (Pottacasey) Creek...being one part of this land being part of a parcell of land that the **said Thomas Bonner bought of Thomas Bonner, deceased,** & the other part of the said land that the said Thomas Bonner took up in his own name the Pattent being dated the Nineth of March 1718.

To Have and to Hold ... & assign affixed our Seals this 14th day of April in the Seventh Year of the Reign of Our Sovereign Lord George of Great Britain, France, & Ireland &c., in the year of our Lord God one thousand seven hundred & twenty one - 1721.

Signed Sealed and Delivered	Thomas Bonner (Seal)
in the presence of us,	Her
Josiah Bridges	Elizabeth X Bonner
William Moore	Mark

Test: John ____?____.

Att a Court held for Chowan Precinct at the Court House in Edenton in Queen Anne's Creek the 18th July 1721 ...**Thomas Bonner & Elizabeth** his wife came unto Court & acknowledge the above deed..Which in motion Ordered to be recorded & is recorded.

Thomas Hessman, Clerk Current

Notice that in the above documents how the name of Thomas Bonner is recorded. First as "William," then as "Thomas" and also as "William Thomas." It is not known whom the above "Thomas Bonner, deceased" was. The above land was situated in the western district of Chowan precinct that was taken from Chowan and designated as Bertie County in 1722. It is not known how William Thomas Bonner was related to Captain Henry Bonner but William Thomas Bonner was living in Virginia and knew of Captain Henry Bonner and trusted him to be his designated attorney. There had to be a close blood kin. William Thomas Bonner finally settled a plantation in Bertie County and died there in 1757.

(WILLIAM) THOMAS BONNER

North Carolina, Bertie County, Nig'l

IN THE NAME OF GOD, AMEN, I Thomas Bonner of the County and Province aforesaid being in my perfect senses and memory, I do to prevent disputes in my family after my desese do make this my Last Will and Testament in manner and form following:

Firstly and principally, I commend my soul to the Hands of Almighty God that gave it; and my Body to be Buried in a Christian like manner.

Secondly, I give to my well beloved son, Thomas Bonner, and his heirs one hundred acres of land, be the same more or less Lying and Being bounded on the road by Hog Pen Branch and the Knee Branch.

3'ly. I give to my well beloved daughter, Ester Moore, two hundred acres of land to her and her heirs bounded by the road and Hinton's Line and Blithenhenden line.

4'ly. I give to my son, Henry Bonner, the sum of one shilling Sterling Money of Great Britain.

5'ly. I give to my daughter, Elizabeth Wheeler, the sum of one shilling Sterling Money of Great Britain.

6'ly. I give to my daughter, Anne Byrde, the sum of one shilling Sterling Money of Great Britain.

7'ly. I give to my daughter, Sarah Wharton, the sum of one shilling, Sterling Money of Great Britain.

8'ly. I give to my daughter, Patience Byrde, the sum of one shilling, Sterling Money of Great Britain.

9'ly. I give to my son, Moses Bonner, the sum of one shilling, Sterling Money of Great Britain.

10'ly. I give to my well beloved wife, Elizabeth Bonner, all the rest of my estate, both real and personal of all kinds whatsoever, to her disposal forever; I also appoint my said wife whole and sole ex'xutrix of this my Last Will and Testament.

In witness whereof, I have set my Hand and Seal, this eleventh day of November in the year of our Lord Christ, one thousand seven hundred and fifty five.

His
Thomas X Bonner
Mark

Signed Sealed and delivered
in the presence of us,
his
Moses M. Bonner
mark
his
Edmond X Byrde
mark
Arthur Moore, jurat
Abraham Blithenden

Bertie County -§

The before written will was exhibited into court and proved by the oaths of Moses Bonner and Arthur Moore two of the subscribing witnesses thereto which was ordered to be certified.

Test: Benjamin Wynns, Clerk Current

This day personally appeared before me, Elizabeth Bonner, and was duly qualified as Executrix to the Last Will and Testament of Thomas Bonner, deceased.

Certified under my Hand this 4th day of April, anno dom 1757.

William Wynns, P. J.

The below is from *Deed Book B-1*, page 251, in Edenton.

Jones
to
Bonner

Be it known unto all men by these presents yet I William Jones of Pamplico Precinct in Bath County in the Province of North Carolina, Planter, do hereby assign ordain authorize constitute & in my stead & place do putt appoint & depute my true & trusty & well beloved friend **Captain Henry Bonner** of Chowan Precinct in the province aforesaid to be my true lawfull Deputy & Attorney for me & in my name & to my own proper use benefit & behoof to ask demand and inquire Sue for recover& receive all such debts duties sum & sums of money due & to be due arreares of rents yearly payments merchandizes legancies money due & to be due open bill of exchange of all other demands whatsoever as now are or hereafter shall be due & payable belonging of to be delivered unto me by or from any person or persons whatsoever & wheresoever & to pay money for me to contract for demise & lett to farm at the accustoms rents or more all or any of my mesuage lands tenements or hereditaments whatsoever & for default of payment or delivery of any rent or rents or other sum of money or other sum of money or other thing or things to me due is to be due or belonging to use all lawfull ways & means for recovery thereof by actions suit arrest bill plaint attachment distress reentry or otherwise fully & amply in every respect as I myself might or could do if I were personally present & to sue implead make answer prosecute & defend in any Court or Courts of Law or equity & before any judge or any justices in any suit matter or cause with me for me or against me as the cause shall require to deal & intermeddle in all actions suits affairs & business any ways touching or concerning me as my agent or factor or otherwise giving & by these presents granting unto my said Attorney full whole & lawfull authority in the execution of all & singular the premises & to substitute & appoint one or more attorney or attorneys in any of the premises & the same again at his pleasure to revoke rattifying & allowing for him effectual all & whatsoever my said attorney shall do or cause to be done.

IN WITNESS whereof I have hereunto Sett my Hand & Seall this 27th day of December Anno Dom 1714.

Sign'd Seal'd & del'd in the presence of, — William I Jones (seal)
Samuel Pattachet (Padgett)
Thomas Jones

The original of the above is in *Deed Book B-1,* page 251 in Edenton.

The below document is in *Deed Book B-1,* page 339 in Edenton.

Bonner
to — A SALE
Bonner

TO ALL XTAIN people to whom these presents shall come, I **Henry Bonner** of the Precinct of Chowan in the County of Albemarle, Gentleman, send greeting know ye yt I the said Henry Bonner for a valuable consideration to be in hand paid at & before ye ensealing and delivery hereof by **William Bonner** of the precinct & province aforesaid have give granted bargained sold aliened ensoff'd & confirm and by these presents do give grant bargain sell aliene ensoss & confirm unto the dais William Bonner his heirs & assigns forever a certain parcell of a tract of land lying situate & being in Chowan Precinct on the North Side of Mattacomack Creek butting and Bounding to the Eastward on the land of the William Bonner to be westward by a line of marked trees to the southward on Mattacomack Creek & to the Northward by one line of marked trees containing one hundred acres be the same more or less the said land being part of a larger tract purchased of John Slocumb ..the said land being part of a larger tract mentioned in a Pattent bearing date of 19th January 1716.

IN WITNESS whereof I have hereunto Sett my Hand & Seal the 17th April 1716.

Signed, Sealed and delivered in the presence of, — Henry Bonner
John Nairne
Thomas Luten, Jr.

Note - The above tract of land was purchased from John Slocumb on 5 March 1714.

The below document is in *Deed Book B-1*, page 571 in Edenton.

Wallstone
to
Bonner

A SALE

To all to whom these presents shall come I William Wallstone of Chowan Precinct, Cooper (note - a barrel maker), sends greetings, know ye yt I the said William Wallstone for a valuable consideration to me in hand paid by **Captain Henry Bonner,** of ye same place the receipt whereof I do hereby acknowledge & of every part & parcell thereof do hereby acquaint exonorate & discharge the said Henry Bonner his heirs...a parcell of land containing two hundred acres by the same more or less lying in Chowan Precinct on the North East side of the Tanyard Swamp in **Green Hall** between the lands of said Henry Bonner and the lands of Edward Champion.....

I bind myself my heirs & c in the sum of fifty pounds current money witness my Hand the 22d day of July 1718.

Signed, sealed & delivered
Robert Hicks

Wm. Wallstone

[The above tract of land was granted to William Wallstone (also spelled Walston) on 17 April 1697, "200 acres on Mattacomack Creek Swamp at Green Hall."]

There are no records describing the types of road in the Colony. One can only imagine that they were mostly cleared paths through the woods and circled the fields. However, the men of the colony were responsible to keep the paths clear and usable. The following explains how the courts handled such an important part of their infrastructure.

"At a Court held for Chowan Precinct 15 October 1717, at the house of William Branch.

"Present: James Beasley; William Charlton; John Jordan; Thomas Garrett; John Dove; John Holbrook; Henry Speller; Thomas Luten, Jr., Esquires, Justices.

"Upon the petition of the inhabitants of Green Hall. Ordered that a road be cleared out from Evan's to John Jones's landing and that Richard Lewis, John Jones, Sr; Francis Branch; Thomas Jones; Henry Jones; Richard Fullinton; Orlando Champion; William Sadler, John Jones, Jr.; Samuel Patchett, William Fallow and **Henry Bonner** be appointed a jury to lay out the same." (Ref: Hathaway, Volume 1, Number 1, page 152.)

The above Richard Lewis was the father of William Lewis who was married to Elizabeth Bonner, daughter of Colonel Henry Bonner.

The judicial system of the North Carolina Colony was strict when compared to the liberal rulings of today's courts. The following can be found in, *The Colonial Records of North Carolina, Volume II,* page 339 for the year 1719.

(Madalin Collar was in Court for the murder of her baby). "She was found guilty of privately delivered of a bastard child born alive and the next morning did bury the child by force against the peace and aginst the Royall Crown and dignity and against the laws and Statues." Madlin Collar pleaded guilty and was found guilty by: Henry Bonner; Henry Speller; Patrick Warde; Thomas Luten, Jr; Thomas Paris; Francis Branch; William Bonner; William Haughton; Lewis Skinner; William Haurth; John Falconer; and Thomas Yates. "She is guilty of Murder and Judged to be Hanged." It is assumed that she was, in fact, hanged.

The tax list for 1721 shows that Henry Bonner paid taxes on 990 acres of land and Thomas Bonner paid taxes on 600 acres. Thomas Bonner lived in now Bertie County.

"Christopher Gale; Edward Mosely; John Lovick, Commissioners of Edenton.

To: Henry Bonner; William Charlton; John Alston; William Badham; John Crisp; Joseph Frasier; James Long, and Joseph Blount, Justices of the Peace for the Precinct of Chowan and their successors and in behalf of the Precinct for their said use for meeting and building a Court House. Lots 58 & 59. 3d May 1723. Test: John Palin & William Badham." (Ref: Hathaway, Volume 1, Number 1, page 122.)

The below can be found in *The Colonial Records of North Carolina, Volume II, 1713 to 1728,* pages 575 and 576.

THE JOURNAL OF THE LOWER HOUSE OF ASSEMBLY

BEGUN THE 1st of NOVEMBER 1725

North Carolina - §

Att a General Biennial Assembly held at Edenton, the 1st of November 1725.

Present in the Lower House

Col. George Pennington; **Major Henry Bonner**; Col Cullen Pollock; Capt. William Downing; Mr. Edmond Porter; Mr. Joseph Jessop; Mr. Thomas Speight; Mr. Charles Denman; Mr. Samuel Phelps; Mr. Samuel Swann; Col. Thomas Swann; Mr. Winright (Wainwright); Mr. McCory Scarboro; Mr. John Baptiste Ashe; Col. Maurice Moore; Col. William Maule; Mr. Arthur Gosse; Mr. James Castellaw; Mr. Isaac Hill; Mr. Thomas Parris.

Col. Maurice Moore is Chosen Speaker, nem: contradicente

Robert Hicks is appointed Clerk; John Falconer (is appointed) Messenger and H. Savage (is appointed) Doorkeeper to this House...

Adjourned till morning 10 a clock.

THE JOURNAL OF THE LOWER HOUSE OF ASSEMBLY

MET IN APRIL 1726

North Carolina - §

Att a General Biennial Assembly held att Edenton the 5th of April 1726 the following members meet at the Usuall Place at Queen Anne's Creek in Chowan Precinct according to Adjornment.

George Burrington, Esquire; **Major Henry Bonner**; Col. Cullen Pollock; Capt. William Downing; Mr. Edmond Porter; Mr. Joseph Jessop; Mr. Samuel Swann; Mr. Charles Denman; Mr. McCory Scarboro; Mr. Robert Morgan; Mr. James Winwright; Mr. Gabriel Burham; Capt. Joseph Sanderson; Mr. Richard Church; Mr. John Woodhouse; Mr. John Baptiste Ashe; Doctor Patrick Maule; Mr. Isaac Hill; Mr. James Castellaw; Mr. Thomas Parris.

Robert Route, Esquire lay'd before the House the following returns: For Chowan (precinct): George Burrington, Esquire; Edmond Porter; Cullen Pollock; William Downing; **Henry Bonner**.

......and upon their return sent the following message to the Upper House. To the Honorable the Governor & Council being the Upper House of Assembly: May it please your Honors: This House is ready to receive such members of your House as it shall be appointed at their Qualifications, per order of the House. Robert Hicks, CDC

Sent per Major Bonner & Mr. Porter.

The above can be found in *The Colonial Records of North Carolina, Volume II, 1713 to 1728*, pages 622 and 623.

Charges of the assembly including that in November last, with attendance & comings and goings from the assembly.

IN THE LOWER HOUSE, CHOWAN

	Days	L	s.
George Burrington	15	7	10
Edmond Porter	15	7	10
Henry Bonner	15	7	10
Cullen Pollock	15	7	10
William Downing	15	7	10

The above George Burrington would be elected Governor of North Carolina.

The below is from *The North Carolina Colonial Records, Volume II, 1713 to 1728,* pages 687, 688, and 689.

North Carolina - §

"To Christopher Gale, Esquire, Chief Justice & the rest of the Justices of the General Court begun & held at Edenton the last Tuesday in March One Thousand Seven Hundred and Twenty Seven:

.......(Edmond Porter)... & also did further contemptously speak of Mr. Thomas Speight and **Major Henry Bonner, both Assistant Justices of the General Court & Members of the Lower House of Assembly at the last sessions** (in 1726) insinuating & declaring & declaring that they were not fitt to be chosen nor should be chosen Burgesses at another election because they had taken a Commission under the Governor..."

MEMBERS OF THE ASSEMBLY OF NORTH CAROLINA

1727

North Carolina - §

At a Genn'll Biennial Assembly held at Edenton began 6th November 1727.

In the Upper House

Sir Richard Everard, Captain Generall & Commander in Chief; Christopher Gale; John Lovick; Edward Mosely; Richard Sanderson; Francis Foster; Thomas Pollock; Thomas Harvey;

Robert West; Edmond Gales; John Worley, Esquires, Members of the Council, being in the Upper House.

In the Lower House

Major Henry Bonner, William Downing; William Badham; Cullen Pollock; Jeremiah Vail; Joseph Jessop; Samuel Swann; Thomas Bell; Richard Skinner, Sr; Samuel Swann; McCory Scarborough; Griffin Jones; Robert Morgan; Gabriel Burham; Richard Church; Jon Etheridge; Thomas Williams; Thomas Davis; Mo Linton; John Baptiste Ashe; Jacob Blount; T. Smith; Mar Franks; Will Hancock; James Wainwright; Enoch Ward; George Pollock; Isaac Hill; Arthur Williams; James Castellaw; Edward Howard; Will Little; Mar. Rowan.

The above names appear as the Preamble to an Act of Assembly confirming the title to a tract to Orlando Champion, which said tract was known as Slocumbs lying ----- about 4 miles North of Edenton, it having been the property of Anthony Slocumb (grandfather of John Slocumb, late of Neuse River in Bath County), who by will entailed the same 620 acres on John Slocumb, his son and the Heirs Male of his body, the said John entered and was seized in fee simple and John the grandson of Anthony sold the same for a valuable consideration to Francis Branch, and Orlando Champion, under said Branch, became the purchaser, and held it for the past 15 years, the said John, grandson of Anthony purposing to settle in fee tayle, other lands at Neuse of greater value to the use of the Last Will and Testament of his Grandfather, aforesaid, the said John the grandson did make a Deed of his lands at Neuse to the use of next Heir but before the said John the Grandson could perfect the Title of the Entailed Lands at Chowan Precinct to the said Orlando Champion the said John the Grandson departed this life & John Slocumb his son & Heir entered into and upon the lands at Neuse and was thereof possessed and accepted of the same in the Room of the Entailed Lands now in the hands of said Orlando Champion, as he now proves and makes appear. Be it therefore Enacted, &c.

Registered, the 20th June per me HENRY BONNER

Captain John Baptiste Ashe, Speaker

Christopher Gale; John Lovick; Edward Mosely; Richard Sanderson; Thomas Pollock; Thomas Harvey; Robert West; Edmund Gale.

The above item is from *Book W, Number 1*, page 344, Register of Deeds Office at Edenton, North Carolina.

The following can be found in *Deed Book* ____, page 492 in Edenton.

Henry Bonner

to A DEED

Orlando Champion

TO ALL TO WHOM shall come I Henry Bonner of Chowan Precinct in the Province aforesaid send greetings &c.

Know Ye Yt, I the said Henry Bonner for & in consideration of the sum of twenty five pounds current money of the said province to me in hand paid before the ensealing hereof by Orlando Champion of the same precinct & province the act whereof I do hereby acknowledge & myself therewith fully satisfied & contended & thereby of every part & parcell thereof do acquitt...forever a parcell of land lying & being in Chowan Precinct on the west side of Slocumb's Creek on the southwest of a branch or swamp issuing therefrom commonly known & called by the name of Filburd's (Filbert's) Swamp beginning at the mouth of the said Swamp running the said line & swamp till it crosses the path which leads to the said Champion's Plantation & contains all the land between the said line & the land of the said Orlando Champion containing by estimation twenty acres...

IN WITNESS WHEREOF I have hereunto sett my Hand & Seal this 21st day of Feb'y 1725.

Signed, sealed and delivered Henry Bonner (Seal)
in presence of,
Robert Hicks
Thomas Jones

The following is from *Deed Book C-1,* pages 495 and 496 in Edenton.

John Jones
to A DEED
Henry Bonner

TO ALL TO WHOME these presents shall come I John Jones of Chowan Precinct in the County of Albemarle and province aforesaid send greetings, &c.

Know yee yt I the said Jno Jones for & in consideration of the sum of one hundred pounds current money of the said province to be well & truly unto the said Jno Jones his heirs ...assigns at four severall payments to at the times hereafter mentioned, viz:

Twenty five pounds by the 25, of this instant January;

Twenty five pounds more by the 25 of December which shall be in year of our Lord 1726;

Twenty five pounds more by the 25 of December in the year 1727 and;

Twenty five pounds more which shall be paid by the 25 of December in the year of our Lord 1728.

By Major Henry Bonner of the precinct aforesaid...confirm unto the said Henry Bonner...all that my plantation or parcell of land lying on the western most branch of Mattacomack Creek in Chowan Precinct bounded to the eastward by the line of marked trees dividing it from the land of Thomas Jones to the westward by the land late in the possession of John Padgett to the northward by the land of the said Henry Bonner & to the southward by a branch of the said creek containing by estimation one hundred and twenty five acres be the same more or less together with all the houses, buildings, gardains, orchards, fencing and all the other appurtenances...provided never the less that the said Jno Jones & Elizabeth his wife shall have the liberty of building, clearing fencing tending and raising stock on the said plantation during their natural lives & shall have one half of the benefits of the orchard and what part of the ground that is now cleared the said Jno Jones thinks fitt to fence & tend.

AND IT FURTHER provided yt the said Henry Bonner may have the liberty of such a part of the barns as shall be sufficient to house what crops of grains & other things he shall make on the other part of the said land not fenced & tended by the said Jno Jones.

IN WITNESS WHEREOF I the said Jno Jones have hereunto putt my Hand and Seal the 8th day of January 1726.

Signed, sealed & delivered John I Jones
Robert Hicks
Elizabeth E Baker
Chowan January Court 1726

The above Deed of Sale was proved by the oath of Robert Hicks one of the evidences thereto & ordered to be Registered.

Test: Robert Foster, Clerk Current

The above document is excellent evidence of the generosity of Henry Bonner which must have had a positive impact of his neighbors. The records also show that John Jones's will was probated in 1727 and his wife was not listed in the will which indicated she died just before John. In the last will and testament of Henry Bonner in 1738, this plantation was left to his son, Thomas, and was called the Jones's Plantation.

The below is from: *Old Albemarle County, North Carolina Miscellaneous Records, 1678-1737,* by Weynette Parks Haun, where the following is found. Copied as is:

"His Excelly John Lord Carteret Palatine and the Rest of the true and absolute Lords propRs. Of Carolina. To all to whom these pRsents shall come Greeting in our Lord God Everlasting KNOW YE that We the said Lords and absolute propRs. According to our Great Deed of Grant bearing Date the first day of May anno Dom: 1668. Given to our County of Albamarle under our Hands and Great Seal of our said Province Do hereby give and grant unto MAJOR HENRY BONNER of our said County a Tract of Land containing One Hundred and Thirteen Acres lying in Chowan Prect: begining at the Head of Mattacomack Creek begining at the side of the Swamp Runing up the sd BONNERS line E.S.E. 320 pole to a White Oak then S. 52W pole to a Saplin Pine in John Jones head line then along his line S.S.W.10 pole to a Pine then W.N.W. 320 pole to the Swamp thence to the first station.

To have and to hold the said Land with all Rights and privileges of hunting hawking fishing and fowling with all Woods Waters and Rivers with all Profits Commodities and Hereditaments to the Same belong or appertaining (Except one half of all Gold and Silver Mines) unto him the said HENRY BONNER his Heirs and Assigns for Ever in as large and ample Manner to all Intents and Purposes as in and by the said Deed is granted or Intended _____ding and Paying unto Us our Heirs and Successors Yearly every twenty Nineth Day of September the ffee Rent of One Shilling for every fifty acres hereby granted to ne Holden of Us our Heirs and Successors in free and common Soccage PROVIDED that if the said HENRY BONNER Shall not Seat and Plant or cause to be Seated and planted thereon within three Years after the Date hereof then this patent to be void otherwise to Stand and be of full force.

Given under the Seal of the Colony the 29th Day of JanRy, Anno Dom: 1730. Witness our trusty and well beloved Councellrs. Who have hereunto sett their Hands. Richd. EVERARD, Jno. PALIN, C. GALE, Edmd. GALE, Robert WEST."

The following is from *Deed Book C-1,* page 728 in Edenton.
North Carolina
TO ALL TO WHOM these presents shall come I Gabriel Cozand of Chowan Precinct in the County of Albemarle and Precinct aforesaid send greetings &c.

KNOW YE YET I the Gabriel Cozand for & in consideration of the sum of Tenn pounds current money of the said province to well & truly paid unto the said Gabriel Cozand his heirs, executors and administrators or assign bargain & sold a certain bit of land to **Henry Bonner** his heirs executors and administrators forever in precinct containing fifteen acres be it more less bounded with Major (Thomas) Luten's line & Richard Lewis's line bounded by a skirt of the Bear Garden pecoson bounded by ye **Hole's** line and Francis Branch's line.

I the said Gabriel Cozand have hereunto putt my hand and seal this 18th of December 1732.

Signed, sealed and delivered Gabriel Cozand
in the presence of,
Jane Phillips
Henry Bonner, Junior

1 January 1734

Gabriel Cozand came this day before me & acknowledge the writ in Deed to Henry Bonner in due form of law.

W. Smith, Clerk Justice

The following very interesting Deed of Sale in from *Deed Book W,* page 280 in Edenton. Reading between the lines of the endorsement it can be seen that the Court was well received of Colonel Bonner and his excellent reputation within the Colony.

Indians
to A SALE
Bonner

TO ALL TO WHOM these presents shall come know ye the we; James Bennett, Thomas Hoyter & Jeremiah Pushing of Chowan Precinct, Indians, for & in consideration of the sum of Eighty pounds current money of North Carolina to us in hand paid before the ensealing & delivery of these presents by Henry Bonner of ye precinct & province aforesaid, Planter, the receipt whereof we do hereby acknowledge & therefore do by these presents have granted bargained & sold alien ensossed & confirm

& by these presents....unto the said Henry Bonner his heirs...forever a certain parcel of land lying in Chowan Precinct beginning at the Miery Branch & running down the Creek Swamp in length a mile & running out in breadth half a mile containing in the whole by estimation three hundred & twenty acres be the same more or less the said land is taken out of a larger tract formerly given to them & their heirs forever by the Honorable Governor & Council of the Province.

TO HAVE AND TO HOLD the said land so bounded as aforesaid unto the said Henry Bonner....

IN WITNESS WHEREOF we the said James Bennett, Thomas Hoyter & Jeremiah Pushing have hereunto set our Hands & Seals this 15th day of December 1735.

Signed, sealed & delivered
in the presence of us,
"At a Council held at
Edenton, 16th December 1735"

James IN Bennett
Thomas TH Hoyter
His
Jeremiah U Pushing
Mark
John I Baley
John R Robins
His
John IR Reding
Mark

Read the Petition of **Col Henry Bonner** set forth that he had purchased of the **Chowan Indians** a certain tract or parcel of land lying & being in ye precinct & praying the same may be confirmed a certain tract of land from the said Nation to the said Bonner which was read & the Indians being interogated thereon declared they had received the consideration money therein mentioned & were therewith fully satisfied whereupon his Excellancy by & with the Advice of the Board was pleased to allow & approve the sale to Col. Henry Bonner.

A true copy,

Nathaniel Rice, Clerk Current

ST. PAUL'S CHURCH, EDENTON, NORTH CAROLINA

"On April 26th, 1736 . Being Easter Monday, the vestry and parishners having met proceeded to chuse a new Vestry agreeable to law and by pole chose William Smith, Esquire; John Montgomery, Esquire; Robert Forster, Esquire; J. Hodgson, Esquire; **Henry Bonner**, Thomas Luten; Edmund Gale; Abraham

Blackall; Joseph Anderson; Henry Baker; John Sumner; Samuel Padgett. Duly qualified themselves vestrymen by taking the Oaths By Law directed, and chosed Abra'm Blackall & **Henry Bonner, Church Wardens** for the ensuring year, then the vestry by plurality of vote chose **Henry Bonner, Jr., Clerk of the Vestry** who was duly qualified by taking the public oaths by law directed. Ordered that a Vestry be held this day fortnight &c. Abraham Blackall, Warden. (Ref: Hathaway, Volume 1, Number 1, page 126.)

"Aaron Blanchard to my kinsman Abraham Blanchard, 250 acres on Indian Swamp. 22 August 1736. Test: **Henry Bonner, Senior; Henry Bonner, Junior**, George Pulley." (Ref: Hathaway, Volume 3, Number 1, page 129.) (Author's note - This is the same Blanchard family whose descendent, Nancy Applewhite, married into the Bonner family in Georgia).

FOOTNOTES

Colonel Henry Bonner's family consisted of the following known children:

1. Son. Henry Bonner, died in 1766. He was the executor of his father's estate.

2. Daughter. Elizabeth Bonner, married William Lewis, son of Richard Lewis. Children: Deborah Lewis, Sarah Lewis, Richard Lewis. It is believed that Elizabeth died between 1739 and 1742. There is mention of a William Lewis that is married to a daughter of Francis Branch in 1742.

3. Daughter, Deborah Bonner, married James Thompson in 1739.

"Deborah Thompson, Chowan. 14th August 1784. Son. Thomas; daughter-in-law, Elizabeth Thompson; grandson, James Halsey. Son, Thomas named executor. Test: Thomas Bonner, Mary Bonner." (Ref: Hathaway, Volume 2, Number 1, page 30.)

The above named Thomas Bonner was Deborah's brother and Mary was Thomas's wife.

Deborah Bonner Thompson's husband, James, passed away in 1764.

"James Thompson, Chowan. 12th January 1764. Son: Henry. Wife: Deborah, sons James and Thomas. Daughters Elizabeth

Halsey,. My small children (unnamed). Test: John Lewis, Henry Bonner." (Ref: Hathaway, Volume 2, Number 1, page 29.) The above Henry Bonner was a brother-in-law to James who had married Deborah, sister of Henry Bonner. John Lewis died in the early part of 1776. His will was probated on 25 June 1776.

4. Daughter, Mary Bonner. Mary never married and nothing is known of her. She is listed in the records as a legatee of her father, in a land deed that was sold for her education and her own Last Will and Testament.

"Mary Bonner, Chowan. Will published 30 January 1759. Probated in July Court 1759. Sister, Deborah Thompson. My two brothers and sisters. Test: John Lewis, Sr., John Lewis, Jr." (Ref: Hathaway, Volume 1, Number 2, page 183.) Notice that Mary's sister, Elizabeth, is not named. Her two brothers were, Henry and Thomas. Her two sisters must have been her nieces, Sarah and Deborah Lewis with whom she lived with as a minor.

5. Son, Thomas Bonner, Known in the legal records after 1767 as "Thomas Bonner, Sr." He may be the Thomas Bonner who married Mary Standing on 14 February 1752. He died in 1785.

"Thomas Bonner, Chowan. 2 February 1785. Wife, Mary. Executors, William Roberts, Richard Hoskins, and Edmund Blount. Test: Mary Badham, William Ellis." (Ref: Hathaway, Volume 1, Number 4, page 519.) Since William Roberts is named it is believed that this Thomas Bonner was a son of Colonel Henry Bonner. William Roberts married his sister-in-law, Elizabeth Hardy Bonner in February 1767.

IV

Section Two

DEBORAH ASTINE

(ca 1652 - 1732)

It is this lady who furnished the blood line to the Bonner family in 1705. It is not known who her parents were although there are hints. The following people immigrated to the New World at a time that she could be related to:

1. Living at James City in 1624 - Robert Austine.

2. Arriving on the ship "Hercules" of Sandwich, Kent in April 1635 - Jonas Austen of Tenderden and Constance, his wife, and children: Jonas Austen, Lidia Robinson and ______ Austen, a little child.

3. Arriving on the ship, "Speedwell" of London to Virginia, 28 May 1635, Edward Austin, 26 years of age.

4. Arriving on the ship, "Elizabeth" from London to Virginia 1 August 1635, John Austin, 24 years of age.

5. Arriving from Southampton to New England in May 1638, Richard Auston of Bishopstroke, (Hants), a tailor 40 years of age, his wife & 2 children and a servant, Robert Knight, a carpenter.

Based on the above and of the fact that a Robert Austin and his wife, Sarah, were living in Perquimans Precinct at the same time as Deborah, tends to make one believe that Robert Austine who arrived in 1624 may be the father of Deborah and Robert. There is no proof. Remember that names were spelled phonetically in those days.

"William Chelsie and Sarah Austen, daughter of Robert and wife Sarah, were married 1 April 1696 by Major Samuel Swann." (Ref: Hathaway, Volume 3, Number 3, page 427.)

Sarah Austen, wife of Robert died 4 February 1697. (Idem, Volume 3, Number 3, page 402.)

Exactly when Deborah arrived in Perquimans is unknown but she came to Perquimans as a married woman.

"Nathaniel Suton and Deborah Astine was married by Mr. Babb, Minister of the Gospel at Nantimum (Nansemond County) in Verginia the 12th of August 1668," (Ref: Hathaway, Volume 3, Number 2, page 200.)

Family Status: Deborah Astine (ca 1652 - 1732)

Husband: 1st: Nathaniel Sutton (ca 1650 - 29 December 1682)

Children:

1. George Sutton (2 March 1669 - 11 March 1699)
2. Joseph Sutton (6 August 1673 - 10 March 1723)
3. Rebecca Sutton (8 August 1676 - after 1719)
4. Nathaniel Sutton (29 August 1681 - 1 April 1725)

THE SUTTON CHILDREN

1. George Sutton
Wife: Rebecca ______.
Children:

a. Rebecca Sutton (14 November 1694 -
b. Richard Sutton (12 September 1697 -
Wife: Mary ____
Children:(1). William Sutton (5 March 1720 -
(2). Richard Sutton (9 December 1722 -
(3). Mary Sutton (23 June 1726 -
(4). Elizabeth Sutton (2 March 1729 -
(5). Sarah Sutton (20 December 1730 -
c. Deborah Sutton (2 January 1699 - 18 December 1728)
Husband: William Wood
When: 8 May 1718 by Dr. Urmstone, Minister of the Church of England.
Children: (1). Richard Wood (30 October 1720 -
(2). Sarah Wood (23 October 1721 - 21 March 1723)
(3). William Wood (2 September 1724 -
(4). Deborah Wood (25 March 1726 -
(5). Rebecca Wood (3 June 1727 -
(6). Elizabeth Wood (18 December 1728 -

Deborah Sutton Wood, born 2 January 1699 - died on 18 December 1728, following the birth of her daughter, Elizabeth.

2. "Joseph Sutton (born 6 August 1673) married Parenthia Durant, daughter of George Durant, the elder and Ann Marwood, on 18 June 1695, by Mr. John Durant, Justice." (Ref: Hathaway, Volume 3, Number 3, page 407.) George Durant was the same George Durant involved in the Culpepper Rebellion of 1677/1679.

Children: a. George Sutton (2 August 1696 -
b. Elizabeth Sutton (15 September 1703 -
c. Parthenia Sutton (8 August 1705 -

3. Rebecca Sutton, born 6 August 1676, married at least two times.

1st: "Jacob Paterson (Peterson), son of Jacob and Rebecca Sutton daughter of Nathaniel and wife Deborah were married 30 September 1695 by Mr. Joseph Sutton, Jr." (Reg: Hathaway, Volume 3, Number 3, page 406.) Rebecca's husband, Jacob Peterson passed away in 1696, although the records are dated 1697.

"Jacob Peterson. Will probated 17 May 1697. Wife: Rebecca. Test: Edward Golff." (Ref: Hathaway, Volume 1, Number 3, page 369.)

"Jacob Peterson, Perquimans. 13 Jan'y 1697. Daughter-in-law, Rebecca Bond (Bird), late wife of my son, Jacob. Daughters, Elizabeth, Constance, Ann. Wife: Mary, executrix." (Ref: Idem, Volume 1, Number 3, page 369.)

"James Cole, son of James of Nancemum in Verginia, and Mary Peterson, relict of Jacob Peterson, Sr., was married 16 July 1698." (Reg: Idem, Volume 3, Number 3, page 408.)

2nd: "John Bird and Rebecca Peterson, relict of Jacob, were married 24 August 1697, by John Burnett, Minister." (Ref: Idem, Number 1, Number 3, page 369.)

"John Byrd & wife Rebecca Adx of the estate of Jacob Peterson, Jr, deceased (1704)." (Ref: Idem, Volume 1, Number 4, page 612.)

"John Bird, Chowan Precinct, 13 September 1716. Probated October Court 1716. Named: Sons, John Bird, born 22 July 1698; Edward Bird, born 6 January 1702; William Bird; Richard Bird. Wife: Rebecca Bayard (Bird); Anne Bird; Richard and __?___ Bayard, child in esse; Wife Rebecca Bayard and John Hardy, exx.

Test: John Crombie, Susanna Williams, Mary Pamvell." (Ref: Idem, Volume 1, Number 2, page 172.)

4. Nathaniel Sutton, born 29 August 1681, may have never married. In his last will and testament he does not mention a wife or children.

"Nath'l Sutton. March 1725. Probated 2 April 1725. Names: John Bird; Ruth Glaister; Joseph, son of my brother Joseph Sutton; Elizabeth Whedbee, daughter of Richard Whedbee; Cousin, Parenthia Sutton; James Anderson, senior; Cousin Thomas Sutton's two children (not named); Cousin George Sutton and Richard Whedbee; Rebecca Carr's children (not named); Brother Richard Whedbee and cousin Thomas Sutton, Executor's." (Ref: Idem, Volume 1, Number 1, page 76.)

Nathaniel Sutton, the elder, was a young man when he died in 1682. He passed away just a few days after publishing his will.

"Nathaniel Sutton, Perquimans. 16th December 1682. Probated 12th March 1683. Sons: Joseph and Nathaniel; cousin, John Gosby; Son, George. Daughter, Rebekkah. Wife, exx. Test: Edward Poulter, John Kinse." (Ref: Idem, Volume 1, Number 4, page 486.)

"Nathaniel Sutton, late of this county, Departed this life ye 29th of Desember 1682." (Ref: Idem, Volume 3, Number 3, page 366.)

Life for the early settlers of the Carolina Colony was not easy. Sometimes death was literally around the next corner because of diseases, wild animals, Indian Wars and raids, coupled with the hazards of the sounds, rivers and creeks; all played a part to shorten a life. Many times food was contaminated and poison to the unaware colonist. Sanitation many times took a back seat to expediency. Often times a settler or a member of his family became ill and went to the nearest home for treatment or medication. Many died at a home, not their own, and were buried there. There are many notations in the records that "x" died at his own house, or "x" died at "x's" house and was buried there. Maybe they were just visiting or traveling on business and became ill and went to the nearest house for treatment, whatever the reason it happened.

"Thomas Foultner Departed this Life ye 12th of November 1683 at the house of Deborah Sutton." (Ref: Idem, Volume 3,

Number 3, page 366,)

Deborah Astine Sutton married second, John Whedbee.

"John Whedby ye son of Richard Whedbee and Elizabeth his wife Late of Virginia and Deborah Suton ye Relict of Nathaniel Suton were married by Mr. John Right, Minister ye tenth of Maye 1685." (Ref: Idem, Volume 3, Number 2, page 206.)

"John Whedbee died on 5 April 1700." (Ref: Idem, Volume 3, Number 3, page 403.)

"A General Court was held in Perquimans September 1700, before ye Honable Sam'l Swann, Sect'y of State, Mrs. Deborah Whedbee administered on ye estate of her husband, Jno Whedbee." (Ref: Idem, Volume 2, Number 2, page 302.)

"John Lilly died 17 July 1701, att ye widow Whedbee's house." (Ref: Idem, Volume 3, Number 3, page 403.)

"Dennis MackClenden married Mrs. Deborah Whedbe (before July 1702)." (Ref: Idem, Volume 1, Number 4, page 609.)

In 1702, the following was recorded in Court in Perquimans County.

"Francis Foster and Joseph Sutton were guardian to Richard Whedbee and Deborah Whedbee, the mother of these children married 2d (actually 3d) Dennis McClenden. John Stepney, Clerk of Court." (Ref: Idem, Volume 3, Number 2, page 256.)

"Joseph Sutton, Guardian of Richard Whedbee (1702)." (Ref: Idem, Volume 1, Number 4, page 610.) Note - Joseph and Richard were brothers.

"At a Court held at the house of James Cole (in 1702) Deborah Whedbee chose Joseph Sutton as her guardian." (Ref: Idem, Volume 1, Number 1, page 609.) Note - Joseph and Deborah were brother and sister.

Perquimans -§

Att a court held att the house of Mrs. Deborah MacClendon

the 9th Day of July anno dom 1706.

Present: The Worpll Captain James Cole,
Thomas Long,
Joseph Sutton, Sr.,
William Long, Esquires, Justices.

Ordered that Nathaniel Nicholson be one of the apprisors of the estate of John Anderson, deceased, in the stead & room of Dennis MacClenden, deceased.

Ordered that this Court be adjourned till the 2d Tuesday in August next ensuring to the House of James Thickpen in Perquimans River & that all process be directed thereto.

His James Cole Mark	His Thos I Long Mark
His Joseph I Sutton Mark	His William W Long Mark

Deborah Astine-Sutton-Whedbee-McClenden's Last Will and Testament is on file at the Archives in Raleigh, North Carolina under the name "Deborah Mackclenden."

DEBORAH McCLENDEN. 28 February 1729. Probated 1732.

IN THE NAME OF GOD, AMEN. I Deborah Mackclenden. Widow of Perquimans Precinct in North Carolina, going in health and perfect in Memory Praise to God for the same & knowing the uncertainty of this Life and desirous to settle my affairs in order doe make this my last will & testament in manner and form following.

That is to say, First I command my soul to God who gave it and my Body to the Earth to be decently buried according to the direction of my executor hereafter named _______ as touching my worldly estate I have as followth - viz: I give and bequeath to my grandson Joseph Sutton six pounds in good species to be paid by my executor.

Item - I give to my son Richard Whedbee all the remaining part of my estate both real & personal be it what kind soever & Lastly,

I do appoint my son Richard Whedbee my sole executor to this my last will & testament revoking all former wills by me heretofore made acknowledging this to be my last will & testament as witness my Hand & Seal this twenty eighth day of February 1728/29.

Signed sealed &	Her
pronounced in the	Deborah O MackClenden
presence of us,	Mark

Charles Denman
James Anderson, Senior
James Anderson, Junior

Perquimans Precinct - At a Court held October the 15th 1732, the written will was proved by oath of James Anderson, Senior and James Anderson, Junior evidences thereto who disposes they saw Charles Denman sign the same as evident the executor being present took the Executor's Oath as the law prescribes.

Test: Charles, Clerk of Court

Since only Richard Whedbee is listed in his mother's will it is believed that he was her only surviving child. If so then daughter Deborah Whedbee who married Henry Bonner in 1705, probably was dead before 28 February 1728/29. Richard Whedbee lived just a few more years and died at the age of 59.

"Richard Whedbee, Perquimans. Probated July Court 1746. Sons, John, Richard, and George. Daughters, Elizabeth Pratt, Deborah Wilkins. Ann Foster. Sons, Benjamin and Joseph. Wife: Hannah, brother-in-laws Christian Reed and Joseph Reed, Executors. Test: Samuel Snowden, Elizabeth Reed and Catherine Davis." (Ref: Hathaway, Volume 1, Number 4, page 509.)

It is known that Richard's first wife, Sarah Durant, died on 4 April 1728. The above document gives the last name of his second wife, Hannah, since he names his brother-in-laws. Therefore, Hannah's last name was Reed.

IV

Section Three

John Whedbee

(ca 1640 - 1700)

In the notice of his marriage to Deborah Sutton, published in Perquimans County, North Carolina, the names of John Whedbee's parents are listed. There is strong evidence that John's father was Richard Whitby who was living at Hogg Island, Virginia in 1624. John had a son that was named, Richard which suggests that a family relationship to Richard Whedbee of Hogg Island. In a Deed of Gift to his children, Richard and Deborah, he names a brother, George Whedbee. Richard, son of John Whedbee, had sons, John and George which suggests that the Richard Whitby of Hogg Island, Virginia was, in fact, his grandfather and that Richard, son of John, was named after his grandfather.

In Virginia there was a notorious Indian Raid in March 1623 where almost one-half of the settlers were killed. In 1624, a census was ordered to see who had been killed and to see who had survived.

"16 February 1624, List of the names of the living in Virginia and of those who have died since April 1623. Living at Hogg Island, Virginia - Richard Whitby." No age was given. (Ref: *The Complete Book of Emigrants 1607-1660,* pages 35 and 41, by Peter Wilson Coldham.)

The first mention of John Whedbee in Perquimans Precinct is when he married Deborah Sutton.

"John Whedbey ye son of Richard Whedby and Elizabeth his life Late of Virginia & Deborah Suton ye Relict of Nathaniel Suton were married by Mr. John right, Minister, ye tenth of Maye 1685," (Ref: Hathaway, Volume 3, Number 3, page 206.)

Children of John and Deborah were:

1. Folke Whedby son of John Whedby and wife Deborah was

borne Jany.6, 1686. (Ref: Idem, Volume 3, Number 2, page 213.) There is no mention of Folke after the announcement of his birth. He was dead before 1697.

2. Richard Whedbee son of John Whedbee & wife Deborah was borne Feb.2, 1687. (Ref: Idem, Volume 3, Number 2, page 215.)

3. Joseph Whedby son of John Whedby & wife Deborah departed ye 12th of Octobr. 1688. (Ref: Idem, Volume 3, Number 3, page 363.) Joseph probably died close to or on the date of his birth.

4. Deborah Whedby daughter of John Whedby & wife Deborah was borne Jany. 28, 1689. (Ref: Hathaway, Volume 3, Number 2, page 216.)

THE WHEDBEE CHILDREN

1. Folke Whedbee died before April 1697.

2. Richard Whedbee married (1st) Sarah Durant. "Richard Whedbee and Sarah (daughter of John Durant and wife Sarah) were married Feb'y. 4, 1709." (Ref: Idem, Volume 1, Number 2, page 204 also see Volume 3, Number 3, page 399.)

Children: a. John Whedbee (23 April 1715 -
b. Sarah Whedbee (23 January 1718 -
c. George Whedbee (19 January 1721 -
d. Ann Whedbee (18 February 1724 -
e. Joseph Whedbee (12 March 1726 -
f. Hezekiah Whedbee (1 April 1728 -

Sarah Whedbee, wife of Richard Whedbee, died on 4 April 1728. Richard then married Hannah Reed.

3. Joseph Whedbee died as an infant on 12 October 1688.

4. Deborah Whedbee married about 1 April 1705, Henry Bonner, in Perquimans County.

"Att a court Holden **** this first Monday in February year of 1688.
Present: Ralph Fletcher, Steward,
Mr. John Barrow,
Mr. John Whitbe
Mr. Robert __?___,
Mr. Thomas Leppers

(Ref: Idem, Volume 3, Number 3, page 429.)

John Whedbee was appointed a Justice as described in a Warrant dated 20 May 1690, as published in the Court Records of Perquimans County:

"Albemarle in the Province of North Carolina.

Wee ye Honble Coll'l Philip Ludwell Gover'r with the rest of the Lds Proprietor of the County & Province grant this Commission of the Peace for ye Precinct of Perquermans in ye afores'd County.

To our Trusty and well beloved Ralph Fletcher, Steward; John Whedbe; Joseph Sutton; William Bundy.

Gent:
The first three whereof to be of the Quorum, three of which beinge, Present, one of them being of the Quorum, shall compleat a Court,

Greeting -Know yee yt wee have assigned you & every of you Justices, Joynylt, & Severally to Keepe or cause to be kept their Majesties, & his Excellencie, the Palatine & Lds Proprietors peace in ye Precinct aforesd;

To keepe or cause to be kept all such Laws, Statues, or Orders as are made or hereafter shall be made Consonant with Loyalty to their Sacred Maj?ties & Fidellity to the Lds Proprietors, by the rules and observations (so neere as may be) to ye Foundamentalls;

To require by ye Oaths of Twelve good and lawful men of the Precinct afore'sd, of all manner of Criminall causes whatsoever (excepting for Treason, Murther, & other offenses punishable unto death) then so proceed agst by finall determination, according to Justice & shall judge all Civill Causes whatsoever.

And in all psonal actions not exceeding the value of fifty pounds Sterlinge, with Appeale;

And you are to Keepe or Cause to be kept ye sd Courts so often as by ye Fundamentall Constitution is prescribed;

In witness whereof Wee ye sd Honble Col'l Philip Ludwell, Gover'r with ye rest of ye Lds Proprietors Deputies have hereunto set their Hands and Affixed ye Seal of the County this Twentieth day of May anno Domini 1690.

(Perquimans	*Philip Ludwell*
	Francis Tomes(Thomas)
County	*Francis Hartley*
	Benjamin Laker
Seal	*Thomas Harris*
	William Wilkerson
here)	*Thomas Harvey*

"At a Court Holden for the Precinct of Perquimans the first Monday in January 1691 at the house of Mary Scott;

Present: Captain Ralph Fletcher, Steward,
Mr. John Whitby,
Mr. William Bundy,
Mr. Joseph Sutton,
Mr. Robert Wilson, Justices.
(Ref: Hathaway, Volume 3, Number 3, page 437.)

Edward, Mr. John Whedby's man Departed this Life on ___date blank__." (Ref: Idem, Volume 3, Number 3, page 364.)

John Whedbee may have begun to experience health problems in the latter part of the 1690's, causing him, in April 1697, to make a Deed of Gift to his two surviving children, Richard and Deborah. The below can be found in, *The North Carolina Colonial Records, Volume I, 1662 to 1712*, pages 485 and 486.

"John Whedby of Perquimans, for: Natural love I bear my son Richard, do give to him a Plan' on North Side of Sutton's Creek - stock of Hoggs, & 3 Negroes belonging to sd plantation, 4 cows & calves, 4 Ewes & lambs, one feather bed and boulster, & 2 blankets, one ring, 29 lbs of pewter & one iron pott."

"To dau Debro, one woman named Sarah, 3 cows 7 calves, 6 ewes 7 lambs, one feather bed & boulster, two blankets, & one ring, 20 lbs of pewter, one iron porrage pott, & an oval table.

"To sd son and dau, "two mares & colts & one horse with thier increase to be divided between them when Debro is 16 years of age, but if they die in Minority to sons of my brother, George Whedby. Ack 13 April 1697."

Test: Caleb Callaway, Ralph Fletcher.

The above can also be found in, *History of Perquimans County,* by Mrs. Watson Wilson, page 47.

"John Whedby died 5 April 1700." (Ref: Hathaway, Volume 3, Number 3, page 403.)

"A General Court was held in Perquimans September 1700 before ye Honable Sam'l Swann, Sect'y of State, Mrs. Deborah Whedbee administered on ye estate of her husband, Jno Whedbee.' (Ref: Idem, Volume 2, Number 2, page 302.)

"Inventory of estate of John Whedbee returned 6th June 1701." (Ref: Idem, Volume 1, Number 1, page 82.)

At a court at ye Hous of Captain James Cole ye second Tuesday in April 1702 for the Precinct of Piquimins.

Present: Captain Ralph Fletcher
Captain James Cole
Mr. William Bartlett (Barcliff)
Mr. Francis Foster
Mr. Samuel Swann

Upon petition of Richard Whedby the He might chuse Mr. Francis Foster His Garden ordered yet Mr. Francis Foster take into his Custodie ye estate of ye said Richard Whedby and an inventory to take of ye sd estate and bring to ye next Court held for Orfens and five Bond for ye estate.

Upon a peticon of George Sutten and Nathaniel Sutten to chuse thare Garden ordered that Nathaniel Nicholson take care of George Sutten he haven chosen Him for his Garden and that Joseph Sutten junior take Nathaniel Sutten into his care He haven chosen him for his garden.

Upon a peticon of Debro Whedby that She may chuse hir Garden and Shee chusen of Joseph Suton, senior.

Ordered that ye sd Sutten take ye sd Debro into his care and hir estate also and an inventory of hir estate to take and bring it to ye next Orfens (court) and give bond for ye estate.

Ralph Fletcher
James Cole
Francis Foster
Samuel Swann, junior.

William Barclift

The above can be found in, *The North Carolina Colonial Records, Volume 1, 1662 - 1712*, pages 563 and 564.

Sometime between 1702 and 1705, the guardianship of Deborah Whedbee, the child, was changed to Dennis McClenden who is now married to her mother. But there was a problem as the following court record shows:

At a court Holden at the house of Captain James Cole on Second Tuesday in July 1702 for the Precinct of Piquimons.

Present: Captain Ralph Fletcher, Judge
Mr. Francis Foster
Mr. William Bartlett (Barclift)

Joseph Sutten, Senior Vars Denis Macklenden and Debro his wife. In a plea of ye case for the estate of Debro Whedby given by Dede of Gift by her father John Whedby ye said Mackelenden is ordered to deliver ye sd estate in kinde as it was given Ales Execution.

Ralph Fletcher
Francis Foster
William Barclift

The above can be found in, *The North Carolina Colonial Records, Volume 1, 1662 - 1712*, page 4.

On or about 1 April 1705, Deborah Whedbee married Henry Bonner. She had just turned 16 years of age. As previously stated, "Deborah," a name for some Bonner women does not show up in the Bonner family until after Deborah Whedbee married into the family. All of the "Deborah" women were named after their ancestral grandmother, Deborah Astine. Note the Sutton, Bonner; Wood, and Thompson families, where some girls were named Deborah.

IV

Section Three

GEORGE DURANT

(1632 - 1689)

George Durant was a figurehead in the establishment of a Colony in North Carolina that established the roots of Government and civilization for the great State of North Carolina. There were settlers before him but they did not have the lasting and staying attributes displayed by this man. Many of those early settlers succumbed to the hardships of the land and went back to Virginia. One of the men who came before George Durant and stayed was Samuel Pricklove. George and Samuel established a strong mutual bond of friendship that endured. George was of the Presbyterian faith and Samuel was a Quaker. They stood together shoulder to shoulder armed with the weapons of the times to defend the cause of freedom as they saw it. For Samuel Pricklove it was against his faith to take up arms but he saw a need and accepted the consequences. As a result, he and George Durant are in the records as the driving force to establish and maintain the first permanent white settlement in what is now North Carolina.

Two of George Durant's descendants married into the Sutton-Whedbee family bloodline.

First - Joseph Sutton, son of Nathaniel Sutton and Deborah Austine Sutton married a daughter of George and Ann Durant, Parthenia Sutton. Joseph was a son of Deborah Astine and Nathaniel Sutton.

Second - Richard Whedbee, half-brother to the above Joseph Sutton, married a granddaughter of George and Ann Durant through their son, John Durant's daughter, Sarah Durant. Richard Whedbee was a son of Deborah Astine-Sutton and John Whedbee. The marriage created an interesting set of family relationships between the two brothers. Think about it.

In the book, *Immigrant Ancestors*, page 771, the following can be found.

"George Durant (born England 1 October 1632. In March 1661, Kelcokomer, a Great Indian Chief of Yeopims deeded to him for a 'valuable consideration' a tract of land bearing the name of Wecameke (a peninsula now called Durant's Neck), this is the earliest records deed in the history of North Carolina; with Samuel Pricklove established the 1st permanent settlement in North Carolina at Durant's Neck in 1661; Atty General, General Council, Albemarle County in 1679; resided at Durant's Neck 1691; an acknowledged leader in public affairs; with (John) Culpepper, led the Culpepper Rebellion against unjust restriction of trade; married 4 January 1658, Ann Marwood of Northumberland County, Virginia."

Family status: George Durant (1632 - 1694)
Married: Ann Marwood (unk - 1695)

Children:1. George Durant (24 December 1659 - 13 September 1671)
2. Elizabeth Durant (11 February 1661 -
3. John Durant (26 December 1662 -
Married: Sarah Jooke on 9 April 1684.
Children: a. George Durant (30 September 1685 -
Married: Hagar Crisp
Children: (1) John Durant (8 July 1714 - 8 October 1721)
(2) Ann Durant (13 September 1716 -
(3) Mary and Sarah Durant (2 December 1718
(4) Elizabeth Durant (12 March 1720 -
(5) George Durant (20 August 1723 -
b. Sarah Durant (ca 1687 - 4 April 1728)
Married: Richard Whedbee (born 2 February 1687 -
c. Ann Durant (16 February 1689 -
d. Elizabeth Durant (28 January 1691
4. Mary Durant (11 February 1665 -
5. Thomas Durant (28 August 1668 -
Married: ___?_____.
Children: George Durant (25 November 1698 -
6. Sarah Durant (17 January 1670-
7. Martha Durant (28 August 1673 -
8. Parthenia Durant (1 August 1675 -

Married: Joseph Sutton about 1695
Children: a. George Suttton (22 August 1696 -
b. Elizabeth Sutton (15 September 1703 -
c. Parthenia Sutton (8 August 1705 -
d. Sarah Sutton (10 October 1711 -

9. Ann Durant (1 April 1681 -

Married: William Barclift, "William Barclift, son of William and Elizabeth Barclift and Ann Durant daughter of George Durant and wife Ann were married on 6 October 1698." (Ref: Hathaway).

"John Durant, son of George Durant and wife Ann, died on 19 January 1699." (Ref: Hathaway, Volume 3, Number 3, page 403.)

"William Stephens and Mrs. Sarah Durant (Relict of John) were married 1st January 1704." (Ref; Idem, Volume 3, number 3, page 410.)

THE OLDEST CONVEYANCE RECORDS IN NORTH CAROLINA ANTEDATING THE FIRST CHARTER OF KING CHARLES BY TWO YEARS

(The original in is *Book A*, pages 374 to 376, Register of Deed Office at Hertford, Perquimans County, North Carolina)

"Know all men by these Presents that I Kilcocanen, King of Yeopim, have for a valuable consideration of satisfaction received with ye consent of my people sold and made over on Raeoke (now Albemarle) Sound on a River called by ye name of Perquimans which issueth out of the north side of the aforesaid sound which land at present bears ye name of Woccomike (Indian for Durant's Neck) beginning at a marked Oak tree which divides this land from ye land I formerly sold to Samuel Pricklove and extending westerly up ye sound to a point of turning of ye aforesaid Perquimans River to a creek called by ye name of Awosrake, to wit, all ye land betwixt ye aforesaid bounds of Samuel Pricklove & the creek thence to ye head thereof. And thence through the woods to ye first bounds -

To have and to hold ye quiet possession of ye same to him & his heirs forever with rights and privileges thereto forever from me or any person or persons whatsoever.

As witness my Hand this first day of March 1661."

Test: Thomas Weamouth — Ye mark of
Caleb Callaway — Kilcocanen

This is a true Copia
by me,
Witness:
Will Lloyd
Thomas Havett (probably Thomas Harvey)

Examined word by word out of ye Original (by) Edward Remington.

Registered the 24th of Octr., 1716
Per: John Stepney, Register

"Know all men by these presents that I Ciskitando, King of Yeopim, do sell unto George Durant a Parcell of land Bounding on Perquimans River at a creek issuing out of ye same beginning at ye aforesaid creek and running down ye aforesaid river to a marked Poplar standing on the side of a Great Swamp which falleth into the river thence running into the woods parallel with ye aforesaid creek. As also up the creek to another Great Swamp which falleth into the same and thence again into the woods parallel with ye River to the bounds proceeding from ye marked Poplar.

To have and to hold ye same land with all belonging to the same to him & his Heirs forever from me or any other soever warranting the same to him a Lawfull Sale as witness my Hand this 4th of August 1661."

Signed & Delivered
in presence of:
Thomas Weamouth
Caleb Callaway

The marke of
Custcutenew

Registered the 24th of October 1716.

The above documents can also be found in Hathaway, Volume 3, Number 3, page 423 and 424.

"At a court held 25 May 1673 at the house of Francis Godfrey.
Present: Hon. Col. John Jenkins, Dept. Sup.
Captain Thomas Cullen
W. F. Crawford (William F. Crawford)
William Jennings
Joseph Scott
Ralph Fletcher

Mrs. Ann Durant, Attorney for Andrew Ball, petitions ye Court for Wages due to said Ball, from ye Barbo two brothers, it being made to appear from under ye Master's hand, yt shews it 10p-14s-6d, ordered that ye said Ball be paid 10p-14s-6d, out of said Barbo two brothers with costs. Alias Exen."

The above documentation established the **historical fact that Mrs. Ann Durant, the wife of George Durant, was the first woman to practice law before a Court in America.** There is a roadside sign outside the town of Hertford in Perquimans County, North Carolina, on highway US 17, marking the occasion.

As a matter of information, the above Joseph Scott, was the same Joseph Scott mentioned in the journal of Reverend George Foxe in 1672.

"A power-of-attorney from George Durant to his wife, Ann Durant, bears date 20 May 1675; it was probably executed at the time George Durant went to England." (Ref: Hathaway, Volume 2, Number 3, page 470.)

George Durant was Attorney General in 1676 and was the Speaker of House of Burgesses (in Perquimans Precinct) in 1679.

GEORGE DURANT SPEAKER OF HOUSE OF BURGESSES IN 1679
DURING THE CULPEPPER REBELLION

George Durant aged 49 years or thereabouts maketh oath in ye year 1679 ye Depot being then Speaker of an Assembly John Harvey Esqr then Governor & being very late in ye night before ye whole body if ye acts could be perfected to be signed by ye Governor & Speaker the Governor did depart home. Ye Burgesses did deliver the Acts into my Custody for ye Governor to Signe to them the rest of ye Lord Deputies and my Self Signed the said Acts in ye parliament before Their departure & I kept ye said Acts in My custody untill ye Governor has Signed them and then delivered ye said Acts into ye Secretary's Office & further the Depot testifyeth that these in ye 58 Art of Say (Votes in elections or any) were not interlyned whilest the said Acts were in My Custody or before ye Governor has signed wch was to ye best of ye Depot knowledge at his own house.

George Durant

(Ref: Hathaway: Volume 3, Number 1, page 40.)

In the book, *History of Perquimans County,* by Mrs. Watson Winslow, page 2, the following is extracted:

"......this migration (in 1653, to the lower Chowan River of Carolina by Reverend Roger Green) preceded the advent of George Durant by eight years, and there can be little doubt in the mind of any one versed in the early history of Albemarle, that many settlers were well established on their own land in Perquimans Precinct before said Durant decided to come to North Carolina. Among these early settlers, no doubt can be enumerated such men as Samuel Pricklove whose land adjoined the land sold to George Durant by Indian Chief Kilcoconewen, King of Yeopin, on 1 March 1661 and Caleb Callaway, who appears as a witness to said deed. The land of said Samuel Pricklove lay around or just below where the town of New Hope now stands. This made him a near neighbor of Durant and they became fast friends. Pricklove was a Quaker but it did not prevent him from following Durant in the Rebellion of 1677-79 even when his association strictly forbade one of the sect to take up arms and other Quakers followed his example also a part of the 'rabble' that helped to depose acting Governor Thomas Miller. The rebellion caused a great deal of unrest in the Colony and the county breathed easier and sat more at ease when Miller finally took passage for Virginia and later went home to England. All unwittingly George Durant struck the first note for American Independence and routed the first unjust tax collector to appear on American soil when he with the 'rabble' drove out Miller and stopped the unlawful Customs receipts in 1677-79."

As previously stated, George Durant was born in London, England on 1 October 1632. He was of Scotch parentage and a Presbyterian by faith. During his life he was one of the most influential planters in all of Albemarle. While living in

Northumberland County, Virginia in July 1658 he made a disposition that he, "came to Virginia in the ship Potomack, age 25 years." That places his arrival in Virginia in 1657. In yet another document, he stated his occupation as a "Mariner."

The family Bible of George Durant, which was printed in 1659, is in possession of the University of North Carolina at Chapel Hill, North Carolina.

The last will & testament of George Durant is as follows:

George Durant, published 9 October 1688, probated 6 February 1694.

"Son, John; Son, Thomas; brother, John Durant of London and his son, Henry; nephew, George son of brother John Durant; wife, Ann. Daughters, Sarah, Mattya (Martha), Portemia (Parthenia) and Ann. Test: John Philpot, Francis Foster, John Cully." (Ref: Hathaway, Volume 1, Number 2, page 203.)

"At a court Holden at the house of Diana Foster - the first Munday in February Anno Do 1694.

Present: Alexander Lillington
Caleb Calloway
John Barrow
Thomas Lepper, Esquires

A will of Mr. George Durant proved in Court by the Oath of Mr. John Philpott & Mr. Francis Foster and that Mr. George Muschamp, Mr. Charles Jones and Mr. John West be appraisers of said Estate.

Mrs. (Ann) Durant enters for her two Grand Children a young sorrell mare with a star in her forehead called Bonner the same mare & her increases to Ann and Elizabeth Waller to them and their heires for ever."

"At a Court Holden (in Perquimans) 28 September in the afternoon 1694.

Present: Daniel Akehurst, Esquire, Secretary
Francis Tomes (Thomas) & Benjamin Laker & Major Samuel Swann & Colonel Thomas Pollock, Esquires, Lord Deputies.

Captain Anthony Dawson &
Mr. John Durant, Assistants

Mrs. Anne Durant shewing that two of the apprisors appointed to apprise the estate of Mr. George Durant, deceased, are by departure or sickness disabled. Craves that others may be appointed in their stead.

Ordered that Mr. John West, **Mr. John Whitby**, Jonathan Bateman and Thomas Hassold or any three of them being sworne before Mr. John Godfrey shall apprise the said estate." (Ref: *The North Carolina Colonial Records, Volume I, 1662 - 1712,* pages 420 and 421.)

"23 January 1695. Ann Durant wife of George, the elder. George Durant, ring etc., Isaac wife (Sarah Durant Rowden) her daughter. Son, Thomas executor. Non Cupative will." (Ref: Hathaway, Volume 1, Number 1, page 41.) There are some records that state George Durant died in 1689. His will was not probated until 1694.

Note for the reader. To be a member of the House of Burgess was to be: "An elected member of the Colonial Legislature."

SAMUEL PRICKLOVE

As previously noted, Samuel Pricklove was involved with George Durant in the uprising of 1677-79. Whether Samuel's legal problems started because he was a Quaker, armed himself and became involved in the Rebellion is not known but in Court in 1680, Samuel is in "deep" trouble.

"Att a General Court held for the County of Albemarle, March 20, 1680.

Present: The Hon. John Jenkins, Governor.

Anthony Slocumb, Captain William Crawford, Major Robert Holden, Esquires
Captain James Blount
Captain John Varham, Deputies Assistants
William Crawford, Attorney of Samuel Blogg of New York

against Samuel Pricklove. Action of Debt.

March 27, 1680. Ordered that Samuel Pricklove stand in the Pillory three hours, and loose his right ear, and be banished this county for ever, and to live in prison without bayle in yrons, or otherwise, until hee shall bee shipped for his transport, and their abroad kept in yrons, till at his place be landed with costs and fees.

Ordered, that Samuel Pricklove, deliver the patent of land possessed by John Burney, and pay costs, that is to say the old patent granted by Sir William Berkeley."

Samuel Pricklove died on 20 April 1692.

PERQUIMANS IS OF INDIAN ORIGIN AND MEANS,
"LAND OF BEAUTIFUL WOMEN"

V

Henry Bonner (4)

(ca 1708 - 1766)

Family Status:
Married: (1st) Sarah Luten
Children: 1. Thomas Bonner (ca 1744 - 1804)
2. William Bonner (ca 1748 - 1770)
3. Henry Bonner (ca 1750 - ?)
Married (2nd) Elizabeth Hardy on 4 January 1758
4. Richard Bonner (ca 1759 - 1781)

It is this Henry Bonner who is believed to be the first born of Henry Bonner and Deborah Whedbee. This belief is based on the facts contained in the last will and testament of Colonel Henry Bonner in 1738. In the will, a grandson, Richard Lewis is left a plantation but a trustee is not assigned to protect the property indicating that Richard was of the age of majority. That would place Richard's birth in or before the year 1717. And that would place Elizabeth's (his mother) birth before the year 1703, probably between 1700 and 1703. Therefore, it is believed that this Henry Bonner (4) was born between 1706 and 1710 with 1708 being the most likely birth year.

Another theory that suggests that this Henry was a relatively young man and had three young sons to raise in the 1750's is the fact that he took a young woman, Elizabeth Hardy, as his wife in 1758. It is believed his first wife was Sarah Luten whom, it is suggested, he married about 1729. There is no hint that they had children before 1744, although they could have and they died in infancy or before Henry Bonner made his will in 1766.

A hint that Elizabeth Hardy Bonner was a young widow is the fact that after Henry died (after 17 July 1766), it is noted in the records that in February 1767, she married William Roberts. As Robert's wife, she gave birth to at least six children, as noted in the last will and testament of Richard Bonner in 1781. As before mentioned, the last will and testament of Henry Bonner (4) has been placed at the beginning of this chapter in order to establish his family at his death. The below document (dated 7 July 1766) was found in the Register of Deeds Office in Edenton, North Carolina where it was used as a Deed of Gift to his family. The Archives in Raleigh, North Carolina has his last will and testament on file and it has the date 17 July 1766. The Deed of Gift document (dated 7 July 1766) has two more pages than the last will and testament in Raleigh. According to the officials in Raleigh, the Deed of Gift document is on file in the mirco film section of the archives. The last will and testament does not name a trustee but the Deed of Gift does.

The following Deed of Gift was found in *Deed Book L,* pages 195, 196, 197 and 198 in Edenton.

Bonner
to
Bonner

North Carolina - Know all men by these presents that I Henry Bonner of Chowan County ye province aforesaid, Gentleman, In consideration of the love and natural regard which I have & bear into my Dearly Beloved wife Elizabeth Bonner also for the same love esteem and personal affection and Regard which I have and Bear into My Dear beloved children, Thomas Bonner, William Bonner, Henry Bonner, Richard Bonner and also for divers good causes and considerations - hereunto especially moving have given granted and confirmed and by these presents DOTH give grant unto the said Elizabeth, Thomas, William, Henry and Richard Bonner all and singular the land hereditaments, improvements, Negroes, good chattles and implements in manner and form as shall be hereafter nominates expresses that is to say:

I give grant and confirm unto my aforesaid Loving wife during her natural life or Widowhood the following Negroes, Viz: Grace, Patte & Solomon, also a roan mare called Starr, one of my best beds and furniture, one square table, two cows and calves, two ewes and lambs, one large Pott of Iron, two large pewter dishes and six best pewter plates, all the earthen Chainey ware and Earthen do (dough) & in like manner the Bosatts? And lastly the use of my dwelling Plantation, That is to say, the half ___?____ with the one half of the Dwelling House during her widowhood.

Now I also give unto my well Beloved **son, Thomas Bonner** , and his heirs and the heirs of his Body lawfull Begotten of his Body forever the one half of my Dwelling Plantation immediately to commence upon the same after my decease and the rest and all thereof after my wife aforesaid forever excepting;

Seventy acres lying on Deep Run known by the name of Old Tom's which I give as aforesaid to my **son Richard**.

I give and confirm as aforesaid unto my **son William my plantation in Green Hall** excepting what lieth beyond Maple Branch toward Richard Hoskins, beginning at the three pines and running a strait line to the Maple Branch thence running up to the Maple Branch to the head thence about north-north-east to Nathaniel Howcott's line which I give as aforesaid to my son Richard his heirs and assigns forever.

I give as aforesaid to my well beloved **son Henry Bonner** his heirs as assign forever my Plantation on the Deep Run Swamp.

I give as aforesaid unto my Dearly Beloved Thomas Bonner my gray mare running in Green Hall.

Also aforesaid unto my son William my Bay known by the name of the Indian, I also give and grant as aforesaid unto my son William all and singular my nursery at the end of the barn of Apple trees to be delivered immediately after my death if demanded by him the said William Bonner or my trustee hereafter mentioned unto him the said William Bonner and assigns also a large box to my wife and the said Henry Bonner all and singular the goods chattles personal estate and the other Real and implements and the other the premises.

I the said Henry Bonner all and singular the real estate personal and all the other implements and premises to the aforesaid, as mentioned to their heirs executors administrators and assigns and all other whatsoever shall of and of all the persons or persons from henceforth shall warrant forever defend by these presents of all and singular real estate good chattles implements and the other the premises whereof I the said Henry Bonner have put into Each and Every of their Hands as Full possession after my decease this now in the ensealing & delivery of these presents.

In the Name of the whole granted premises, I have hereunto set my Hand and Affix my Seal this Seventh day of July 1766.

Signed Sealed and delivered Henry Bonner (Seal)

in presence of,

Jeremiah Halsey, Jurat
Henry Thompson
William Matthews

And all the Rest of my personal estate after my lawfull debts are paid my desire that it may be equally distributed between my four children, Thomas, William, Henry and Richard Bonner - I also nominate constitute and appoint my loving Cousin Captain Thomas Bonner also my Dear Brother Thomas Bonner, to be after my decease to be the only Trustees on my children's behalf and Executes & fully file the same to the best of there knowledge untill he are they may arrive at the Lawfull age to obtain there estates real & personal rattifing and confirming this and only this to be my last will and desire.

Acknowledged and Declared Henry Bonner (Seal)
the day & date,
also in presence of us,

Jeremiah Halsey
Henry Thompson

NORTH CAROLINA
Chowan County July Inferior Court, 1766
Present: His Majesty's Justices
Deed of Gift from Henry Bonner to Elizabeth Bonner, Thomas Bonner, William Bonner, Henry Bonner and Richard Bonner was duly proved in Open Court according to Law by the Oath of Mr. Jeremiah Halsey and ordered to be registered.

Test: Thomas Jones, Clerk Current
Registered: 6 February 1767.

A careful reading of the above Deed of Gift shows that Henry's brother, Thomas and his Cousin Thomas Bonner were nominated to the trustees to the estates left to his four minor children. Note that ALL of Henry's children were not of age in July 1766. It is not known who "Cousin Thomas" was. However, an examination of the documents for the period will show that it was one of three persons named "Thomas" who were living in the area.

First - and the most unlikely was Thomas Bonner, son of Sheriff Thomas Bonner, in Beaufort County.

Second - and less likely also, was Thomas Bonner, son of (William) Thomas Bonner of Bertie County and

Thirdly, and most likely, was Thomas Bonner, brother of John Bonner. Thomas and John Bonner lived adjacent to the family of Henry Bonner and it is thought that the father of Thomas and John may have been Will Bonner and it is believed that Will and Colonel Henry Bonner were brothers. But the records are silent on this theory!

The above Cousin Thomas Bonner may have been the Thomas Bonner who passed away in Perquimans County in 1766. In the book, *History of Perquimans County*, page 287, the following is found:

"Jeremiah Halsey, for an Audit of Thomas Bonner's estate, who was guardian of Joshua & Thomas Long (orphans of Thomas) & William Stepney (orphan) of John)." 20 October 1766. (Author's note - Notice the date of this document occuring after the will of Henry Bonner was published. It is the feeling of this author that this Thomas Bonner was the brother of John Bonner).

The reader will also notice that Jeremiah Halsey was a witness to the will of Henry Bonner who died in July 1766. The true question is, "Was this Thomas the son of Colonel Henry Bonner or the brother of John Bonner?" The records leave us in the dark.

The proof that Henry Bonner (died 1766) was married to a woman named Sarah (believed to be Sarah Luten) is contained in the below document. It can be found in *Deed Book C-1*, page 683 in Edenton.

Henry Bonner
to
George Martin

To all to whome these presents shall come I Henry Bonner of Chowan Precinct in the Province aforesaid send greetings &c.

Know ye yet I said Henry Bonner for & in consideration of the sum of four hundred and twenty pounds to me in hand paid at or before the ensealing and delivery of these presents by George Martin of the aforesaid precinct, Gentleman, whereof I do hereby acknowledge & by myself to be therewith fully satisfied & contented & paid have given granted bargain sold aliened ensossed conveyed & confirm assign & sett over & by these presents do for myself my heirs exers, adms, give grant bargain sell alien ensossed convey confirm assign & sett over unto the said George Martin his heirs or assigns all yet my Plantation or Tract of land lying & being in the precinct of Chowan on the north side of Mattacomack Creek;

Beginning at the bottom of a Little Marsh between Philburd's (Filbert's) Creek and a small branch yet along Philburd's Creek ...through the said Philberd's Creek...to a Red Oak standing on the East side of the Main Road so along the Main Road to a Marked Forked Red Oak standing on the said Philburd's line so along Philburd's or Rowden's line to a White Oak in Orlando Champions line yet along Orlando Champion's line to his Corner tree yet along his said line to a Marked Red Oak near the Head of a Branch yet down the Westside of the said Branch to the first Station;

Containing by estimation three hundred & twenty acres be the same more or less together with all houses, outhouses, edifices, orchards, Gardens & all other appends privileges & commoditys of what nature & kind so ever thereon being belong or in any wise appertaining....

In Witness whereof I have hereunto Sett my Hand & Seal this 6th day of April 1732.

Signed sealed & delivered   Henry Bonner (Seal)

in Presence of,
George Nicholas
April 7th 1732

The above Deed was acknowledged by the subscriber, Henry Bonner & **also Sarah the wife of the said Henry Bonner** acknowledges her right of dower to the Lands before me.

John Palin, Clerk Justice
Lett it be registered.

As noted in the last will and testament of Colonel Henry Bonner, he left instructions that funds be furnished for the education of his two minor daughters, Deborah and Mary. True to his obligation, Henry Bonner, the son, sold property in order to comply with the wishes of his father as noted below.

NORTH CAROLINA

Bonner
to
Craven

This indenture made the tenth day of November in the year of our Lord one thousand seven hundred and thirty nine;

Between Henry Bonner of Chowan County in the province aforesaid, Gentleman, executor of ye last will and testament of Henry Bonner, his late father, deceased, of the one part and James Craven of Chowan County aforesaid, Gentleman, of the other part.

Whereas the Lords and Proprietors of Carolina by their Patent bearing date ye nineteenth day of January Anno Damo 1716...did grant unto the said Henry Bonner, the father, a tract of land containing five hundred and twenty acres lying in Chowan Precinct on the North side of Mattacomack Creek abutting and bounding as therein...

And whereas the said Henry Bonner by his last will and testament Bearing the date the twenty first day of September in the year of our Lord one thousand seven hundred and thirty eight did among other things order and direct his executor thereafter mentioned to dispose of all the rest and residue of his real estate and the money arising therefrom to be laid out for the Educating and Maintaining his two daughters, Deborah and Mary, in their minority as by the said will duly proved and recorded in the said province relation being thereto also had may more fully and at large appear and whereas the said James Craven hath agreed with the said Henry Bonner party hereto for the absolute purchase of one hundred and seventy acres of land part of ye said five hundred and twenty acres in the above recited Patent mentioned.

Now this indenture witnesseth that the said Henry Bonner party to these presents for in consideration of the sum of one hundred and fifty seven pounds Current Money of the province ... all that piece or parcell of land containing by estimation one hundred and seventy acres be the same more or less situate laying and being in the said County of Chowan being a part and parcell of the said five hundred & twenty acres in the above recited Patent mentioned adjoining on John Bonner, Abraham Blackall & Joseph Anderson.

IN WITNESS whereof the said Henry Bonner hath hereunto set his Hand and Seal the day and year above mentioned.

Signed, Sealed and delivered
in presence of, Henry Bonner (Seal)
William Luten
James Arthaud

Received ye day & year within of the within named James Craven the sum of one hundred and fifty seven pounds Current Bills of North Carolina being the full consideration within mentioned to be by him unto me paid, per Henry Bonner.

Witness:
William Luten
James Arthaud

NORTH CAROLINA
Chowan County July Court, 1741
Present: His Majesty's Justices

To James Craven - These may certify that the within Deed of Sale from Henry Bonner was duly acknowledged by him in open court and motion is ordered to be Registered.

Test: James Craven, Clerk Current
Registered July the 31st 1741 (by) James Craven, Register.

The above document is from *Deed Book A-1,* pages 14 and 15 in Edenton.

The above mentioned Land Patent is noted below as it pertains to the above:

"(to) Henry Bonner, 19 January 1716, 520 acres on North side of Mattacomack Creek on Filbert."

"Commissioners of Edenton:
John Hodgson, William Smith, Edmund Gale
To: Henry Bonner. Lots 31, 33 & 39. New plan of Edenton, 29 December 1736." (Ref: Hathaway, Volume 1, Number 1, page 126.)

There is confusion as to whom Henry Bonner was first

married before Elizabeth Hardy. It appears by the records that it was Sarah Luten, evidenced by the fact that he was married "to a Sarah" in 1732 and supported by the following facts:

"Henderson Luten's children: James, Ephraim, Henderson and Sarah married Henry Bonner, and another child died before the father." No date. (Ref: Hathaway, Volume 2, Number 3, page 470.)

A William Bonner, probably the son of (William) Thomas Bonner of Bertie County married Sarah Luten 21 August 1744. Bond was furnished by William Luten and witnessed by George Parris. (Ref: Hathaway, Volume 1, Number 2, page 236.)

"William Bonner married one of the daughters of Henderson Luten, deceased, so stated in a petition for a Negro belonging to said estate. There were four heirs: William Luten was one of them and executor of the estate." (dated 1745.) (Ref: Hathaway, Volume 1, Number 3, page 455 and 456.)

"(In 1747) Ephraim Luten orphan of Henderson, 14 years of age placed under tuition of William Bonner, who married his sister." (Idem, Volume 1, Number 3, page 457.)

"Henderson Luten, 1744. Sarah, James, Ephraim and Henderson Luten, heirs of Thomas Luten." William married Sarah, above. (Idem, Volume 2, Number 2, page 266.)

"William Bonner married a daughter of Henderson Luten, niece of William Luten. Henderson Luten left five children but one died shortly after himself." (Idem, Volume 2, Number 3, page 469.)

All evidence points to the fact that William Bonner and Henry Bonner married different Sarah Lutens. There is at least twelve years difference in the two entries. The records are not confused enough to suggest that William and Henry were the same man. An interesting clue is in the lines: "Henry Bonner was married to Sarah Luten, daughter of Henderson Luten, who had a child who died before the father and William Bonner married Sarah Luten, daughter of Henderson Luten who had a child who died shortly after the father."

The below William Bonner was probably the son of (William) Thomas Bonner of Bertie County.

"William Bonner, published 15 September 1775, probated

November Court 1775. Sons: William, John, George, Miles and Thomas if child in esse. Daughters, Penelope White, Sarah Billups, Martha Bonner and Ann Bonner. Wife, Ann. Son, William ½ my lots in Edenton, N. C., also ½ of the land giving to my brother, Thomas Bonner. Grandson, William Dorsey. Wife, James Moore and son, William, Exrs. Test: William Matthews, Peter Yeates, John Yeates." (Ref: Idem, Volume 2, Number 4, page 329.) It is believed that this William Bonner married Sarah Luten in 1744. Notice that he has a daughter named Sarah. It is also believed that this same William Bonner married Ann Moore of Tyrrell County. "William Bonner married Ann Moore of Tyrrell County in 1760."(Source: Hathaway).

"Thomas Bonner (son of William) married Elizabeth Virgin on 4 May 1802. Bond: Miles Bonner." (Hathaway, volume 2, Number 3, page 374.)

The records show that a Thomas Bonner died in Granville County, North Carolina in 1828. He might have been the same Thomas who married Elizabeth Virgin and was the son of (William) Thomas Bonner.

"Married In Tyrrell County on 16 July 1764, Frederick Dorsey and Penelope Bonner." No bondsman. (Ref: Idem, Volume 3, Number 1, page 107.) Frederick passed away and Penelope remarried. Note the above Penelope White.

An interesting document noting that Henry Bonner (died 1766) was an officer in the Militia is contained in the following. It can be found in *Deed Book A-1*, pages 244 and 245 in Edenton.

Henry Bonner
to
Thomas Luten

This indenture made the tenth day of September in the year of our Lord one thousand seven hundred forty three between Henry Bonner of Chowan County in North Carolina of the first part and Thomas Luten of the same place of the other part.

Witnesseth that the said Henry Bonner for and in consideration of the sum of Fifty pounds Current Money of Carolina to him is paid before the Ensealing and Delivery of these presents by the said Thomas Luten the receipt whereof the said

Henry Bonner doth hereby acknowledge and thereof clearly acquit...and confirm unto the said Thomas Luten...one certain tract or parcell of land containing thirty acres be the same more or less laying and being on the North side of the Tanyard Branch at Green Hall in Chowan County.

In witnesseth whereof the said Henry Bonner hath hereunto Sett his Hand and Seal the day and year above written.

Signed sealed and delivered Henry Bonner (Seal)
in the presence of us,
William Lewis
Francis Penrich

Rec'd the day and year above mentioned of the said Thomas Luten the sum of Fifty pounds being the consideration money above mentioned by me.

William Lewis
Francis Penrich Henry Bonner

Chowan County - April Court Anno Dom 1744
Present: His Majesties Justices

This may certifie that the within Deed of Sale of land from **Captain Henry Bonner** to Thomas Luten, Esquire, was duly acknowledged in open court & on motion was ordered to be Registered.

Test: Edmund Hatch, Clerk Current
Registered May 2d 1744, James Craven, Reg.

The below document is the Deed of Sale from Henry Bonner to William Bonner. This William Bonner was probably the son of (William) Thomas Bonner of Bertie County and married Sarah Luten in 1744. The document can be found in *Deed Book C-2,* page 175 in Edenton.

Henry Bonner
to Deed
William Bonner

To all to whom these presents shall come greetings, Know ye that I Henry Bonner of Chowan County for and in consideration of the sum of One Hundred & Thirty Pounds Current money of North Carolina to me in hand paid by William Bonner of the

County & province aforesaid the receipt whereof I do hereby acknowledge myself fully satisfied contented & paid & thereof to William Bonner his heirs...& assign forever one Lott or half acre of land in the Town called Edenton or two half Lots no. 37 & 38 equally divided by a line from the main County Road across the said two Lotts together with all privileges.....

In witness whereof I have hereunto Set my Hand and Seal this 20th day of January Anno Domminue 1743.

John Luten — Henry Bonner (Seal)
His
Nathaniel N Howcott
Mark

North Carolina, Chowan County January Court 1744
Present: His Majesty's Justices

These may certify that Henry Bonner came into open court & acknowledged the written Deed & acknowledged the within Deed of Sale to William Bonner in due form of Law & on motion is ordered to be registered.

Test: Richard McClure, Clerk Current
Registered: April 29th 1749, James Craven, Regt.

From Miscellaneous Papers.

"William Bonner came into Court and undertook to move the warehouse and place, and underpin the same on the Court House lot or such part of said Lotts as the Commissioner of Edenton shall direct, &c. (1749)." (Ref: Hathaway, Volume 1, Number 3, page 452.)

The following is from *Deed Book H-1*, page 161 in Edenton.

Bonner
to
Garrett

North Carolina - To all to whom these presents shall come I Henry Bonner of Chowan County & in province aforesaid send greetings. Know yee that I Henry Bonner for & in consideration of the sum of twenty-five pounds Bill money of the province aforesaid to me in hand paid at & before the ensealing & delivery of these presents by Richard Garrett of the County aforesaid the receipt whereof I do hereby acknowledge & my self to be herewith fully satisfied contended & paid have given & set over..unto the said Richard Garrett...

One tract of land containing six hundred and forty acres lying and being in Bertie County called Meherring...beginning at a Pine in the head of Chinkepin then said 80 west 320 pole to a Pine then 80 west to the center of Three Pines then 20 east 116 pole to a Pine on Chinkpin Swamp then up the said Swamp to the first station which said land was granted by a Patent bearing the 6th day of August 1719 to have and to hold the said Plantation...

In witness whereof I have hereunto set my Hand and Fixed my Seal this 28th day of January 1749.

Signed Sealed & Delivered Henry Bonner (Seal)
in presence of us,
William Branch
Jesse Copelia (?)
Acknowledged before me ye 16th October 1755.
Let it be Registered. James Hassel, Clerk Justice
Registered, 20th of June 1757 (by) George Disbrane.

The exact month and day Henry Bonner died in 1766 is unknown. He made his Last Will and Testament on 17 July 1766, and a Deed of Gift to his family on 7 July 1766. He was dead before 6 November 1766, therefore he may have died between 17 July and 31 August 1766. His will was probably probated in September and it was probably during October his widow petitioned the Government to recover damages to her estate caused by the Government in the execution of two of her slaves. On 6 November 1766 that petition was acted upon.

REPORT OF THE COMMITTEE OF PUBLIC CLAIMS,
HELD AT NEW BERN, ON THURSDAY, THE
6th OF NOVEMBER, 1766

Present: The Honorables; Lewis Henry DeRosset, John Sampson, Henry Eustace McCulloh, Esquires, Members of the Council.

Richard Caswell, Samuel Benton, John Frohock, Edward Vail, John Barrow, William Haywood, John Bradford, John Pain, Cullen Pollock, Thomas Repress, Thomas Lloyd, Samuel Spencer, Esquires, Members of Assembly.

Elizabeth Bonner, Administratrix of Henry Bonner, of Chowan County, deceased, was allowed her claims of One Hundred and sixty pounds for two Negroes, named, Cato and Peter, executed in Edenton and valued to that sum, as by certificate from the court who tried them ...160 0 0.

As previously stated, Henry Bonner (4) had four children named in his will in July 1766. William and Richard died young and judging from the records, never married. Thomas died in Clarke County, Georgia and Henry's life after 1766 is not documented in the records clear enough to place his identify. He probably was the Henry Bonner who was married to Leah Jordan. Since Thomas's eldest son was named Jordan there must have been a close relationship between the Bonner and Jordan families. Therefore, Jordan Bonner was probably named to honor the Jordan family of Chowan County.

"William Bonner, Chowan County. 1775. (Important note - The year 1775, may have been the date of probate or settlement of his affairs in court. See Chapter VI for a more precise statement stating his passing). Named: Thomas Bonner, Henry Bonner, Richard Bonner." (Ref: Hathaway, Volume 2, Number 2, page 257.)

Evidenced by the above, William was the first of his siblings to pass away.

It appears from the way Richard Bonner's will was worded that it is highly probable that Elizabeth Hardy Bonner was his mother or he was so young at the marriage of his father to Elizabeth that he was bonded to Elizabeth as firmly as if she were his birth mother.

"Richard Bonner, 1781. Brothers: Thomas Bonner, Henry Bonner. William Roberts, Sr., William Roberts, Jr., Liles Roberts, Sarah Roberts, Elizabeth Roberts, Miriam Roberts and Penelope Roberts." (No witness or test) (Ref: Idem, Volume 2, Number 2, page 257.

The Henry Bonner who died in Chowan in 1797, was probably the brother of Thomas Bonner, who was living in Georgia at the time of Henry's death.

"Henry Bonner, Chowan County. Published 24th March 1795, Probated December Court 1797. Wife: Leah Bonner. Daughters, Nancy, Elizabeth, Sarah, Fanny Satterfield (married James Satterfield on 5 March 1795). Son, John (died 1832). Son, William Bonner and Miles Elliott named executors. Test: Thomas Jones, John Fife." (Ref: Hathaway, Volume 1, Number 4, page 519.)

Leah Bonner's father was Jacob Jordan as proved in the following:

"Jacob Jordan, Chowan County, 24 June 1795. Wife: Elizabeth. Daughters, **Leah Bonner**, Rachel Elliott, Patience Elliott. Sister-in-law, Sarah Valentine. Executors, wife, Elizabeth and Nicholas Stallings. Test: Nathan Parker, Ann Earl, Jr., Mary Stallings." (Ref: Hathaway, Volume 2, Number 1, page 5.)

It was the above Jordan family that confused Dr. James C. Bonner when he wrote about the wives of Jordan Bonner. The Leah Bonner that James Bonner wrote of was the wife of Henry Bonner of Chowan County, N. C., and the Rachel Bonner that Dr. Bonner wrote of was, in fact, Rachael (Moon) Bonner, Jordan's second wife.

It is a historical fact that Elizabeth (Hardy-Bonner) Roberts, Mary Bonner (wife of Thomas Bonner, Sr.) and Lydia Bonner (daughter of Mary and Thomas, Sr) attended the Edenton Tea Party on 25 October 1774 to protest the high taxes on British tea.

It is this Henry Bonner (died 1766) that some records of the DAR show as being born ca 1702. There is no proof and analysis of the records suggest a date closer to 1710 as the true year his birth.

Other Bonners of Chowan whose relationship to the Henry Bonner clan of Green Hall is unclear include the following:

Men of whom almost nothing is known of is John Bonner and his brother Thomas Bonner of Chowan. They lived adjacent to the Henry Bonner family in Green Hall and may have been children of Will Bonner, mentioned in the records in the 1700's.

The following is from *Deed Book B-1,* page 437 in Edenton.

Fallow to William Bonner assignment of a Sale of 50 acres of land purchased of David Lee called Wallowing Root.

Know all men by these presents yt I William Fallaw of the Precinct of Chowan province of North Carolina for and in consideration of the sum of seven pounds & ten shillings to me in hand paid by William Bonner of the same place do by these presents for me my heirs executors & administrators & assigns over all my right title & interest of in & unto the lands mentioned in the Deed of Sale unto William Bonner his heirs and assigns forever as witness my hand yt 21st of February 1716.

Seal'd & del'd
in presence of, William W Fallaw
Robert Heicks (Hicks)
John Howcott.

It is believed that the above William Bonner was also known as "Will" and was a brother of Colonel Henry Bonner.

The following is from *Deed Book B-1,* page 451 in Edenton.

Whitmarsh
to A BOND
Bonner

Know all men by these presents yt I John Whitmarsh of Colleton County in South Carolina, Merchant, am held & firmly bound unto William Bonner of Albemarle County in the Province of North Carolina, Cooper, in ye full & just sum of Thirty pounds current money of ye said province which said sum I bind my self my heirs executors administrators firmly by these presents to payments ye said William Bonner his heirs executors, administrators or assigns seal'd with my Seal & Date this 3d day of June 1716.

The condition of the above obligation is such yt if the above John Whitmarsh shall well & truly deliver at the dwelling house of Colonel Edward Mosely in Chowan Precinct in North Carolina aforesaid, One Indian boy about the age of eight or nine years to & for the only proper use benefit & behoof of the said William Bonner on or about the last of October next ensuring the date hereof then his obligation to be void else to remain in full force & ventue.

Seal'd & Del'd
in presence of,
Richard Albans
Robert Hicks

John Whitmarsh

This William Bonner was probably also "Will". The exact date of William Bonner's death is not contained in the records. But, he was probably dead before 1740.

The below document is from *Deed Book E-1*, pages 123, 124 and 125 in Edenton.

John Bonner
to
Thomas Bonner

To all to whome these presents shall come I John Bonner do send greetings. Know ye that I the said John Bonner of the County of Chowan and Province of North Carolina, Planter, for and in consideration of love good will and affection which I have and do bear towards my loving brother, Thomas Bonner of the county and province aforesaid have given and granted and by these presents do freely clearly and absolutely give and grant unto the said Thomas Bonner his heirs executors administrators or assign forever one Mesuage or tract of land situate lying being in the province aforesaid on the Wallowing Root Swamp in Green Hall by estimation one hundred and thirty acres be the same more or less situate and bounded as followeth, viz:

Beginning at a Red Oak standing on the Wallow Root Swamp No 17 West 56 poles to a Maple then No 17 West 10 poles to a Rad Oak (at) Henry Bonner's Corner then along his line No 40 West 260 poles to a Popplar (at) Henry Bonner's corner then No 5 East 76 poles to a Gum standing on Wallowing Root Swamp then up the various courses of the said Swamp to the first station.

I the said John Bonner for myself my heirs executors and administrators do convenant and ingage the above described premises to him the said Thomas Bonner his heirs and assigns aginst the unlawful claim and demands of any person or persons whatsoever.

In witness whereof I the said Jno Bonner have hereunto Sett my Hand and Seal this 18th day of April 1740.

Signed Seal and Delivered John Bonner (Seal)
in the presence of us,
William Hoskins
James Wooden

North Carolina -§
Chowan County - April Court Anno Dom 1746
Present: His Majesty's Justices

This may certify that the withing Deed from John Bonner to Thomas Bonner was acknowledged in open court in due form of law and on motion was ordered to be registered.

Test: James Craven, Clerk Current
Registered: May the 10th 1746, by James Craven.

The above tract of land was sold to Nathaniel Howcott by Thomas Bonner in 1760 which is probably why Nathaniel Howcott was a witness to the wedding of Elizabeth Hardy Bonner and William Robert in 1767 since he was a "next-door" neighbor.

Notice the description of the land in the below document and compare it to the tract that John Bonner gave his brother, Thomas, in 1740, above.

The below is from *Deed Book K-1,* pages 216 and 217 in Edenton.

Bonner
to
Howcott

This indenture made 28th day of August of 1760 between Thomas Bonner of Chowan County in North Carolina of the one part and Nathaniel Howcott of the County aforesaid of the other part:

Witnesseth that the said Thomas Bonner for and in consideration of the sum of Thirty Pounds proclamation Money to him is paid before the ensealing and delivery of these presents the receipt whereof the said Thomas Bonner doth hereby acknowledge & thereof & of every part & parcel doth clearly acquit exonerate & discharge to said Nathaniel Howott...

A certain tract or parcel of land situate lying and being in the province aforesaid on the Wallowing Root Swamp in Green Hall containing by estimation one hundred & thirty acres be the same more or less butted and bounded as follows, viz:

At a Red Oak standing on the Wallowing Root, (then) to a Maple, then to a Red Oak (on) Henry Bonner's Corner, then along his line to a Popplar (at) Henry Bonner's Corner, then to a Gum on the Wallowing Root Swamp, then up various courses of the said Swamp to the first station.

In witness whereof the said Thomas Bonner have hereunto Set my Hand & Seal the day & year above written.

Signed, Sealed and Delivered   Thomas Bonner (Seal)
in the presence of,
Thomas Hoskins
Thomas Eggleston

North Carolina
Chowan County October Inferior Court 1761
Present: His Majesty's Justices

Deed of Sale from Thomas Bonner, Esquire to Mr. Nathaniel Howcott was duly proved in Open Court according to law & ordered to be registered.

Test: Thomas Jones, Clerk Current
Registered: 4 September 1762.

The following is from *Deed Book A-1,*. pages 111 and 112 in Edenton.

Craven
to

Bonner

North Carolina - To all people to whome these presents shall come I James Craven of Edenton in the Province aforesaid, Gentleman, sendth greetings know ye that I the James Craven for & in consideration of the sum of two hundred pounds before the ensealing & delivery to me well truly paid by John Bonner of Chowan County aforesaid, Planter, the receipt whereof is hereby acknowledged have given grant.... unto the said John Bonner his heirs..One tract piece or parcel of land situate lying & being in the County of Chowan containing by estimation fifty six acres be the same more or less being one third part of a larger tract of one hundred seventy acres of land **purchased of Henry Bonner** to be divided equally between the John Bonner, Joseph Anderson and Abraham Blackall as each of them have an equal width on the main road and as back in proportion to the shape or form of the aforesaid tract of one hundred seventy acres and this John Bonner his part....

In witness whereof I the said James Craven have hereunto Set his Hand and Seal the third day of June Anno Domo 1742.

Signed sealed and Delivered   James Craven (Seal)
in presence of,
William Hoskins
Miles Gale

July Court 1742
Present: His Majesty's Justices

These may certify that the within Deed was then and there Duly acknowledged in due form of law and on motion was ordered to be registered.

Test: James Craven, Clerk Current
Registered August the 10th 1742 (by) James Craven, Regr.

The following is from *Deed Book F-1,* pages 231 and 232 in Edenton.

James Craven
to   DEED
John Bonner

This indenture made the fourth day of March one thousand

seven hundred & forty nine between James Craven of Edenton in North Carolina, Gentleman, of the one part and John Bonner of Chowan County in the said Province, Planter, of the other part.

Beginning at the __?__ tree joining upon William Hoskins land and the land that was formerly Nicholas Crisp running thence as to include one acre of ground or land and also all trees woods common of pastures...

In witness of the said James Craven hath to these presents set his Hand and Seal the day and year first above written.

Signed sealed and delivered James Craven (Seal)
in the presence of us,
Edmund Hatch
Thomas Bonner

North Carolina - Chowan County at a Court begun opened and held for the County at the Court House in Edenton on the third Thursday in April Anno Domo 1750.

Presents: His Majesty's Justices

These may certify that the within Deed of Sale of one acre land lying and being in the said County from James Craven, Gentleman, to John Bonner, Planter, then proved in open court in due form of law by the oath of Thomas Bonner, one of the subscribers evidences thereto and on motion was ordered to be Registered.

Test: Will Mears, Clerk Current
Registered the 4th May 1750 per James Craven, Registering Clerk

---

The below is from *Deed Book F-1,* pages 229 and 230 in Edenton.

James Craven
to DEED
John Bonner

This indenture made the tenth day of March in the year of our Lord one thousand seven hundred and forty nine between James Craven of Edenton in the Province of North Carolina, Gentleman, of the one part and John Bonner of Chowan County in the province aforesaid of the other part.

Witnesseth that the said James Craven for and in consideration of the sum of one hundred and twelve pounds ten shillings current money of the Colony of Virginia to him in hand... (A certain) plantation or tract of land containing fifty acres be the same more or less situate lying and being in Chowan County in the province aforesaid commonly called or known by the name of Arkill's Plantation except the Burial place thirty square reserved for the wife of William Branch's family being the Plantation I bought of William Arkill adjoining to Edenton, George Liles and the said John Bonner and Joseph Anderson, Esquire as by Deed of Lease and __?__ from William Arkill to the said James Craven having dates eighteenth and nineteenth day of October last, duly registered in the Register Office of Chowan County....

In witness whereof the said James Craven hath to these the presents Set his Hand and Seal the day and year first above written.

Signed Sealed and delivered James Craven
in the presence of us,
Edmund Hatch
Thomas Bonner, Jurat

Received the day and year first within mentioned of the within named John Bonner the sum of one hundred and twelve pounds ten shillings current money of the Colony of Virginia the full consideration money within mentioned to be paid by him unto me, L112:10:00.

Witness: Edmund Hatch James Craven
Thomas Bonner

North Carolina - Chowan County at a Court begun opened and held for the said County a the Court House in Edenton on the third Thursday in April 1750.

Present: His Majesty's Justices

These may certify that the within Deed of Sale of fifty acres of land in said County commonly known and distinguished by the name of Arkill's Plantation from James Craven, Gentleman, to John Bonner, Planter, was then and there approved in open court in due form of law by the oath of Thomas Bonner one of the subscribing evidences thereto and on motion was ordered to be registered.

Test: Will Means, Clerk Current

Registered May the 4th 1750 per: James Craven, Regr.

JOHN BONNER'S WILL

In the name of God, Amen. The eleventh day of November and the year of our Lord God, one thousand seven hundred and fifty three.

I, John Bonner of Chowan County, in the Province of North Carolina, Planter, being very sick and weak in body, but of perfect mind and memory, thanks be given unto God for it, therefore calling unto mind the mortality of my body and knowing that it is appointed for all men once to die do make and ordain this my Last Will and Testament.

That is to say, principally an first of all I give and recommend my soul into the hands of God that gave it; and my body I recommend to the earth, to be buried in decent Christian Burial at the discretion of my executors nothing doubting but at the general Resurrection I shall receive the same again by the mighty Power of God; and as touching such worldly estate wherewith it hath pleased God to bless me in this Life, I give, demise and dispose of the same in the following manner and form;

Imprimis, I give and bequeath unto my godson, Thomas Eccleston (also spelled Eggleston), two Negroe boys, Jack and Cato, six cows and calves & my riding horse to be deliver'd him when he comes of age, and if he should die without heir lawfully begotten of his body, the same to return to my brother, Thomas Bonner.

Item. I give and bequeath to my cousin, William Howcott, one Negroe boy named, Bob and if he should die without heir, the said Negroe boy to be divided between his two sisters, Elizabeth and Mary Howcott.

Item. I give and bequeath to my cousin Edward Howcott one Negroe girl named, Grace and if he should die without heir, the said girl to be divided between the aforesaid Elizabeth and Mary Howcott.

Item. I give and bequeath to my sister, Sarah Howcott, one gold ring.

Item. I give and bequeath to my sister, Martha Howcott, one gold ring.

Item. I give and bequeath to my brother, Thomas Bonner, my plantation whereon I now live and all the land that I have now in my possession, likewise all the rest and residue of my worldly estate, (Except such as is herein before mentioned.)

I likewise constitute and appoint the aforesaid Thomas Bonner my sole executor of this my last will and testament; I likewise leave John Benbury and HENRY BONNER as Trustees to see that my will is fulfilled according to my desire. And I do hereby utterly disallow, revoke, disannul all and every other former testaments, will, legacies and bequests and executors by me in any ways before named, willed and bequeathed ratifying and confirming this and no other to be my last will and testament.

In witness whereof I have hereunto set (my) Hand and Seal the day and year above written.

John Bonner (Seal)

NB - The above word (my) was interlined before the signing and sealing of this will. Signed and declared by the said John Bonner as his last will and testament in the presence of us,

Jeremiah Michener
John Smith x
George Liles
Thomas Bonner, Qualified

North Carolina - Chowan County -§ January Court 1754

These may certify that George Liles appeared in open court and made oath that he saw John Bonner, sign seal publish and declare the within to be and contain his last will & testament and that he was then and at that time of sound & disposing mind and memory and that also saw John Smith & Jeremiah Mitchener, sign there names thereto at the same time. Then appeared Thomas Bonner, Exr., to the within will and was duly qualified by taking the oath by law appointed.

Ordered that the Secretary of said province have notice that letters testamentary issue thereon as the law directs.

Test: Will Halsey, Clerk Current
(Authors note - NB is for "Nota Bene" which means "look

carefully or beware". Also the term "cousin" was sometimes used for nephew or niece.)

The below Thomas Bonner is believed to be the brother of Henry Bonner (died 1766). There is ample evidence to prove the point.

The below is from *Deed book Q,* pages 165, 166, and 167 in Edenton.

Thomas Bonner, Esquire
to DEED
Thomas MacKnight, Esquire

This indenture made the twenty second day of December in the year of our Lord, one thousand seven hundred and seventy-four, between Thomas Bonner Esquire, Late Sheriff of Chowan County in the province of North Carolina on the one part and Thomas MacKnight, Esquire, of Pasquotank County within the province aforesaid of the other part.

Whereas, in virtue of a Writ of our Lord the King duly issuing out of the Superior Court for the District of Edenton bearing date the twenty fifth day of October in the Eighth Year of the Reign of our Lord the King directed to the Sheriff of Chowan County aforesaid commanding him that the goods and chattles, lands, & tenements of Francis Brown in this Baliwick he should cavets be made, two hundred and eighty one pounds, eight shillings being the balance of the damages which Thomas MacKnight lately of that Court recovered against him and also one pound nineteen shillings taxed and adjudged to the said Thomas MacKnight as well for detention of his said damages as far as his costs and charges in his suit in that behalf expended for as by the said Writ remaining filed and of record in the court may more fully and at large appear and also in virtue and pursuance of an Act of the British parliament passed in the Fifth Year of the Reign of his late Majesty King George the Second entitled, "An Act for the More Easy Recovery of Debts in His Majesty's Plantations and Colonies in America," on which the said Writ is founded the said Thomas Bonner then Sheriff on the twentieth day of March in the year of our Lord one thousand seven hundred and sixty nine did enter open and take possession of the water grist mill and lands thereto belonging of the said Francis Brown lying on the Yeokim Creek in then the County of Chowan aforesaid and after due and legal notice the said Thomas Bonner set up the same at vendue or public sale and the said Thomas MacKnight did then and there bid and offer for the said water grist mill and lands thereto belonging the sum of forty seven pounds proclamation money which was then the best or largest sum that __?__ or offered by any person for the said water grist mill and lands thereto belonging.

Now this indenture witnesseth that the said Thomas Bonner for and in consideration of the said sum of forty seven pounds proclamation money to him in hand paid the receipt whereof is hereby acknowledged...

In witness whereof the said Thomas Bonner hath hereunto set his Hand and Seal the day and year first within written.

Signed, sealed & delivered   Thomas Bonner (Seal)
in the presence of,
Lydia Bonner
Alexander Gellatly, Jurat

Received 22 December 1774 of the within named Thomas MacKnight the sum of forty seven pounds proclamation money being the full consideration money within mentioned to be paid by him to me.

Witness:
Alexander Gellatly   Thomas Bonner
North Carolina

Chowan County December Inferior Court of Pleas & Quarter Session 1774
Present: His Majesty's Justices

Deed of Sale from Thomas Bonner, Esquire, Late Sheriff of this County to Thomas MacKnight, Esquire, was duly proved in Open Court by the Oath of Alexander Gellatly one of the subscribing evidences thereto; and ordered to be Registered.

Test: Thomas Jones, Clerk Current
Registered 5th January 1775 (by) Alexander Gellatly, Regr.

The above Lydia Bonner was probably the daughter of

Thomas and Mary Bonner who married Joseph Blount, Jr., on 15 July 1775.

It is of interest to note that the dividing line between Chowan and Perquimans Counties was adjusted between 1769 and 1774, as mentioned above.

The below document is from *Deed Book Q*, pages 104, 105, 106, and 107 in Edenton.

James Jones
to
Thomas Jones

This indenture Quadripartite made the thirteenth day of February in the Fifteenth year of the Reign of our Sovereign Lord George the Third, King of Great Britain, France & Ireland & in the year of our Lord one thousand seven hundred & seventy five, between James Jones of Chowan County in the province of North Carolina, Planter, of the first part, Thomas Benbury of Chowan County within the Province of North Carolina, Esquire, of the second part, Alexander Gellatly of Edenton within the province of North Carolina of the third part and Thomas Jones of Edenton in the province of North Carolina, Attorney-at-Law, of the fourth part.

Witnesseth, that for and in consideration of the sum of ten pounds Sterling money of Great Britain by the said Thomas Jones and five shillings of like lawfull money by the said Thomas Benbury to the said James Jones, in hand paid at or before the sealing & delivery of these presents the receipts hereof or of which paid several sums of ten pounds and five shillings to the James Jones doth hereby acknowledge...unto the said Thomas Benbury his heirs and assigns all that tract or parcel of land lying and being in the County of Chowan in the Province of North Carolina aforesaid on the west side of the said James Jones land which his father, William Jones, of Chowan County in the province of North Carolina, bought of John Hodgson, Esquire;

Beginning at a Gum at the side of the old field commonly called OLD TOM'S then running a south east course to COLONEL THOMAS BONNER'S land, then along the old line between the said Thomas Bonner and the said James Jones and the said Thomas Jones and the said James Jones to the first station and also lying on the east side of the said James Jones land which his father the aforesaid William Jones, deceased, bought of aforesaid John Hodgson, beginning at the west corner of the said James Jones plantation and running south west or west course, to Colonel Thomas Bonner's land then along the old line between the said James Jones and William Badham, then along the Deep Run to the first station, containing in the whole one hundred acres...

In witness whereof the said parties to these presents hereunto interchangeably set their hands and affixed their seals, the day and year here before mentioned and expressed; being the fifteenth day of February in the year of our Lord one thousand seven hundred and seventy five.

Signed, sealed and delivered
in the presence of;
Thomas Bonner
James Flood
Nathaniel Bonner

Be it remembered that the above named James Jones, at the time of the execution of the above or within deed did enter into and upon the premises comprised in the said deed or some part thereof in the name of the whole and after seisen and possession thereof by him had and taken did give and deliver the seisen and possession thereof, or part thereof in the name of the whole unto the above named Thomas Benbury, to be held to him the said Thomas Benbury his heirs and assigns according to be true intent and meaning of the said deed.

In the presence of;
Thomas Bonner, Jurat — James Jones (Seal)
James Flood — Thomas Benbury (Seal)
Nathaniel Bonner — Alexander Gellatly (Seal)

North Carolina - Chowan County March Inferior Court of Pleas and Quarter Sessions 1775

Deed of Quadripartite from James Jones to Thomas Jones was proved in open court by the oath of Thomas Bonner, Esquire, one of the subscribing witnesses thereto and ordered to be registered.

Test: Thomas Jones, Clerk Current

It is not known who the above Nathaniel Bonner was. He is

not mentioned in the records before or after the above document. He may have been a son of the within named Thomas Bonner.

The below is from *Deed Book Q*, pages 198 and 199 in Edenton.

Thomas Jones
to   Deed
Thomas Bonner

This indenture made the fourteenth day of February in the year of our Lord one thousand seven hundred and seventy five between, Thomas Jones, Esquire, of Edenton in the province of North Carolina, Attorney-at-Law of the one part and THOMAS BONNER, SENIOR of the County of Chowan in the province of North Carolina, ESQUIRE, of the other part;

Witnesseth that the said Thomas Jones for and in consideration of the sum of five pounds proclamation money to him in hand paid by the said Thomas Bonner at and before the ensealing and delivery of these presents the receipt whereof is hereby acknowledged hath granted bargained sold...

Fifty acres of land lying in the east side of James Jones's land which William Jones, father of the said James Jones bought of John Hodgson, Esquire;

Beginning at the east corner of the said James Jones Plantation and running south west or west course to the said Thomas Bonner?s land then along the old line between the said James Jones and William Badham then along the Deep Run to the first station.

Witnesseth whereof the said Thomas Jones hath hereunto set his Hand and Seal the day and year first above written.

Signed, sealed & delivered   Thomas Jones (Seal)
in the presence of;
Alexander Gellatly
Thomas Benbury
James Jones

Received 14th February 1775 of the within named Thomas Bonner the sum of five pounds proclamation money being the full consideration money within mentioned to be paid by him to me. I say received by me, Thomas Jones.

Witness:
Thomas Benbury
Alexander Gellatly
James Jones

North Carolina - Chowan County March Inferior Court of Pleas and Quarter Sessions 1775

Present: His Majesty's Justices

Deed of Sale from Thomas Jones to Thomas Bonner, Senior was duly acknowledged in open court and ordered to be registered.

Test: Thomas Jones, Clerk Current
Registered 29th March 1775 (by) Alexander Gellatly.

When the last three documents are compared to each other, it can be ascertained that Colonel Thomas Bonner, Thomas Bonner, Senior, and Sheriff Thomas Bonner are the same man, being the son of Colonel Henry Bonner, died 1738.

As I read into the legal records of Chowan, Bertie, and Perquimans Counties, I was struck by the number of times a certain family would appear that had ties to the Bonner family. Many of the marriages were between cousins from where the families had intermarried many years previously.

Such was the case of Reverend Clement Hall. He was the First Rector of St. Paul's Church in Edenton and the Plantation where he lived was sold to him by Thomas Bonner, Sr. For reasons not stated Thomas Bonner, Sr., and his wife Mary made Perquimans County their main residence in the 1750's. That fact is proved by a land sale of Thomas Bonner, Jr., and his wife Margaret in the 1770's of property that fits the exact description of a plantation that was purchased in 1752 by Thomas and Mary Bonner and was sold by Thomas and Margaret to Julius Branch in 1775. When Thomas and Margaret took possession of the Perquimans County Plantation is not recorded.

Richard Hoskins (born 1740) was the son of William and Sarah

Whedbee Hoskins. Mrs. Sarah Whedbee Hoskins was born 13 February 1717. She was a daughter of Richard Whedbee (son of John and Deborah Astine Sutton Whedbee). Another of Richard's daughters was Ann Whedbee who married Francis Foster, Clerk of Chowan Precinct, and later Clerk of Bertie County. Francis and Ann Whedbee Foster's daughter Frances Foster on 19 July 1742 married Clement Hall, an Attorney-at-Law, who shortly after the marriage went to England and received orders in the Church of England and on his return to Chowan County was called in 1745 as the 1st Rector of Saint Paul's Parish, Edenton, North Carolina. It was his only Parish, he died in 1758 on his plantation located about three miles North of Edenton. (Ref: Hathaway, Volume 3, Number 1, page 116.)

The above information is interesting not only for naming the 1st Rector of St. Paul's Parish but also in establishing the location of the plantation in reference to Edenton. Additionally, the Plantation that Rev. Clement Hall lived on was purchased from Thomas Bonner (Sr) the brother of Henry Bonner (died 1766.) Attorney Thomas Jones of Edenton came into possession of Clement Hall's plantation, and in 1775, at Thomas Jones death, it was willed to his kin.

The below document is from *Deed Book H-1*, pages 271, 272, and 273 in Edenton.

Bonner
to
Hall

North Carolina - This indenture made the Nineth day of September in the Thirty-First year of the Reign of Our Sovereign Lord King George the Second & in the year of our Lord one thousand seven hundred & fifty-seven between Thomas Bonner of Perquimans County in the province of North Carolina, Planter, & Mary his wife of the one part & Clement Hall, Rector of St. John Parish in Chowan County & province aforesaid of the other part;

Witnesseth; that the said Thomas Bonner for and in consideration of the sum of ninety five pounds proclamation money to him in hand paid by the said Clement Hall at or before & delivery of these presents the receipt whereof he doth hereby acknowledge & there by & every part & parcel thereof doth acquit

& discharge the said Clement Hall his heirs...

All that tract or parcel of land containing by estimation one hundred twenty five acres be the same more or less situate lying and being in Chowan County aforesaid butting and bounding on outermost Branch of Mattacomack Creek & on Robinson's, Bonner's, Blackall's & Hall's lines also all houses, buildings, woods, water courses, profits, commodities & involvement to the said tract of one hundred twenty five acres...the said Clement Hall his heirs & assigns forever and lastly the said Mary Bonner doth by her becoming party to these presents...

In witness whereof the parties have hereunto set their Hands & seals the day and year first above written.

Signed Sealed and delivered
in presence of,
Timothy Truelove
Thomas Freeman
Angline Freeman

Thomas Bonner (Seal)
Mary Bonner (Seal)

North Carolina - Chowan County April Court 1758

Present: His Majesty's Justices

Deed of Sale from Thomas Bonner and Mary his wife was duly acknowledged in open court according to law and at the same time Mary Bonner was privately examined & renounced her right of dowry to the said land.

Test: Thomas Jones, Clerk Current
Registered 11 of May 1758 by George Disbanes, Regr.

It is believed that Thomas Bonner, (Sr) married Mary Standing in Chowan County on 14th February 1752.

"Thomas Bonner, Chowan. 2 February 1785. Wife, Mary. Executors, William Roberts, Richard Hoskins and Edmund Blount. Test: Mary Badham, William Ellis. (Ref: Hathaway, Volume 1, Number 4, page 519.)" The aforementioned William Roberts married Elizabeth Hardy Bonner in February 1767 and was this Thomas's brother-in-law. Lydia Bonner Blount, wife of Edmund Blount, Jr., died before 1780 and therefore is not mentioned here.

"Mary Bonner, Chowan. 2 August 1789. Grandson, John Blount. Granddaughter, Mary Blount. William Littlejohn and Samuel Dickinson, trustees. Brother, Jonathan Roberts, my deceased husband's brother, William Bonner; John Brickell son of my sister Mourning Brickell, Joseph Littlejohn son of William Littlejohn, Ann Littlejohn, daughter of said William; sister, Lydia Shepard, William Littlejohn and Samuel Dickinson, Executors. Test: John Little, Elizabeth Little, William Bateman." (Ref: Idem, Volume 1, Number 4, page 519.)

The above Mary Bonner was not the wife of Thomas Bonner, son of Colonel Henry Bonner, unless there are many records of the period missing. She was probably the wife of Thomas Bonner, son of William Bonner who died in 1775 who also had a son named William.

Some marriages concerning Bonners of Chowan County that are of interest to this work are as indicated below:

1. 21 August 1744 William Bonner married Sarah Luten. (B) William Luten & (W) George Parris.
2. 14 February 1752. Thomas Bonner married Mary Standin. (W) James Craven and (B) William Luten.
3. 4 January 1758. Henry Bonner married Elizabeth Hardy. (No bondsman).
4. 21 February 1767. William Roberts married Mrs. Elizabeth Bonner. (B) Nathaniel Howcott.
5. 6 May 1767. Thomas Bonner married Margaret Jones. (B) Thomas Carroll and (W) Thomas Jones.
6. 5 November 1773. Henry Bonner married Esther Worley. (B) Thomas Bonner.
7. 15 July 1775. Joseph Blount, Jr., married Lydia Bonner. (B) Joseph Blount and (W) Thomas Jones.
8. 14 June 1779. Henry Bonner married Elizabeth Williams. (No Bondsman).

VI

Thomas Bonner

(ca 1744 - 1804)

Family Status: Thomas Bonner (ca 1744 - 1804)
Wife: Margaret Jones, (ca 1750 - ca 1828)
When: 6 May 1767 in Edenton, North Carolina
Children:

1. Jordan Bonner (12 December 1767 - 8 May 1841)
2. Zadock Bonner (17 June 1769 - 1848)
3. Deborah (Nancy) Bonner (1772 - after 1860)
4. Whitmel Bonner (ca 1775 - 1819)
5. Thomas Bonner (1779 - 1862)
6. Mary Elizabeth Bonner (1779 - after 1865)
7. Allen Bonner (1781 - 1828)
8. Willis Bonner (ca 1785 -
9. Josiah Bonner (5 May 1787 - 9 December 1851)
10. Daniel M. Bonner (ca 1789 -

This Thomas Bonner was the main subject that Dr. James C. Bonner wrote of in his manuscript, *Migration Pattern of the Descendants of Thomas Bonner - A Family History*. Dr. Bonner's main emphasis on the Bonner family was after Thomas had moved to Georgia and settled in Greene County, (later Clarke and presently Oconee) in the Dove's Creek community. When I found that Thomas had married in Edenton, North Carolina in 1767, I decided to research the family in North Carolina and connect them to the Bonner family of Georgia through legal documents. That way there would never be "second" guessing about who his ancestors were.

When I first traveled to Edenton and looked at the Marriage Bond Book of 1767, I immediately found Thomas and Margaret Bonner. However, the book had his name stated as "Thomas Bonner, Jr." and I began research for Thomas Bonner, Sr. The

Thomas Bonner, Sr., I found did not match the profile to be the father of Thomas Bonner, Jr. After much research, I made a comment that I had found the perfect family for Thomas, Jr., but the father's name was Henry not Thomas. Almost three years later I found a single line in an old genealogy magazine that stated that Thomas Bonner, Jr., was in court in 1769 concerning business about his father, "Henry Bonner, deceased". With that piece of information, I arranged a schedule that gave me a full day of research in Edenton. There I found conclusive evidence backed by legal documents that, in fact, Thomas was a son of Henry. That was when the fun started. After compiling many documents, I still could not prove that Thomas Bonner of Chowan County was the same Thomas Bonner who died in Clarke County, Georgia in 1804. At the time I had the proof in my files but I did not know it. Dr. James Bonner stated, in his work, that an unknown daughter of Thomas Bonner had married Richard Vandiford. That unknown daughter was the connection I needed to prove the family connection. A descendant of Jordan Bonner sent me information that he had obtained from within his family about a daughter of Jordan Bonner who wrote, in 1900, a letter outlining her family. In that letter she stated that Deborah Bonner had married Richard Vandiford. I found out later that Deborah, in her adulthood, was known as "Nancy" which was interesting. The records show that after Deborah Bonner, born 1772, went by the name of Nancy, the name "Nancy" shows up in some branches of the Bonner family of her sibling's children and the name "Deborah" disappears.

The name Thomas Bonner, Jr., came about because of the tradition of that era. When Colonel Henry Bonner died in 1738, he left a minor son, Thomas, to live with his older son, Henry. When Thomas, son of Henry, was born ca 1744, there became two Thomas Bonners in the same house. It was the tradition of the time that the eldest would become known as Senior and the youngest Junior, regardless of their kin status. When Henry made his Will in July 1766, he designated his brother Thomas and his Cousin Captain Thomas Bonner to be trustees to his sons which suggests that none of his sons were at the age of majority.

The following can be found in the *Marriage Bond Book,* page 17, located in the Register of Deeds Office, Chowan County Court House, Edenton, North Carolina.

Groom	Bride	Date of Bond	Bond/Witness
Bonner, Thomas, Jr.	Margaret Jones	6 May 1767	(B) Thomas Carroll (W) Thomas Jones

---

The below is a copy of the complete Marriage Bond that Thomas Bonner and Margaret Jones swore to as their marriage contract. The original is on file in the North Carolina Archives in Raleigh, North Carolina.

MARRIAGE BOND

North Carolina, Chowan County

Know ye all men by these presents that we, Thomas Bonner and Margaret Jones, all of the county and province aforesaid are held and firmly bound unto our Sovereign Lord the King, in the penal sum of Five Hundred Pounds, to the which payment well and truly to be made we bind ourselves, our heirs, Exrs, Admrs., and assigns, jointly and severally by these presents.

Sealed with our Seals and dated this 6 May, 1767.

Whereas Thomas Bonner hath applied for a License pursuant to an Act of Assembly of this Province entitled, "An Act for Preventing Clandestine and Unlawfull Marriages," to be joined together in the Holy Estate of Matrimony with Margaret Jones of the County aforesaid.

Now the condition of this obligation is such, that if there appears no lawful cause to obstruct for which the aforesaid license was desired pursuant to the true interest and meaning of the aforecited act, then the above obligation to be void, else to be and remain in full force and virtue.

Thomas Bonner (Seal)
Margaret Jones (Seal)
Surety: Thomas Carroll.

The above Thomas Carroll is an unknown person to this writer. His name does not appear anywhere in the records of

Chowan County except in the marriage bond of Thomas and Margaret. It would really be interesting to know his relationship to the family.

In the manuscript written by James C. Bonner, he made the premise that the parents of Margaret Jones were Nathan and Elizabeth Slaughter Jones. That has been proven to be wrong. Below is a copy of the Slaughter Family Bible pages that puts that premise to rest and proves it to be false:

Ezekiel Slaughter (RS) (ca 1724 - 1792) was born in Virginia and married his cousin, Sarah Butler.

Children:

1. Mary (born 15 October 1748) married Edward Worsham.
2. John (RS) (born 9 May 1750) married Mary Hedrick.
3. Sarah (born 10 June 1751) married Peter Roberts.
4. **Elizabeth (born 11 June 1753) married Nathan Jones.**
5. Judeth (Judea) (born 17 October 1754) married Daniel Gill.
6. Ezekiel (born 30 April 1756).
7. Samuel (born 3 April 1758) married Frances Gill.
8. Nancy Ann (born 5 July 1760) married ____ Stilwell.
9. Susannah (born 14 January 1764) married Samuel Hawkins.
10. Patty (born 23 July 1764) married John Gill.
11. Rueben (RS) (born 4 November 1766) married (1st) Ann ___.,(2d) Mary Lawson.
12. Lucy (born 30 April 1769) married Wiley Clark.

The "RS" above denotes Revolution Service. From the above, it can be seen that Elizabeth was too young to be the mother of Margaret Jones. However, the Bonners and Slaughters were close friends and neighbors in Georgia, as noted:

"Last Will and Testament of Ezekiel Slaughter, Greene County, Georgia. To my daughter, Mary Worsham; My son, John Slaughter; My daughter, Salley (Sarah) Roberts; My daughter, Bettey (Elizabeth) Jones; My daughter, Judea (Judith) Gill; My son, Samuel Slaughter, tract of land on Banister River; My daughter, Ann Stillwell; My daughter, Susannah Hawkins; My daughter, Patty Gill, one hundred acres on Powell's Creek; My son, Reuben Slaughter; Grandson, Ezekiel Slaughter; Daughter, Lucy Slaughter; My wife, Sarah Slaughter; Three grandchildren, Ezekiel Gill,

Ezekiel Hawkins, Ezekiel Slaughter. Appoint my loving wife, Sarah Slaughter, Rueben Slaughter, Samuel Slaughter, Executors. Ezekiel Slaughter (Seal). **Witness: Thomas Bonner, Jordan Bonner,** Richard Parker. Dated: 20 June 1792. Proven 21 August 1792. Recorded: 23 August 1792." (Note - The part of Greene County where the Bonners and Slaughters lived became Clarke County in 1802. Today that area is in Oconee County.)

The parents of Margaret Jones, wife of Thomas Bonner, may never be known. There were many Jones families in the Edenton area of Chowan County during the time that Margaret lived there. One document that does give a hint as to whom she was a daughter of is a Deed dated I June 1768 in which Thomas Bonner (Jr) sells to Thomas Jones 640 acres of land in which Thomas Bonner (Jr) retains 320 acres according to the deed. Therefore the best possibility, and it is only a guess, is that Margaret was a daughter of Thomas Jones, the Chowan County Clerk of Court, or why would he purchase 640 acres and allow Thomas and Margaret to retain 320 acres of it? Thomas Jones's occupation was Attorney-at-Law; he not only witnessed legal court documents but purchased many of the plantations that Thomas and Margaret Bonner sold. Additionally, it will be noticed that Thomas Jones owned a plantation that shared a boundary line with the Bonner family. However, a reading of all of the Wills made by a Jones of that era, does not lend a clue as to which man was her father. Thomas Jones passed away in 1775, and he did not name Margaret in his will. This writer has speculated that since Jordan was not a nine month baby there may have been a scandal about the circumstance of the birth. Was Margaret disowned by her father, whomever he was? Remember that the Bonner and Jones families were prominent people in the Carolina Colony. I suspect that Attorney Thomas Jones was her father. His brother was Chief Justice Frederick Jones who today is well known in the legal circles of North Carolina.

There are no documents about Thomas Bonner (died 1804) prior to July 1766. He first appears in his father's will dated 7 July 1766 and again in his fathers Deed of Gift dated 17 July 1766. The Deed of Gift is more detailed in that it names the trustees of the estates for the children's behalf.

The below document is listed here because the land was disposed of by Thomas and Margaret in 1775 and has been noted previously. It was purchased by Thomas (Sr) and Mary, his wife in 1752. When Thomas (Jr) and Margaret took possession is not recorded. It was the last piece of property sold before their move to South Carolina about 1778. The original can be found in the Register of Deed office, Hereford, Perquimans County, North Carolina.

Luten
to
Bonner

North Carolina - This indenture made this eighteenth day of September in the year of our Lord one thousand seven hundred & fifty two between James Luten of Edenton in the province aforesaid of the one part & Thomas Bonner of Chowan County in the province aforesaid of the other part.

Witnesseth that the James Luten for & in consideration of the sum of one hundred pounds current money of the Colony of Virginia to him in hand by the said Thomas Bonner the receipt whereof the said James Luten doth hereby...(sell) unto the said Thomas Bonner his heirs & assigns forever all that tract plantation & parcell of land lying on the North side of Yeopins River in Perquimans County being the land the said James Luten purchased of Henry Warren as by Deed bearing date the 7th of December, one thousand seven hundred & fifty...containing by estimation three hundred acres be the same more or less & also all houses, trees, woods, under woods, commons of pastures...

In witness whereof I have hereunto set my Hand and affixed my seal the day & year above written.

Signed, Sealed and Delivered James Luten
Edmund Hatch
Thomas Bonner

Received the day & year mentioned of the within Thomas Bonner the sum of one hundred pounds current money of the Colony of Virginia being the full consideration money within mentioned as witness my hand.

Witness:
Edmund Hatch James Luten
Thomas Bonner

Perquimans County, April Court Anno Domo 1753

Present: His Majesty's Justices

These may certify that the above Deed of Sale & the above receipt from James Luten to Thomas Bonner was duly proved in open court by the oath of Edmund Hatch as evidence thereto & on motion is ordered to be Registered.
Test: Edmund Hatch

Registered in the Register's Office of Perquimans County this 19th day of April A.D. 1753.
Test: John Harvey, Regrt.

Soon after the death of his father in 1766, Thomas Bonner began to dispose of the family plantations he inherited. No records have been found showing that he purchased property in his own name to increase his holdings. It can be speculated that early in the marriage with Margaret Jones they had plans to immigrate to the lands south of North Carolina.

The below is from *Deed Book N-1,* pages 215 and 216 in Edenton.

Thomas Bonner, Junior
to
Thomas Jones

This indenture made the first day of June in the year of our Lord, one thousand seven hundred and sixty-eight between Thomas Bonner, Junior of Chowan County in the province of North Carolina, Gentleman, of the one part and Thomas Jones, Attorney-at-law, of the same county and province of the other part.

Witnesseth that the said Thomas Bonner for and in consideration of the sum of one hundred and fifty pounds to him in hand paid by the said Thomas Jones at and before the sealing and delivery of these presents and the receipt whereof of the said Thomas Bonner doth hereby acknowledge the said Thomas Bonner hath granted bargained and sold aliened and confirmed and by these present, doth grant bargain sell...

One moiety of a certain plantation lying and being in Chowan County containing six hundred and forty acres of land **it being the**

said plantation which was devised to the said Thomas Bonner, Junior by his father, Henry Bonner, deceased by his last will and testament bearing the date seventh day of July in the year of our Lord One thousand seven hundred and sixty six in fee simple.

In witness whereof the said Thomas Bonner hath hereunto set his Hand and Seal the day and year first above written.

Signed, sealed and delivered Thomas Bonner, Junior (Seal)

Samuel Dunscomb
John Norcum
Thomas Bonner

Be it remembered that on the fourth day of June in the year of our Lord one thousand seven hundred and sixty eight it was agreed by and between the said Thomas Bonner, Junior and the said Thomas Jones that a partition line should began so as to distinguish the respective tracts of land that is to say to run a line through the tract of land containing six hundred and forty acres which was done by a line of Marked Trees running in the following manner to wit:

From a Gum standing at Thomas Jones' corner **formerly Clement Hall's,** near the Deep Ponds from therein North eighteen degrees West hundred & twelve poles to a Red Oak at the head of Poplar Branch and it was likewise agreed by the said Thomas Bonner, Junior should take the land containing three hundred and twenty acres lying to the Westward of the said line and the said Thomas Jones should take the land lying to the Eastward of the said line of Marked Trees.

In witnesseth whereof the said Thomas Bonner, Junior and the said Thomas Jones have hereunto set their Hands and Seals the day and year first within written.

Witness: Samuel Duncomb Thomas Bonner, Junior (Seal)
John Norcom Thomas Jones (Seal)
Thomas Bonner

Received the fourth day of June one thousand seven hundred and sixty eight of Thomas Jones the sum of one hundred and fifty pounds proclamation money being the full consideration money within mentioned.

Witness: Samuel Dunscomb

John Norcom
Thomas Bonner

Thomas Bonner, Junior

North Carolina. October 2d 1768. The within Deed of Bargain Sale of Land from Thomas Bonner, Junior to Thomas Jones was proved according to the Oath of Captain Samuel Dunscomb.

Registered, 20 March 1769 (by) Frederick Blount, Rgr.

The below document is from *Deed Book N-1,* page 209 and 210 in Edenton.

Bonner
to
Bonner

North Carolina - Know all men by these presents that I Thomas Bonner of Chowan County in the province aforesaid for divers good causes and consideration me moving thereunto but more especially for the love and natural affection I bear **unto my brother William Bonner** his heirs and assign forever all my plantation tract or parcel of land commonly known by the name of Turkey Neck lying on the South side of the Wallowing Root Swamp in Chowan County bounded on one side on Richard Hoskin's land and John Luten's land and Nathaniel Howcott's land together with all the profit commodity & hereditaments to the same belonging or any wise appertaining.

To have and to hold the said land and plantation and all and singular the appurts belonging unto the said William Bonner and his heirs & assigns forever full and ample manner as I myself could or might have done and for a certainty of this being my act and deed I have hereunto put my Hand and Seal this 14th day of December 1768.

Signed, sealed and acknowledged
in the presence of;
Jeremiah Halsey
Jacob Boyce
Elizabeth Halsey

Thomas Bonner, Junior (Seal)

North Carolina - Chowan County, December Inferior Court of Pleas and Quarter Sessions, 1768.

Deed of Gift from Thomas Bonner, Junior to William Bonner was duly acknowledged in Open Court according to law by Thomas Bonner and ordered to be Registered.

Test: Thomas Jones, Clerk Current.
Registered 25th July 1769 (by) Alexander Gellatly. Reg.

The above Elizabeth Halsey was married to Jeremiah Halsey. She was a daughter of James and Deborah (Bonner) Thompson.

The below document is from *Deed Book O-1,* pages 104 to 108 in Edenton.

Thomas Bonner, Junior and Margaret, his wife
to DEED
Thomas Jones

This indenture made the Nineth day of October in the year of our Lord one thousand seven hundred and sixty nine between Thomas Bonner, Junior and Margaret his wife of Chowan County in the province of North Carolina of the one part and Thomas Jones of Edenton in the province of North Carolina attorney-at-law of the other part;

Whereas Henry Bonner late of Chowan County within the province of North Carolina, Planter, in and by his last will and testament bearing date the seventh day of July in the year of our Lord one thousand seven hundred sixty six duly caveted and attended; Did thereby give and devise to the said Thomas Bonner and his heirs of his body lawfully begotten of body forever;

The one half of his dwelling Plantation, situate lying and being in Saint Paul's Parish in Chowan County within the province of North Carolina, the one half of which said dwelling plantation contains by estimation three hundred and twenty acres be the same more or less bounded in the following manner;

That is to say, beginning at a Red Oak on Poplar Branch, joining the land commonly called Cleland's, now in the possession of James Luten's then down the said Poplar Branch to Mattacomack Creek, then down the various courses of the said Creek to John Henley's line so up his line to Thomas Jones (formerly Clement Halls) line to a corner Gum, so along the partition between Thomas Bonner and Thomas Jones to the first station. **It being that part of the said Henry Bonner's Plantation whereon he the said Bonner lived.**

AND whereas His Majesties in Nature of an Ad Quid Damnum hath issued out from the Secretary's Office of the province of North Carolina aforesaid for the Docking of the Estate Tail, simited to the said Thomas Bonner by the will of the said Henry Bonner.

Whereby the Sheriff of Chowan County in pursuant of the Directions of the Act of the General Assembly in that case made and provided in the Twenty Second year of the Reign of our Late Sovereign Lord George the Second, King of Great Britain an act intitled, "An Act Directing the Method for Cutting or Docking Intails of Small Estates", was commanded that by good and lawful men of the County of Chowan aforesaid he should diligently inquire if it might be to the damage or prejudice of our said Lord the King or others, if the aforesaid Thomas Bonner should sell the aforesaid three hundred and twenty acres of land situate, lying and being in Saint Paul's Parish in the County of Chowan within the province of North Carolina aforesaid, whereof the said Thomas Bonner was seized as Tenant in Eutail, by the last will & testament of the aforesaid Henry Bonner, deceased, and if to the damage or prejudice and to what prejudices or damage to others, and of what value the said land with the improvements thereon made is in good lawful money of the Kingdom of Great Britain and whether the same be parcel or contiguous to other lands whereof the said Thomas Bonner or seized as tenant infutail and that the said Sheriff of Chowan should send the Inquisition thereof, distinctly and firmly made into the Secretary's Office of the province of North Carolina under the said Sheriff's Hand and Seal and the Hands and Seals of those whom the said Sheriff should made such Inquisition without delay.

And Whereas in pursuance of the Writ in Nature of, Ad Quod Damnam aforesaid and of the Act of Assembly aforesaid an Inquisition hath been made on the plantation of the said Thomas Bonner, Junior.

AND, Samuel McGuire, Moses Blanchard, Thomas Bauhus, Joseph Rodgers, William Simpson, Thomas Ellis, Charles Jordan, John Simpson, Micajah Chappel, Thomas Gooding, Martin Hurdle, Zebulon Mansfield, William Spivey, William Munns and John Padgett, having been duly summoned, returned and qualified according to the direction of the Act of Assembly, aforesaid did value the said land in the Writ, in the nature of Ad Quod

Damnum aforesaid mentioned to the sum of Forty Five Pounds Sterling money of Great Britain and likewise did further on their oaths say, that the said land was not contiguous to other intailed lands as by the said Last Will and Testament of the said Henry Bonner, Writ in Nature of an Ad Quod Damnum and inquisition so made in consequence thereof, none remaining of record in the Secretary's Office of the province aforesaid relation thereto being had more fully at large the same may and doth appear.

Now this indenture witnesseth that the said Thomas Bonner, Junior and Margaret his wife in pursuance of the act aforesaid, impowering the said Thomas Bonner, Junior to dock the estate aforesaid and of the below recited proceeding directed and injoyned by the aforesaid act and also for and in consideration of the sum of Forty Five Pounds lawful money of Great Britain to him the said Thomas Bonner, Junior and Margaret his wife in hand well and truly paid by the said Thomas Jones at and before the ensealing and delivery of these presents, the receipt whereof the said Thomas Bonner, Junior and Margaret his wife do hereby acknowledge and consess and thereof & therefrom do acquit exonerate and discharge the said Thomas Jones his heirs executors and administrators forever by these presents have granted bargained sold aliened and confirmed and by these presents do grant bargain sell alien and confirm unto the said Thomas Jones his heirs and assigns forever; all that before mentioned Three Hundred and Twenty acres of land situate lying and being in Saint Paul's Parish in Chowan County as aforesaid be the same more or less bounded as aforesaid with all the appurtenances thereunto belonging or in any wise appurtaining.

To have and to hold the aforesaid Three Hundred and twenty acres of land with all and singularly the appurtenances thereunto belonging unto the said Thomas Jones his heirs and assigns forever unto the only proper use and behoof of the said Thomas Jones his heirs and assigns forever.

In witness whereof the said Thomas Bonner, Junior and his wife have Hereunto set their Hands and Seals the day and year first within mentioned.

Signed, Sealed and delivered
in the presence of us, Thomas Bonner, Junior (Seal)
Thomas Bonner

Jimmy Walton
Thomas Benbury
Henry Thompson

Received the Nineth day of October in the year of our Lord one thousand seven hundred and sixty nine the full and just sum of forty five pounds good and lawful money of Great Britain being the full consideration money within mentioned.

Witness:
Thomas Bonner — Thomas Bonner, Junior
Jimmy Walton
Thomas Benbury
Henry Thompson

Chowan County - I John Hodgson, Esquire, one of the Members of the Inferior Court of the said county being appointed by the said court privily to examine the within names Margaret, the wife of Thomas Bonner, Junior whether she the said Margaret doth fully acknowledge the within Deed and voluntarily assent thereto.

Do certify that upon such examination taken agreeable to the Direction of the severall acts of assembly, in such case made the said Margaret did declare that she did freely acknowledge the same and voluntarily assented thereto. Given under my Hand and Seal the twenty third day of March in the year of our Lord one thousand seven hundred and seventy.

John Hodgson (Seal)

North Carolina - Chowan County March Inferior Court of Pleas and Quarter Sessions 1770

Present: His Majesty's Justices

Deed of Bargain and Sale under the Act of Assembly of the province of North Carolina for Docking Futails of Small Estates from Thomas Bonner, Junior and Margaret his wife to Thomas Jones was duly acknowledged by the said Thomas Bonner, Junior and Margaret his wife to be their Act and Deed in Open Court and ordered to be Registered.

Test: Thomas Jones, Clerk Current — Joseph Hewes
Cullen Pollock
Thomas Bonner
William Boyd

Registered 7th April 1770 (by) Alexander Gellatly, Regr.

The following is from *Deed Book O-1,* pages 217 and 218 in Edenton.

Thomas Bonner, Junior and Margaret his wife
to DEED
Thomas Jones

North Carolina - This indenture made the Nineth of October in the year of our Lord one thousand seven hundred and sixty nine between Thomas Bonner, Junior, Planter, and Margaret his wife of the Parish of Saint Paul in the County of Chowan within the province of North Carolina of the one part and Thomas Jones of Edenton in the province of North Carolina attorney at law of the other part.

Witnesseth that the said Thomas Bonner for and in consideration of the sum of forty five pounds good and lawful money of the Kingdom of Great Britain to him in hand paid by the said Thomas Jones at and before the ensealing and delivery of these presents the receipt whereof the said Thomas Bonner hath granted...unto the said Thomas Jones his heirs and assigns forever all that tract or parcell of land situate lying and being in the Parish of Saint Paul in the County of Chowan within the province of North Carolina.

Beginning at a Red Oak on Poplar Branch joining the land commonly known as Cleland's now in the possession of James Luten's heirs then down the said Poplar Branch to Mattacomack Creek then down the various courses of the said Creek to John Henley's line, so up his line to Thomas Jones (formerly Clement Hall's) line to a corner Gum, so along the partition between Thomas Bonner and Thomas Jones to the first station being the **land his father Mr. Henry Bonner lived on during his lifetime,** containing by estimation three hundred and twenty acres...

In witness whereof the said Thomas Bonner, Junior and the said Margaret have hereunto Sett their Hand and Seals, the day and year first written within.

Signed, sealed and delivered
in the presence of us,
Thomas Bonner
Jimmy Walton
Thomas Benbury
Henry Thompson

Thomas Bonner (Seal)
Margaret Bonner (Seal)

Received the Nineth day of October in the year of our Lord one thousand seven hundred and sixty nine the full and just sum of forty five pounds good and lawfull money of Great Britain being the full consideration money within mentioned.

Witness: Thomas Bonner, Junior
Thomas Bonner
Jimmy Walton
Thomas Benbury

Chowan County - I John Hodgson, Esquire one of the Members of the Inferior Court of the said County being appointed by the said Court privily to examine the within named Margaret, wife of Thomas Bonner, Junior whether she the said Margaret doth freely acknowledge the with Deed and voluntarily apert thereto;

Do certify that upon examination taken agreeable to the divations of the several acts of assembly in such case made the said Margaret did declare that she did fully acknowledge the same voluntarily assigned thereto.

Given under my Hand and Seal the twenty third day of March in the year of our Lord one thousand seven hundred and seventy.

John Hodgson (Seal)

North Carolina - Chowan County March Inferior Court of Pleas and Quarter Session 1770

Present: His Majesty's Justices
Deed of Bargain & Sale from Thomas Bonner, Junior and Margaret his wife to Thomas Jones was duly acknowledged by the said Thomas Bonner, Junior and Margaret his wife to be their act and deed, in open court and ordered to be registered.

Witness:
Joseph Hewes
Cullen Pollock
Thomas Bonner
William Boyd

Test: Thomas Jones, Clerk Current
Registered: 21st May 1770, Alexander Gellatly, Reg.

The below document is from *Deed Book P-1,* pages 7 and 8 in Edenton.

Thomas Bonner, Junior
& Others to DEED
Joseph Blount

North Carolina - This indenture made the twenty first day of September in the year of our Lord one thousand seven hundred and seventy between Thomas Bonner, Junior and Margaret his wife, and William Roberts and Elizabeth his wife of Chowan County of the part of the first part and Joseph Blount of Edenton in the county aforesaid of the other part.

Witnesseth that the said Thomas Bonner, Junior and Margaret his wife and William Roberts and Elizabeth his wife for and in consideration of the sum of four hundred pounds proclamation money to the said Thomas Bonner, junior doth hereby acknowledge and thereof in hand before the ensealing and delivery of the presents by the said Joseph Blount as the receipt whereof the said Thomas Bonner, Junior acknowledges and thereof and of every part and parcel thereof doth hereby acquitt, esonate, and discharge the said Joseph Blount his heirs executors and administrators and assign and every one of them by these presents forever hath given grant bargain ____, _____, empowers, ____, by these presents all that tract or parcel of land containing eight hundred thirty acres more or less the said **Thomas Bonner, Junior now dwells situate and being in Green Hall** and known by the name of Turkey Neck being all the land that was given to William Bonner, brother of the said Thomas Bonner by their father Henry Bonner's will bearing the date the seventh day of July One thousand seven hundred and sixty six may more fully appear which said **land fell to the said Thomas Bonner, Junior Heir-at-law by the death of the said William Bonner** the said Joseph Blount to have and to hold the said tract or parcel of land and singular the ____ hereby bargain and sold with their appurtenance to him and the said Joseph Blount his heirs and assigns forever the said Thomas Bonner, Junior and Margaret his wife and William Roberts and Elizabeth his wife doth hereby grant for themselves and their heirs that they the said Thomas Bonner, Junior and Margaret his wife and William Roberts and Elizabeth his wife the said tract or parcel of land above bargained and sold and all and singular the appurtenances unto the said Joseph

Blount his heirs and assigns against them the said Thomas Bonner, Junior and Margaret his wife and William Roberts and Elizabeth his wife and their heirs and assigns and against all and every person or persons whatsoever shall and will warrant and forever defense by these presents and that the said tract of land is Free and Clear of all encumbrances whatsoever quitt rents excepted.

In witness whereof Thomas Bonner, Junior and Margaret his wife and William Roberts and Elizabeth his wife have hereunto set their Hands and Seals the day and year first above written.

Sealed and delivered	Thomas Bonner, Junior (Seal)
in the presence of,	Margaret Bonner (Seal)
Henry Thompson	William Roberts (Seal)
	Her
John Payton, Jurist	Elizabeth X Roberts
	Mark

Test: Robert Hardy, Clerk of Court

Received the twenty first day of September 1770 from Joseph Blount the sum of Four Hundred pounds proclamation money being the consideration within mentioned, by me, Thomas Bonner, Junior.

Witness:
Henry Thompson
John Payton
Robert Hardy

Chowan County - I Robert Hardy, Esquire, one of the Members of the Inferior Court of the said County being appointed by the Court privately to examine Elizabeth Roberts within named the wife of William Roberts doth fully acknowledged the with Deed and voluntarily assents thereto, Do Certify that upon such examination __?__ agreeable to the several Acts of Assembly in such canonade the said Elizabeth did declare that she did fully acknowledge the same and voluntarily assents thereto.

Given under my Hand and Seal the twenty first day of December in the year of our Lord one thousand seven hundred and seventy.

Rob Hardy

Edenton - 29th October 1771, Margaret Bonner one of the within subscribers being in Open Court appeared and acknowledged the within is a true account to be her act and deed she being privately examined according to law. Let it be registered,

Test: M. Howard, Clerk Current
Registered, 3 December 1771 (by) Alexander Gellatly, Regr.

The above document gives the date of 21 September 1770 stating that William Bonner is already dead. It will be remembered that on 14 December 1768 William Bonner took possession of the above plantation. William passed away sometime between the two dates. He was the first of the brothers to pass away. The above Henry Thompson was a son of James and Deborah Bonner Thompson. It is believed that the above Joseph Blount was the father of Joseph Blount, Jr., who married Lydia Bonner in 1775.

The following document can be found in the Register of Deed Office, Perquimans County, Hereford, North Carolina. The deed book number is not listed because when the document was found it was not thought to be significant to the history of Thomas Bonner, Jr. As it turns out it was probably the very last Deed of Sale made by Thomas and Margaret Bonner prior to their relocation to South Carolina. Thomas Bonner, Sr., purchased the property in 1752 and there are no records as to when Thomas, Jr., and Margaret took possession of it. It might have been a wedding present.

Bonner
to
Branch

This indenture made this twenty fourth of April one thousand seven hundred and seventy five between Thomas Bonner, Junior of Chowan County and Julius Branch of Perquimans County and province aforesaid of the other part.

Witnesseth that for and in consideration of the sum of two hundred and forty five pounds proclamation money...sell unto the said Julius Branch his heirs and assigns all that mesuage tract of land lying and being in the County of Perquimans aforesaid on the North side of Yeopin River bounded as follows;

Beginning at a Red Oak by the River thence no twenty one degrees East one hundred and fifty poles to a Pine Tree thence

South twenty one degrees west three hundred and twenty eight poles to a Gum by the Swamp of the River thence to the first station containing by estimation three hundred acres be the same more or less...

Thereunto belonging or any ways appertaining together with all buildings, house, orchards, meadows, pastures, ponds, and springs of water...

In testimony, I have hereunto set my Hand and Seal the day and the day and year above written.

Signed sealed and delivered — Thomas Bonner, Junior
in the presence of
Josiah White
Nazareth Bunch
Solomon Bunch

Margaret Bonner the wife of Thomas Bonner doth by these presents freely and willingly give yielded up and surrenders all her rights of Dowry and forever of thirds and to the above devised premises unto him the said Julius Branch.

In witness whereof I have hereunto set my Hand and Affixed my Seal this 15th day of June 1775.

Witness: — Margaret Bonner (Seal)
Josiah White
Nazareth Bunch
Solomon Bunch

Perquimans County July Inferior Court 1775
Present: His Majesty's Justices

This certifies that the within Deed of Sale from Thomas and Margaret Bonner to Julius Branch was proved ib Court by the affirmation of Josiah White and on motion ordered to be registered.

Test: Miles Harvey, Clerk Inferior Court

Registered in the Registering Office of Perquimans the 1st day of June 1776.

Test: Thomas Harvey, Regr.

The available records show that Thomas and Margaret Bonner disposed of 2,090 acres of land between 1768 and 1775 for the amount of 840 pounds, "current money."

I thought it ironic that the very last document I found in the Court records about Thomas and Margaret Bonner would be the document that legally connected Thomas Bonner of Chowan County, North Carolina to be the same Thomas Bonner of Clarke County, Georgia. The Georgia records show that an unknown (to James C. Bonner) daughter of Thomas and Margaret was married to Richard Vanderford. I had found a document in Edenton where Thomas Bonner, Junior had purchased a Negro girl named Rose in the name of Deborah, who was less than six years of age. I had possession of the document for about two years and could not conclude how it fit into the Bonner family history. And the reason was because I did not know the name of the unknown daughter married to Richard Vanderford. About 1993, I started a correspondence with Darrell Harrington of Stonewall, Mississippi. He had a copy of a letter written by a daughter of Jordan Bonner, (Wilmoth Almira Bonner, born 1826 - died 1924) that she wrote in 1900 in where she listed all of her father's siblings. In that letter she stated that a sister of Jordan, Deborah, had married Richard. When I received that bit of information, I made the family connection that I was looking for.

The below document is from *Deed Book Q*, page 243 in Edenton.

John Lewis
to   DEED OF SALE
Deborah Bonner

North Carolina - Know all men by these presents that I, John Lewis of Chowan County and province aforesaid, Planter, for and in consideration of the sum of Thirty Pounds proclamation money to me in hand **paid by Deborah Bonner, daughter of Thomas Bonner, Junior**, of the County and province aforesaid, Planter, whereof I do hereby acknowledge the receipt and myself therewith satisfied, have bargained and sold and delivered unto the said Deborah Bonner, she, her heirs, executors, admins, or executors, administrators and assigns against all and all manner of persons shall warrant and forever defend by these presents.

IN WITNESS whereof I have hereunto set my Hand & Seal this 20th day of March 1776.

Signed, sealed and delivered   John Lewis (Seal)
in presence of us,

(No names listed)

Received the day and date within mentioned the sum of Thirty Pounds proclamation money in full for a Negro girl Rose, witness my hand.

John Lewis

North Carolina - Chowan County March Inferior Court of Pleas and Quarter Session 1776

Present: His Majesty's Justices

Deed of Sale of a Negroe girl from John Lewis to Deborah Bonner, daughter of Thomas Bonner, Junior was acknowledged in Open Court according to law; Ordered to be Registered.

Test: Thomas Jones, Clerk Current.
Registered 30th May 1776 (by) Alexander Gellatly, Regr.

The exact date Thomas and Margaret moved to South Carolina is not recorded but it was after March 1776 and before sometime in 1779 since it is recorded, in the 1860 Georgia census, that Thomas Bonner (1779 - 1860) was born in South Carolina. Additionally, exactly where the family lived in South Carolina from 1779 to about 1786 is also unknown but it can be surmised that it was in Upper South Carolina since that is where Colonel Benjamin Roebuck's Regiment was formed and Thomas was a member of that Regiment during the Revolution. Thomas and Margaret may have lived with or near the present town of Gaffney, South Carolina since that is where Benjamin Bonner, grandson of (Sheriff) Thomas Bonner of Beaufort County, North Carolina had a plantation. Thomas and Margaret may have lived with, or near, Benjamin Bonner. Thomas was allowed bounty land north of present day, Gaffney, South Carolina in Cherokee County, near the North Carolina line. There must have been a relationship between the two Bonner families. It also needs to be noted that about 1810 Jordan Bonner moved to the western area of Alabama in Choctaw County near the present town of Toxey. A grandson of Benjamin Bonner of South Carolina purchase a plantation about three miles from Jordan Bonner in Choctaw County near the present town of Gilbertown. Was it just coincidence or was it close kinship?

The records of South Carolina show that Thomas Bonner, (who was born in Chowan County, North Carolina and died in

Clarke County, Georgia) fought in the American Revolutionary War while living in Upper South Carolina. The following can be found in the State Archives in Columbia, South Carolina.

"On 18 July 178__ (blurred but thought to be 1784), Thomas Bonner, for Militia duty, since the Fall of Charleston in Roebuck's Regiment of Anderson's Return." At the top of the document is "No. 11A and '#3369.'"

It has been suggested that Thomas Bonner may have been captured during the Fall of Charleston by the British. There is no proof.

For serving his country in those trying times, Thomas Bonner was granted Bounty land located north of present city of Gaffney, South Carolina. He probably never lived on it because the land was granted in September 1784 and in December 1785 he had designated it be sold. By June 1787 he had already moved to Georgia, in what was then Greene County.

Maps are located in the Archives in Columbia, South Carolina and they show the exact location of the Bounty land granted to Thomas Bonner. The below is from those documents.

"On 4th September 1784, Thomas Bonner was granted 140 acres of land in the District of Ninety-Six east of the Old Boundary on both sides of Cherokee Creek of Broad River."

"On 4th September 1784. Thomas Bonner was granted (for 3 pounds 10 shillings) a tract of 150 acres of land situate in the District of Ninety-Six on both sides of a Branch of Cherokee on waters of Broad River."

In *Deed Book B,* pages 3 & 7, as published in, *Spartanburg County/District of South Carolina, Deed Abstracts,* on page 13, by Pruitt the following is found;

"4 December 1785, Thomas Bonner (Spartanburg) to Vardrey McBee; power of attorney to convey 2 tracts of land to William Tate, Esq., in fee simple; first tract 150 acres and second tract 144 acres; land is on Cherokee Creek and South Side of Broad River; both were granted to Thomas Bonner. Witness: William Tate, Sr., Thomas Camp and William Tate. Signed: Thomas Bonner."

"16 June 1787. **Thomas Bonner (formerly of South Carolina now Georgia)** to William Tate, Senior, Esquire (Spartanburg); for

100 pounds Sterling sold 150 acres on both side Cherokee Creek Waters of Broad River. Granted 1 May 1786. Witness: Ola Trimmer and J. Thomson. Signed: Thomas Bonner by Attorney Vardrey McBee,"

"16 June 1787. Thomas Bonner (formerly of South Carolina now Georgia) to William Tate, Senior, Esquire (Spartanburg) for 60 pounds Sterling sold 143 acres on both side of Cherokee Creek waters of Broad River, granted 1 May 1786. Witness: Ola Trimmer and J. Thomson. Signed: Thomas Bonner by Attorney Vardrey McBee."

(Author's note - The above Thomas Bonner was a gggg grandfather of this writer. Recently, it was found that the above William Tate, Sr., was also a gggg grandfather of this writer through his McConniell family).

Vardrey McBee was a Captain in Colonel Roebuck's Regiment. During his service, Thomas Bonner may have served under McBee.

The above document shows that by 16 June 1787, Thomas Bonner was a resident of Georgia. In the book, *Some Georgia County Records, Volume 2 extracted from Greene County, Georgia, Deed Book 1,* page 233, the following can be found:

"15 October 1789. Robert Flournoy of Wilkes County to **Thomas Bonner of Greene County** for 500 pounds, 200 acres in Washington County now Greene County on the South side of Powell's Creek bounded South by Benjamin Gilbert & said Flournoy, West by Hardwick, North by said Bonner and partially by Robert Flournoy. Signed: R. Flournoy. Witness: Leaven Maddux, **Zadock Bonner, Jurdan Bonner**. Proved by Jurdan Bonner 18 March 1791 before Michael Rogers, J. P. Registered: 20 July 1792."

Thomas Bonner, son of Henry Bonner, was born in the Green Hall section of Chowan County, North Carolina. He passed away on 30 December 1804, probably very suddenly because he did not make a Will or if he left a Will it was never located. He died very much in debt and it stands to reason that if he thought he was not healthy and had not died suddenly he would have left a death bed will. Remember that he came from a family of lawyers.

The following can be found in the State Archives in Atlanta,

Georgia.

STATE OF GEORGIA, Clarke County

Know all men by these presents that we, Jordan Bonner, Zadock Bonner, Phillip Allen, G. (Gabriel) Hubert are held & firmly bound unto their Honors the Judges of the Court of Ordinary for the said County & their successors in office in the just & full sum of Fifteen Thousand and None Dollars for the payment of which sum the said Judges & their successors in office we bind ourselves, our Heirs, Executors, and administrators in the whole & for the whole sum jointly & severally firmly by these presents sealed with our Seals and dated this fifteenth day of February 1805.

The condition of the above obligation is such that if the above bound Jordan Bonner & Zadock Bonner Administrators of the good chattals & credits of Thomas Bonner - Late of this County, deceased, do make a true & perfect inventory of all & singular chattals & credits of said deceased which have or shall come to the hands possessions of said Jordan & Zadock or into the hands possession of any other person or persons for _?_ & the same so made do ecibet into the said Court of Ordinary when they shall be thereunto required & such goods & chattals do well & truly administer according to law & do make a just account of their acting & doing therein when they shall be thereunto required by the said Court of Ordinary for said County & all the rest of the goods chattals & credits which shall be found remaining upon account of the said Administration the same being first allowed of by the said court shall deliver & pay to such person or persons respectfully as are in(s)tilled to the same by law & if it shall hereafter that any Last Will & Testament was made by the deceased & the same proved before the Court & the Executors obtain certificate of the probate thereof & the said Jordan Bonner & Zadock Bonner do in case if required render & _?_ deliver up the said Letters of Administration then this obligation to be null & void.

Signed, sealed & acknowledged
in Open Court
Registered: C. Smith, CCO

Jordan Bonner
Zadock Bonner
Phillip Allen
G. Hubert

The above G. Hubert was Gabriel Hubert who would later become the father-in-law of Josiah Bonner, the youngest son of

Thomas Bonner.

GEORGIA - Clarke County

We the undersigned Heirs and distributors of Thomas Bonner, late of this County, deceased, do Hereby Certify that we are willing & desirous that the Honorable Inferior Court should make an order for the sales of at public auction, one of the following tracts of land, to wit; One containing one hundred and twenty three and a half acres on the waters of the Appalachia River and one tract containing fifty acres having a Grist Mill thereon - both tract granted to David Meriwether, according to the provisions of the act in such case made and provided for the benefit of the heirs and creditors of the said deceased.

Signed:
Jurden Bonner, Admr.
Zadock Bonner, Admr.
Edmund Duke, Jr.
Thomas Bonner
Richard Vanderford
Whitmel Bonner
Allen Bonner.

GEORGIA - Clarke County
To the Honorable the Justices of the Inferior Clarke County Court;

The Petition of Jordan Bonner and Zadock Bonner, rightfully showeth that they were duly appointed Administrators of the goods & chattals rights and credits which were of Thomas Bonner, late of this county, deceased, was considerably in debt, and that your petitioners have not been able or yet to make enough out of the personal estate to discharge the said debt; that your petitioners concur it would be advantageous to all interested in the said estate, to have the lands properly sold according to the provisions of the act in such case made & provided, that they have preparatory and with a view to this application already advertised a notice for nine months in one of the publick Gazattes of this State; that all the heirs and distributors of the said Thomas Bonner, deceased, as aforesaid, how have arrived at the year of manhood have signified their assent and which is herewith presented to the Honorable Court & therefore your petitioners pray that your honors will make an order enabling us the Administrators to dispose of the lands described in the said Advertisement, to wit; One hundred and twenty three and a half acres lying on the waters of the Appalachia granted to David Meriwether **adjoining Zadock Bonner & Thomas Bonner**, and fifty acres of land on the River Appalachia having a grist mill thereon, **adjoining Allen Bonner** & others at Publick auction for the benefits of the heirs and Creditors of the said deceased. And your petitioners are in duty bound with ever pray, &c.

(Signed)

Jordan & Zadock Bonner

The above document gives the place of residence for Allen, Zadock and Thomas Bonner in the fall of 1805 as still living in Clarke County. Note the first document is dated 15 February 1805 and they advertised for nine months a desire to sell the subject property, which places the date of the above document as about November 1805.

GEORGIA - Clarke County - Inferior Court

On the petition of Jordan Bonner and Zadock Bonner, Administrators of good &c of Thomas Bonner, deceased, stating that it would be advantageous to the Heirs & Creditors of the said deceased, to dispose of by publick auction two tracts of land belonging to the said estate, to wit: One tract containing one hundred and twenty three and a half acres lying and being on the waters of the River Appalachia also one tract containing fifty acres having a grist mill thereon on the said River, both tracts granted to David Meriwether and as appearing to the court from the assent of the major part of the heirs and representatives and their __?__ exhibitors that such sale would be beneficial for the Heirs & Creditors of the said deceased.

It is ordered that the said tracts of land above mentioned be by the said Administrators sold at publick auction for the benefits of the Heirs & Creditors according to the Provisions & terms of the Act in such case made and provided.

William Strong, Inferior Justice

John Floyd

Records of the sale show that at public auction on 10 September 1806, Jordan Bonner purchased the 123-1/2 acres of land for $340.00 and Richard Vanderford purchased the 50 acre tract with grist mil for $1,000.00 on 12 months credit.

PART TWO

MIGRATION PATTERN OF THE
DESCENDANTS OF
THOMAS BONNER
A FAMILY HISTORY
by
JAMES C. BONNER
of
THE WOMEN'S COLLEGE OF GEORGIA
(Now)
GEORGIA COLLEGE
MILLEDGEVILLE, GEORGIA

PREFACE

This study began more than forty years ago before it appeared in its present form. At that time my only purpose was to satisfy my own curiosity about who these people were and where they came from. My principal source of information consisted of oral and written communications from older people that I had known.

Beginning about 1935 I began a serious study of History and subsequently acquired two graduate degrees in this field of knowledge. The research necessary for writing several historical books and monographs gave me a more mature concept of family history than I would have acquired otherwise. I tended to agree with Thomas Carlyle's statement that "history is the essence of innumerable biographies." While the biographies given here are only thumbnail sketches and they generally do not go beyond the nineteenth century, their total impact on the imagination transcends mere personal and local interest.

Historical research has taken me to dozens of libraries throughout the Southeast and sent me delving into numerous archival holdings where I continued to collect notes on family history, but often in a somewhat desultory manner, to be sure. In the meantime I acquired the unofficial status of family historian. This entailed a responsibility to answer as graciously as possible many queries which came to my desk. To conserve my time for more productive pursuits, I decided to assemble the principal substance of my date in this form for distribution. I have found it necessary to make a small charge to cover the cost of production. Only 150 copies of this brochure have been produced, of which this is copy number 62.

James C. Bonner
Professor of History
Women's College of Georgia
(Now Georgia College)
Milledgeville, Georgia
June 1964

Note - Dr. James C. Bonner was born in 1904 and passed away in 1984. There is a reading room at the library at Georgia College named in his honor.

CHAPTER I

BACKGROUND AND EARLY MIGRATIONS, 1066 - 1776

The family name of Bonner is of Norman-English origin. The original bearers of the name probably came to Britain during the Norman Conquest in the eleventh century. The name appears in France as Bonheur and Bonnaire, the former word meaning "good humor" and the latter meaning "of good manners" or "good disposition." The stem of the word "Bon" is from Latin "bonus" which means good, gracious or kind. The word is quite common throughout western Europe. Bonn, which is the present capital of West German Republic, is one of many examples. The name Bonner is frequently found in English history and literature. Representatives of the family are numerous today in France, Germany, England and Northern Ireland as well as in America and the British Dominions.

An English genealogist, Jerome A. Ringrose, has given what is perhaps a reliable history of the Bonner name in England. According to this authority, the most remote ancestor of the English Bonners was Quentin de Riddell, ancestor of the noble house of Buchanan-Riddell. It was Quentin de Riddell who first bore the Ensign of Bonner and from whom descended the noted Bishop Edmund Bonner of the Middle Tudor period.

There are several charters in the House of Riddell dated in the Reign of King Henry VIII wherein the same persons are called Riddell in the body of the documents and Bonnaire (Bonner) in the margin. When two families bear the same Coat-of-Arms as was the case of Riddell and Bonner, the younger family (which in this case was Bonner) in all probability descended from the older. Immediately after the death of Bishop Bonner, we find his cousin, William Bonner of Banbury, Oxfordshire, Clerk in Holy Orders, fighting in the courts for his interest in certain estates acquired by purchase from the Bishop. This William Bonner married Alice Gorham of Glapthorne (1568) and resided chiefly at "Elmsmere," a splendid mansion in the Parish of the Blessed Mary of Bow, in Cheapeward, London. William Bonner came off victorious at the Lord Mayor's Courts and held this splendid estate at a time when he was the younger son of an illustrious but impoverished family and the property eventually passed by marriage to George Lennard of Stratfield Bay, in Hampshire.

Reverend Anthony Bonner, brother of William, bore a son, Anthony, whose son Anthony was born at Quinton in Gloucestershire, having married Marian Vaughan. Their children were, Richard (born in 1615); Thomas (born in 1617); and Ellen (born in 1624), Thomas apparently had no children and Ellen married Honorable Edward Wells. By this time most of the Bonners renounced Catholicism and embraced the Protestant faith.

Richard Bonner, the elder son of Anthony and Marian Bonner who was born at Quinton in 1615 had long been absent from the Gloucestershire home of Bonners at the death of his wealthy cousin, Thomas Coombe, for Richard had left England for Virginia at the age of 20 and arrived in James City, Virginia in March 1636. He married there and had considerable issue.

William Bonner of Elmsmere had a son, John Bonner, who resided at Hinckley in Leicester at the time of his father's death. He married Mary Walker at the Parish Church of Hinckley in 1607 and he left six sons and four daughters. One of these Michael Bonner married Alice Wilson, at Howby in 1629. Joseph Bonner, another son, married one of the Macdonalds of Hinckley. John's brother, Thomas Bonner, also married at Hinckley, Anne Botfishe of Sheasley, and they had several children.

Joseph's eldest son, John, married Mary Burton at Hinckley in 1699 and they had 12 sons and several daughters. Of this issue one son, Richard Bonner of Hinckley, Gentleman, was married in 1719 to Anne Taylor at the near-by Church of All-Saints, Leicestershire and he the father of Captain John Bonner.

Returning again to the main stem of the family, we find that Anthony Bonner, the elder (mentioned above as brother of William Bonner) had a brother who formed a most illustrious alliance with the Tates of de la Pre Abbey, he having married Elizabeth (daughter of William Tate) who was born in 1671 at this historic Northamptonshire Mansion. She was then co-heiress and direct descendant of the Noble House of Tate.

Sir Bartholomew Tate who received the honor of Knighthood from King Henry VIII was the original purchaser of the monastery lands of de la Pre Abbey in the County of Northampton. His grandson, Sir William Tate, married in 1597, Elizabeth, the eldest daughter and Heiress of Edward, the eleventh and last Baron Zouche of Haryngworth. The Zouche family was descended in the whole line from the Sovereign Princes of Brittany, **a fact which gives the American House of Bonner, a Royal Descent.** On the south side of the chancel at Hardingstone there today is an altar tomb probably in memory of the late Sir William Tate, who is known to have left fifty pounds for the creation of such a structure. This tomb has a canopy surmounted by a crest. The arms are now almost obliterated but they are unmistakably that of Bonner.

The Bonners arrived early on the American continent. One of the better known of the early immigrants came to Boston in 1678 and later settled at Cambridge, about 1697. He was Captain John Bonner (born 1642) the son of John Bonner of London. Captain John Bonner married Mary Clark (second marriage) who died in 1697. In 1705, he sold his house in Cambridge and moved back to Boston where he died on 30 January 1725 at the age of 83 years. He is buried in the Old Granary Burying Ground in Boston and the Coat-of-Arms found on his tomb bears the following description:

"Quarterly gules and sable, a cross pattee quarterly ermine and ox. On a Chief of the last a demi-rose streaming rays between two pelicans vulning themselves of the first. Crest - A talbot's head argent, collared azure. Studded edged and ringed or.

Motto: Semper Fidelis"

The obituary of John Bonner, written at the time of his death, depicts him as "A gentleman very skillful an ingenious in many arts and sciences, especially in navigation, drawing molding of ships, etc., one of the best acquainted of coasts of North America of any of his time, of great knowledge and judgement of marine affairs, was very much consulted, relied upon by the government as principal pilot of our marine expeditions and with diligent care and faithfulness discharged his trust." By his second wife, who was a daughter of the famous Elder Clark of Cambridge, he had several children, but a son and a daughter only survived him. His children were: Jane (died 1686); Jonah (died 1687); Mary (1668-1699) and Jane apparently named for her older sister who had died. The second Jane was born 2 May 1691 and later went to London. Other children were: John, born 6 December 1693 who was baptized in Boston but also went to London. Sarah (died 2 December 1721) and Thomas born in Cambridge on 6 January 1695 and was buried in South Carolina where he died 3 June 1719, at age 24.

The presence of members of the Bonner family in various other American colonies prior to the Revolution is evidenced by numerous records. One of these is an Old English document, dated

March 1636, which mentions Richard Bonner, "belonging unto the Friendshippe of London att Ankere in the Themes bound for Vergenia." Again, in 1623, James Bonner, aged 20, arrived in "Charles Cittie" in the Truelove. On the passenger list of the port of London for the year 1635 is the name of John Bonner, age 18, as among those bound for the Barbados in the Expedition. The record further states that, "The men have taken the oaths of allegeance and supremacie and have been examined by the Minister of the Town of Gravesend touching their Conformity to the Orders of Discipline of the Church of England." This may be the same John Bonner whose arrival in Virginia was mentioned in another document, dated 1638. Others arriving at various times were: Thomas (in 1638); Richard Bonner (in 1643); and **Henry Bonner, his wife and two children (in 1664).**

There is a legend concerning the Bonner family in America which traces the American branch to three brothers - James, Richard and Robert - who arrived early in the 17th century. They were said to have established a home on the banks of the James River where Robert, according to legend, was drowned within a year or two of his arrival when a boat loaded with salt capsized in a storm on the river. Richard and James married and left issue. This "three brothers" tradition, so common in American genealogy is completely without historical validity. All documentary evidence indicates that the original immigrants of this name were numerous; they settled in more than one of the colonies, and they arrived in America at various periods throughout the first two centuries of its history.

After the Revolutionary War, which officially ended in 1783, there was a marked decrease in the number of representatives of this family who arrived in America from England. In keeping with the general pattern of American immigration, many of the post-Revolution Bonner emigrants came from countries other than England. One of these was Robert Bonner who was born at Rambleton near Londonderry in North Ireland on 28 April 1824, son of Andrew and Marian Russell Bonner of Scotch-Irish descent. He came to the United States in 1839 and settled at Hartford, Connecticut following an uncle who had arrived earlier. He later moved to New York in 1844 where he owned and published the *New York Ledger* and became the owner of famous race horses. One of the organizers of the Scotch-Irish Society in America, Robert Bonner died in 1899. He had three sons, Robert E.; Frederick, and Allen. This family is said to be related to the Bonners who migrated to America at an earlier date. **Robert Bonner, the editor, was host to some of the Carroll County, Georgia, Bonners who** visited him in New York in the latter half of the nineteenth century. However, no documentary evidence has been found to establish the exact kinship between these two families.

The fact that Robert Bonner was a nationally known figure in the period before and immediately following the Civil War and that he was known to have to come to America from Ulster in the North of Ireland has given force to a strong tradition that the Bonners of Carroll County are of Irish or Scotch-Irish origin. However, the facts indicate that the family is by and large of English and Norman descent, including those who came to America directly from North Ireland. The presence of the Bonners in North Ireland can be traced from the middle of the 17th century when Thomas Bonner, an Englishman, acquired by Royal grant, a considerable estate in Ulster (under Act of 17, Charles I, Chapter 33, A. D. 1642). This Thomas Bonner was the forerunner of a very considerable clan in the North of Ireland, men of whom the native Irish looked upon as interlopers and exploiters and whom they opposed by every means within their power.

The so-called Scotch-Irish were lowland Scotch who were encouraged to settle in Ulster, in addition to a few Welshmen and Englishmen. Those who came to America of English extraction often were younger sons of noblemen. The term "Scotch-Irish" did not come into general use until around 1820 when it was used to distinguish this group from the Catholic Irish who were of Celtic origin. After 1820, the latter began to arrive in America in large numbers from souther Ireland. Up to this time the Scots, Welsh and English living in Ireland called themselves Irish. These facts help to explain the confusion which often has arisen concerning the national origin of many American families among which is the Bonner family.

All of the families in the United States by the name of Bonner are perhaps distantly related with the possible exception of members of the Pennsylvania branch who appear to be of German origin. For example, among the list of German passengers on the *Loyal Judith* arriving in the Pennsylvania colony on 25 November 1740 is the name "Casspar Boner" age 20 from the Palatine. Elsewhere the name was written possibly by an English speaking clerk as "Jasper Bonner," thus illustrating an early anglicizing of the German spelling. Rudolph Bonner, also from the German Palatinate, arrived in Philadelphia in 1732 on board the *Johnson Galley*. Adam Bonner, age 40 was among the German Protestants arriving in South Carolina in 1765. Arriving at approximately the same time was William Bonner, age 42; his wife Mary, 57; John, James, and Rebecca, ages 16, 14, and 4, respectively. On the first census of Pennsylvania (in 1790) there were 30 families by the name Benner, nine whose name was spelled Boner and eight who spelled it in the traditional fashion, Bonner. However, it should be noted that uniformity in the spelling of a name is by no means a reliable index to a family relationship. Ignorant and careless recording officials and illiteracy on the part of others have given origin to a wide variety of renditions of the same name. This writer has seen records of the same person written on various occasions as Boner, Benner, Bonner and Bonney.

Before the Revolution the name of Bonner was found in all of the American colonies with the exception of New York which was settled by the Dutch and taken by the British about the middle of the 17th century. Even in 1790 there were no persons by this name listed on the census of New York State. Virginia had the largest concentration of families by this name. The great majority of those living in the Carolina and Georgia in 1790 deem to have migrated southward from the older colonies of Virginia and Maryland.

Early in the 18th century, for example, three came from the Chesapeake region to North Carolina. * Their names were: Thomas, James and William Bonner. James, who died single, founded the town of Washington in eastern North Carolina. William settled in another county some distance away, probably Chowan. Thomas settled one mile north of Washington on what he called Bonner Hill and is buried near the site of his old dwelling. The engraving on his tombstone indicated that he died on 7 April 1765 at the age of 75 years. He had been High Sheriff of Beaufort County, a member of the North Carolina Colonial Assembly and a Colonel in the Militia. His wife Abigail bore him eight children; Henry, Thomas, Elizabeth, Sarah, Abigail, Mary, Ann and James. Of these, Thomas and James were Colonels in the Revolutionary War. Most of the Bonners in eastern North Carolina are descended from one of these brothers. The family bears an excellent reputation in that part of the state. For he most part they were substantial planters and hard-working farmers. Among them are physicians, lawyers, judges, professors and a member of the United States Congress, Herbert Bonner. * *

In every southern state and in most of the middle and far western states are members of this family who trace their forebears from the Virginia seed-bed. Early in the 19th century, for example, John and Thomas Bonner migrated from Virginia to Tennessee, settling in Madison and Wilson counties, respectively. John had served in the Virginia militia during the Revolution, but Thomas, who was born in 1769, was too young for Revolutionary service. The will of their father, John Bonner, Sr is recorded in Surrey

County, Virginia under the date 1804. This particular family apparently is descended from the Richard Bonner who arrived in James City, Virginia on *The Friendshippe* in March 1636. A century after the arrival in Tennessee of this branch of the family, James Allen Bonner, representing another branch of the family which in 1828 had begun to settle in Carroll County, Georgia and moved with his brother, William, and other relatives to Tennessee where they acquired a large uncleared tract of land and founded the settlement of Bonnertown, in Lawrence County just north of the Alabama line.

In the early part of the 19th century, Henry Bonner, Jr., grandson of John Bonner (born 1699) left Surrey County, Virginia for Illinois when that region was still a territory. Having married a Quaker, Polly Vaughan, they are said to have left the South to avoid a slave holding society. There are dozens of families in the Middle West who are descendants of this branch. This name appears among the Illinois companies who fought in the Mexican War. They were among General William T. Sherman's legions who devastated Georgia in 1864. Some marched past the graves of their Virginia ancestors as they maneuvered with Grant in the Campaigns around Richmond.

Several migrations of Georgia Bonners to California are known. An old newspaper account relates the story of Colonel Seymour B. Bonner of Georgia, who commanded a wagon train to the California gold fields in 1849. One of the most unusual stories of the era of the California gold rush tells of a self-styled, "Judge Bonner", who meted out justice to outlaws with an iron hand. Representing himself as a legal court official, he took a sizeable fee from the communities who employed him. This writer has speculated on the possibility that William Bonney, the teen-age western outlaw known as "Billy the Kid" may have been a distant kinsman of this spurious judge. * * *

Various branches of the Bonner family are known to have migrated to Georgia directly from the Old Dominion. William Bonner who died in Prince George County, Virginia in 1796 had three sons who settled in Hancock County, Georgia not far from the present site of Milledgeville. Through a power-of-attorney given in Hancock County on 26 December 1796, Robert Hicks Bonner and Hubert Bonner appointed their brother, James, "to sell land for them in Prince George County, Virginia, formerly property of their father, William Bonner." From 1798 to 1813 no less than thirteen family heads by the name of Bonner appear on the records of Hancock County alone. They are; James, Jordan, Richard, Jeremiah, Hubbard, Hubert, Chappell, Robert H., Thomas

M., Pleasant, Hamilton, Alexander and Henry. These thirteen men all of whom were landowners in Hancock County are known to represent three separate branches of the family and even in 1800 these three were probably no more related than second cousins.

Jordan was the son of Thomas Bonner who migrated from South Carolina to Greene County soon after the Revolution. Hamilton Bonner and his wife came to Georgia from North Carolina in 1803. He was the son of Jeremiah Bonner of Prince George County and his wife was Mary Boisseau of French Huguenot descent. John Bonner, the son of Hamilton, was among the early progressive planters in Hancock County where his father settled and is buried at "Bonner Hill" near White Plains. Still another branch of the family prominent in Hancock County was that of Captain Richard Bonner (1754-7 January 1813). Born in Dinwiddie County, Virginia and a veteran of the Revolution, he arrived in Hancock in 1784 and engaged in a wagon train business. Richard was the son of # Henry Bonner (born 1724) and Nancy Cate Bonner. Nancy Cate was the only child of Richard and Sarah Wyatt and she was a descendant of the Reverend Hant Wyatt, who came to Jamestown, Virginia with his brother, Sir Francis Wyatt, at the time the latter became Governor of the Colony in 1621. Captain Richard Bonner's grandfather, according to tradition, was John Bonner (born 1700) of Martin Brandon in Surrey County, Virginia, whose father in turn was also named John.

Another William Bonner (1781-1852) moved from Virginia to Wilkes County, Georgia some time after the Revolution. The son of Joseph and Susan Bonner, he was married on 27 April 1809 to Nancy Chapell (1791-1852) daughter of John and Sarah Chappel of Washington County. They later moved to Troup County in western Georgia and are buried in ther Thomas Harris Cemetery near Standing Rock in Chambers County, Alabama. They were the parents of seventeen children, thirteen of who survived them.

The Bonner-Chappel relationship is apparently still another branch of the Georgia family which is known to have originated in Dinwiddie County, Virginia. Thomas S. Bonner was born in Dinwiddie County in 1793, the son of Chappel Heath Bonner and his wife, Priscilla. Chappel Bonner came to Hancock County, Georgia in 1802 and died there in 1806, at which time Robert H. Bonner was appointed guardian of Thomas, James and Polly P., "orphans of Chappel Bonner." Robert H., appears to have been an uncle of these children, as were Hubert and James Bonner. If this surmise is correct, Chappel Bonner was the son of William Bonner of Prince George County, Virginia. William's father in turn probably was John Bonner. (A land deed of Prince George County in 1827 transferred title from John "to my son, William.")

Thomas S. Bonner was married to Patsy Cleveland in Morgan County in 1814. A deed record of that year shows that he moved to Morgan from Jasper County in the same year of his marriage and acquired lots 246 and 247 in the Fifteenth District which was just north of Little River not far from the homestead of Thomas Bonner (born 1779) described in a subsequent chapter. Thomas S. Bonner represented Morgan County in the Lower Branch of the State Legislature in 1821 and was a Senator from that county in 1823. In the meantime one of his sisters, Mary Pleasant Bonner (1791-1854) had married Joseph Stovall of Milledgeville where they lived in an elegant house near the Governors Mansion. They owned an extensive plantation in Baldwin and Wilkinson Counties and thirty-nine slaves.

Thomas S. Bonner's will was probated in Morgan County in 1869. His children were: Thomas, James, Benjamin, William Smith, Leonidas, Franklin, Pleasant Stovall, Marcus Aurelius and Judson. Most of the above children remained in Georgia. However, William Smith (9 February 1821 - 6 March 1907) married Mary Elizabeth Durden in Morgan County in 1851 and a little later with his brother, Marcus Aurelius, moved to Northern Louisiana, settling near Homer in Claiborne Parish. Among William Smith Bonner's descendants in 1963 is Judge William N. Bonner of Houston, Texas.

It is significant to note that this writer has never found a record indicating that a single member of the Bonner family came to Georgia directly from England or from any other country. All appear to have arrived from one of the older colonies or states. They came largely from Virginia by way of the Carolinas where some remained permanently and others for only a generation or two. Several of the latter group arrived in Georgia before the 1780's. This was a pattern of the early western migration which followed the expansion of the plantation system. The magnet which attracted them was the presence of cheap and abundant land in a virgin wilderness. There were six of the names on Georgia's roster of the American Revolution, all of whom apparently had moved into the lands around Augusta ceded by the Indians in the cessions of 1763 and 1773. These are: Captain Robert Bonner, George, Henry, Joseph, Richard, Sherwood and William. Some of these doubtless were brothers and cousins of * * * * Thomas Bonner who fought in Roebuck's South Carolina Regiment, and about whom detailed information is recorded in the following chapter.

The below data is 1995 update information to the work of James C. Bonner in this chapter.

* The information in this paragraph does not hold up when compared to the history of Beaufort County. The James Bonner mentioned herein did not found the City of Washington, N. C. The James Bonner who founded the City of Washington was the son of Sheriff Thomas Bonner who died in 1765. A William Bonner was, in fact, living in Chowan County. (Sheriff) Thomas Bonner was in Hyde Precinct of Bath County, N. C., by 1715 where on 8 January 1715 he was a witness to the Will of William Barrow who lived in "Hide" precinct of County of Bath. Sheriff Thomas Bonner's remains were removed from his plantation and placed in the church yard cemetery of the Episcopal Church, (beside his son Colonel James Bonner who founded the city of Washington), in downtown Washington, North Carolina.

* * A bridge connecting the outer banks islands of Pea and Bodie is named the "Herbert C. Bonner Bridge" in honor of the Congressman who passed away in the 1960's.

* * * William H. Bonney was an alias of Billy the Kid.

Henry Bonner (1724 - 1822) of Sussex County, Virginia was a Colonel in the American Revolution from Virginia. He died in Warren County, Georgia.

* * * * Thomas Bonner was born in Chowan County, North Carolina and only had three brothers (Richard, William and Henry) and no sisters. Two brothers died before the Revolution (Richard and William) and there is no data that Henry served in the Revolution although he may have and if he did it was from North Carolina.

The below is new information about Chappel Bonner and Chappel Heath Bonner that was not available to James C. Bonner in 1964, as follows; they were, in fact, uncle and nephew.

Chappell was a brother of Chappel Heath Bonner's father, Frederick Bonner of Dinwiddie County, Virginia. Chappel Bonner was born ca 1766 in Dinwiddie County and was married there on 13 August 1787 to Priscilla Smith. Chappel Heath Bonner (born 23 June 1786) was born in Dinwiddie County and died in Georgia. He married Nancy Pelham about 1807.

The below Thomas Bonner (born ca 1735) may have been a brother of Henry Bonner (1724 - 1822).

THOMAS BONNER

Thomas Bonner was born ca 1735 and died before 19 July 1793 in Dinwiddie County, Virginia.

First Wife: unk
Children:

1. Frederick Bonner (4 November 1758 - 23 March 1 married Elizabeth Smith.
2. **Chappel Bonner** (ca 1760 - 1806) married Pricilla Smith.
3. Susannah Bonner married Samuel Lee.
4. Joan Bonner married Hicks Bonner.

Second Wife: Jane _____.

5. Elizabeth Bonner married Thomas Bonner (son of John Bonner of Sussex County, Virginia)
6. Rebecca Bonner married Haitable Peebles.
7. Jane Bonner married Epps Reeves.

FREDERICK BONNER

Frederick Bonner was born in 1758 and died in Dinwiddie County, Virginia.
Wife: Elizabeth Smith (23 April 1756 - 23 July 1818)
When: 28 September 1779
Children:

1. Davis Smith Bonner (born 20 October 1780) married Elizabeth Reynolds.
2. Nancy Bonner (born 21 October 1782) married Reverend John Sale about 1804.
3. Mary Bonner (born 23 June 1784(died before adulthood.
4. **Chappell Heath Bonner** (born 23 June 1786) married Nancy Pelham.
5. Martha Bonner (born 7 July 1780) married Samuel Pelham.
6. Stith Bonner (born 21 November 1790) married Marie Mercer in June 1819.
7. Elizabeth Bonner (born 29 April 1793) married John Taylor.
8. Frederick Bonner (born 11 November 1796) married Elizabeth Mercer.

CHAPELL BONNER

Chapell Bonner was born ca 1760 in Dinwiddie County, Virginia. He passed away before 15 December 1804 in Hancock County, Georgia.

Wife: Priscilla Smith
When: 13 August 1787 in Sussex County, Virginia.
Children:

1. Thomas Bonner
2. James Bonner
3. Polly P. Bonner

"15 December 1804 - Priscilla Bonner, Admnx of Chappel Bonner, dec'd."
"Richard P. Brown, gdn for Polly P. Bonner, 7 April 1806."
"Hubert Reynolds, gdn for Thomas Bonner, 1 December 1806."
"Robert H. Bonner, gdn for Thomas Bonner and Jarrus (James?) Bonner, 7 April 1806."
"John Herbert and Hubbard Reynolds, adms of Robert H. (Hicks) Bonner, dec'd 1 December 1806."

SUSANNAH BONNER

Susannah Bonner was born about 1770, probably in Dinwiddie County, Virginia.

Husband: Samuel Lee (born about 1759, son of Thomas Lee)
When: Before 1790

Children:

1. Thomas Lee, born 1791
2. Chappel Lee
3. Ludowick Lee
4. Richard Lee

Note: Samuel Lee had been married previously.

Wife: unk
Children:

1. Littleberry Lee, about 1780
2. Mary Lee married Jeremiah Clements.

JOAN BONNER

Joan Bonner was born about 1777 in Dinwiddie County, Virginia.

Husband: Hicks Bonner, son of John Bonner of Sussex County, Virginia.
Children: unk

(Note - It is believed that Hicks Bonner and Thomas Bonner who married Elizabeth, Joan's sister, were brothers).

The above information of the Bonner family comes from records of Virginia and of Georgia, including, *Tidewater Virginia Families*, by Virginia Lee Hutcheson.

CHAPTER II

THOMAS BONNER

(ca 1744 - 1804)

It is this Thomas Bonner who, with his numerous descendants, is described in some detail below. The Bonners identified largely with the history of Carroll County, Georgia are known to have descended from him. This Thomas Bonner, who was born probably in 1744 came to Greene County, Georgia from South Carolina in 1788. There is a court record reproduced in a previous chapter which shows that he was married to Margaret Jones in Chowan County, North Carolina on 6 May 1767. # A reminiscence of his great grandson, George A. Bonner, largely substantiates this conclusion. # # Margaret Jones probably was a daughter of Nathan Jones who died in Greene County in 1798. Nathan's wife, Elizabeth, was a daughter of Ezekiel Slaughter, a Quaker whose death occurred sometime earlier. The Bonner, Slaughter and Jones families in Greene County were contiguous as were the Jones and Bonner lands later in Clarke County. Nathan Jones and his brother Jonathan are listed as heirs of John Jones (who lived in the Wrightboro township north of Augusta) in a will probated on 1 January 1783. At that time the Jones family had land in South Carolina as well as in Georgia,

The date of Thomas Bonner's birth has been determined from known facts concerning his marriage, the birth of his oldest son and the age which his children reached maturity.

As already indicated Thomas Bonner served during the Revolution in Roebuck's South Carolina Regiment which was recruited In and around Newberry County. This was in the Old Ninety-Six District in what was then the western frontier of that State. In 1784, just after the close of the Revolution, he was granted two plots of land in Ninety-Six District, one for 150 acres on the "East side of the Old Boundary on both sides of a branch of Cherokee Creek, waters of Broad River, surveyed 5 September 1784," and one covering 143 acres with the same location and description. This land was on the state's extreme frontier, just above the "Ninety-Nine Islands" and four miles north of Gilky's Mountain. It was near the later site of Spartanburg. Since this was military bounty land it is not likely that Thomas Bonner ever actually settled it. He held it only a short time. In 1785 he granted one Vardrey McBee a power of attorney to sell both tracts. In June 1787 both tracts were sold to William Tate for a total of 160 pounds Sterling. The deed record fixes this as the date at which Thomas Bonner must have arrived in Georgia, for it identifies his as "formerly of the State of South Carolina, now of the State of Georgia."

In his trek to Georgia, Thomas and his family evidently followed a well-traveled route of migration which finally brought them to rest in approximately the same latitude, as his old home in South Carolina, some 25 miles north of the fall line, in what was then Greene County, Georgia. The earliest record in Georgia of Thomas Bonner is that of a land warrant dated 13 November 1788 and executed in February of 1789 in which Henry Graybill granted to him, "181 acres of Oak and Hickory land" on Powell's Creek, near where that stream flows into the Ogeechee River. This land lay in the extreme southern part of what later became ,Taliferro County, which was created out of territory of the original County of Greene in 1825. His farm lay just three miles north of Powellton and the Hancock County line. On 15 October 1789, through a deed executed by Robert Flournoy of Wilkes County and recorded in Greene County Courthouse 20 July 1792, Thomas acquired an additional 200 acres adjoining his original tract. The consideration was "five hundred pounds lawful money" of the State of Georgia and the land acquired lay "in Washington now Greene County on the South fork of Powell's Creek."

The tax returns of Greene County indicate that Thomas Bonner paid a tax in 1788 on "30 pounds of property in Captain Cain's District." The tax, also given in English denomination, came to "Eight Shillings and nine D." His returns were the same for 1789. In 1793, however, he returned for taxes 359 acres No, three Oak and Hickory land adjoining James Alford on the Ogeechee. By 1796, he had apparently sold this land and for the next four years he paid only a poll tax. During the time that he lived in Greene County, from 1788 to 1800, his three oldest sons and his two daughters reached maturity, for the names of Zadock, "Jurdan" and Whitmal appear on the tax books during the latter part of the period.

On 20 December 1801, Thomas Bonner was a witness to a warranty (made by David Meriwether of Wilkes County) transferring to his son, Zadock Bonner of Jackson County title to 650 acres in that county, "on the waters of the Appalachee bounded southeasterly by said Appalachee and on all other sides by vacant land when surveyed in 1785." Jackson County was created from the southern part of Franklin County in 1796.

Franklin, an original County, was created in northeastern Georgia in 1784, was one of the principal recipients of Revolutionary War veterans. A military reservation in the southern part, later embraced by Jackson County, was set up between the Oconee and Appalachee Rivers. It was in this area that the Bonners finally settled.

In an act of 1801, Clarke County was created from the territory lying in the southern part of Jackson County. The Appalachee at that time not only was the western boundary of the new County of Clarke but it also marked the western limits of the white settlement. The Appalachee River was not confirmed as the western boundary of the ceded lands until 1790, after which date the Creek Indians ended their warfare on the white settlers along the Appalachee-Oconee frontier, this so-called "Oconee War" at its height in 1786-88, was one in which the Bonners must have been deeply involved. The Indians frequently crossed the river, drove off cattle, burned houses and plundered the countryside. On a visit to the Dove"s Creek community in 1952, this writer talked to some of the older inhabitants who remembered many "old fort houses" which stood along the east bank of the Appalachee, one of which was standing as late as the visit in 1952. It was probably in such a house that Thomas Bonner and his neighbors lived in the early part of the preceding century.

Zadock's Bonner's tract of 650 acres on the Appalachee became the land on which his father Thomas, his brothers and perhaps his two brothers-in-law finally settled. While no record have been found of the transfer of title from Zadock to other members of the family, the original tax book of Clarke County (in 1802) shows 297-1/2 acres of No. 3 land originally granted to Manuathes adjoining land of Absalom Otrey on the Appalachee River. The following year the tax return was the same except that the name Meriwether is substituted for Manuathes. The latter appears to be the name of an Okfuskee Chief to whom this land may have once been pre-empted. Thomas Bonner's 297-1/2 acres is also described as adjoining 229 acres "originally granted to Meriwether," belonging to his son, Allen Bonner; 100 acres "granted to Bonner" belonging to his son, Whitmal, and 246-1/2 acres "originally granted to Meriwether" belonging to his son-in-law, Richard Vanderford.

In fact, five of Thomas's sons were old enough to have their names on the tax books, as well as his two sons-in-law, Edmund Duke and Richard Vanderford, who were close neighbors on the Appalachee River at this time. It appears that Thomas acquired his land, as did his sons, largely from the 650 acres purchased from

David Meriwether (the original grantee) make by Zadock Bonner in 1801. The original Meriwether grant on file in ther Office of the Secretary of State embraced several thousand acres in Upper Georgia.

From other sources and through records of subsequent returns, the Bonner lands have been more accurately described as "lying on Dove's Creek" which runs into the Appalachee just north of and in the vicinity of what later became Hebron Church. This tract in 1963 can be more accurately described as lying in Oconee County (created from Clarke in 1875) just north of US Highway 78 as it crosses the Appalachee River from Monroe to Athens, Georgia. Here Thomas Bonner operated a corn mill in connection with other activities dwelt in this community for almost 30 years. By 1825 all of them, except Allen, had departed for the newer counties farther westward, which were opened to settlement by the various land lotteries held in Georgia between 1803 and 1835.

It was here in Dove's Creek settlement the elder Thomas Bonner died just after Christmas of 1804, at the approximate age of 60 years. Here also died his wife, Margaret Jones Bonner, his daughter-in-law Rachel, wife of Jordan Bonner, his son Allen, whose death occurred there in 1827 and perhaps others. No Bonner cemetery has been located in this vicinity. It is possible that after they were interred in a common family plot which after 1830 became lost to the memory of any person in the community. Such family cemeteries in this area often succumbed to the encroachment of cotton fields during the period of expansion of the plantation economy from 1800 to 1860. Also following the contraction of cotton-growing in the area after 1930 and the wholesale abandonment of arable farms, many such plots have reverted to wilderness.

One of the earliest records on file in the Clarke County Courthouse involves the administration of the estate of Thomas Bonner who died just three years after the county was crested. His older sons, Jordan and Zadock, were joint administrators and gave bond for $15,000.00. They were dismissed at the May term of Court in 1819, at which time it is assumed the youngest child and heir had reached maturity. The records of administration of this estate provides some insight into the economic status of Thomas Bonner at the time of his death. Among his personal property were: 4 horses, 5 oxen, 13 cows, 15 head of sheep, 25 hogs and 3 litters of pigs. In addition he possessed goats, geese, ducks, and beehives. The productions of his farm included cotton, wool, flax, corn, tobacco, wheat and potatoes. Among his possessions were three saddles and one cart. Only three books were listed among the goods and chattles sold at auction in March 1805. His land alone sold for $1,350 including the grist mill on the Appalachee. His personal property brought an additional $1,600 although there is no record of his owning slaves at the time of his death.

There were at least ten children in the family. Since Thomas died intestate, those who had reached maturity at the time of his death in 1805 can be easily identified from existing administration records. Those who signed the petition to have his land sold and listed as "Heirs and distributors" of his estate were; Jordan, Zadock, Thomas, Whitmal (also spelled Whitmel, Whitnel and Whitmil) and Allen. Also included were; Edmund Duke, Jr and Richard Vanderford (also spelled Vandever in a few places) as sons-in-law, were also listed as "heirs and distributors." This was consistent with Georgia law at that time.

The petition stated that there were heirs who had not yet "arrived at the years of manhood." Further evidence of minor children is found in the accounts against his estate among which was a doctor's bill dated 24 September 1804 for attendance upon his wife and son. A careful study of all the records available in the county indicates that there were three minor children in the family in 1805, all of whom either were his sons, or minor sons of a deceased older son. Their names were; Willis, Josiah and Daniel. On the tax books, these names always appear next to those of the Bonner brothers who were administrators of their father's estate and hence there is little doubt of them being the minor heirs mentioned in the petition of 1805. Josiah is known to have been born 5 May 1787 and the fact that Willis appeared on the tax books first in 1808 would indicate that he was perhaps a year or two older than Josiah. Daniel appeared as the payer of a head tax in 1810, thus placing his birth at 1789. It is possible that only Daniel was born after his parents moved to Georgia. It was not until 1850 that census records listed the state of one's birth.

Not much is known of the younger brothers, Willis and Daniel, after about 1820 when their names disappeared from the records of Clarke County. Neither was an extensive landowner there, nor is there a record of their marriage in Clarke County. However, these names are very prominent in the land records of Old West Florida, which lay in the southern part of the present states of Alabama and Mississippi. In all probability these brothers joined the migration to more fertile lands in the Southwest, which had assumed gigantic proportions by 1820. The name Daniel M. Bonner appears on the Clay County, Georgia census for 1860 as owner of 1,700 acres of land. It is possible that an investigation of other records of this county would identify him as the younger brother of the Clarke County clan.

Very little is known about the two girls who married in Clarke County. The Dukes had left the settlement on the Appalachee River by 1823. The Vanderfords were still there at the middle of the century when Richard Vanderford died in 1847. The Dukes and Vanderfords had accompanied the Bonners from Greene County to Clarke; the Duke and Vanderford families appear to have come to Georgia from Anson County, North Carolina. The latter name is common to many parts of North Carolina at the middle of the twentieth century. The Clarke County records carry the name both as Vandiford and Vandiver.

On the Carroll County census records for 1860 the names of "Ed Duke" and his wife Mary. It is significant to note that Ed (Edmond - Edmund) was then 79 years old and his wife was 81 and the place of the latter's birth was South Carolina. The long geographic proximity of the Duke and Bonner families which began in the Carolinas and continued across Georgia to the southwest, is typical of the migration pattern which prevailed in the Lower South in the century which preceded the Civil War. Thus "Ed Duke" (born 1781) who resided in Carroll County in 1860 is the same "Edmund Duke" who appeared on the Clarke records at the beginning of the century and later on the Morgan County records. His wife, Mary (born 1779) was the daughter of Thomas Bonner who died at Dove's Creek settlement in 1804. Because of the close relationship between the Duke and Bonner families, a short sketch of the family is included in this work.

Edmund Duke was the only member of his family whose name appeared on the early Greene County platbooks. It is assumed that he is the father of Edmond Duke who was born 1781 and married Mary Bonner about the beginning of the nineteenth century. Other Greene County records show the marriage of; Robert Duke to Patty Holloway in February 1800; Isham Duke to Elizabeth Sherrell in October 1806; and Green Duke to Ann Robinson in August 1800. These appear to have been the older brothers of Edmond Duke, Jr.

As early as 1802, William and David Duke were neighbors of the Bonners on Dove's Creek and Barber's Creek in Clarke County. Later, in 1812, Henry and Edmund Duke (born 1781) appeared on the tax books in the same district (Funderburk's) the latter being listed just above the name of Willis Bonner. The Dukes appear to have been among the early emigrants from North Carolina to Wilkes County between 1763 and 1780.

@ The will of Henry Duke was probated in Wilkes County in

April 1780, wherein Thomas Duke and James Duke are listed as his brothers and Charles, Thomas, Henry and Mary are given as his children. Henry Duke, Senior must have died relatively young at the time of his death in 1780 for his parents were still living at that time, although their names are not recorded. James Duke of Wilkes County died in 1789 and Edmund Duke, Senior was one of the heirs, having sold at that time his legacy consisting of 287-1/2 acres on Richard Creek in Washington County.

Edmund Duke, Junior (born 1781) who became the husband of Mary Bonner (born 1779), lived in Clarke County from about 1800 to 1820 when he moved to Morgan County. Here in 1830, he, (Edmund Duke, Jr) was administrator of the estate of John P. Duke. Legates of John P. Duke were; John, Henry, Thomas, David and Nancy Duke, the last having married Greenberry Darnell in January 1829. Thomas Duke had married Nancy Morgan in Jackson County in 1808. Henry Duke had married Polly Norris in 1806 and David B. Duke had married Sally Tallant in 1810. All of these marriages occurred in Jackson County, the original county from which Clarke was crested.

About 1841, Edmund Duke, Jr., left Morgan County and seems to have sojourned for a brief period in Troup County before coming to Carroll County where he acquired land in the tenth district (near the present site of Bethesda Church) and owned one family of slaves. He died about 1866 on lot No. Eleven.

Coming to Carroll County along with Edmund Duke some time before the Civil War were his kinsman; Thomas Duke (1800 - 1866) who is buried on lot No. 143 in the fifth district; James H. Duke (3 December 1808 - 19 February 1879) who is buried at Old Camp Church; William Duke (son of Edmund and Mary, born 1812). William Duke had twin sons (born about 1837) whose names were Albert and Alfred. The former who became the father of Henry Duke who died in Carroll County in 1926. The census of 1860 for Carroll County lists a total of ten Duke men who were over 21 years of age. The oldest of these was Edmund Duke, then 79 years old. The others were: Thomas Duke (1800-1866) and his sons, Washington Duke (born 1821); William Duke (born 1812); Zebulon Pike Duke (born 1835); A. H. (Alfred) Duke and A.J.P. (Albert) Duke; James H. Duke (born 1809); Ward Duke (born 1832) and Thomas F. Duke (born 1838). All of these were farmers except Washington Duke who was a blacksmith. The elder Thomas Duke was also a Primitive Baptist Clergyman.

An interesting aspect of the Carroll County Duke family is an unsuccessful attempt by one of the descendants, Thomas Duke in 1927 to share in the $2,000,000 legacy made by James B. Duke of

Durham, North Carolina to be divided among the heirs of Taylor and Dicey Jones Duke. The latter two were the parents of the tobacco tycoon, Washington Duke for whose family Duke University was named.

In subsequent chapters the children of Thomas Bonner will be covered.

The below information is the 1995 update from the original work of James C. Bonner.

The reminiscence of George A. Bonner coupled with the fact that, while in North Carolina, Thomas Bonner purchased a slave girl for his daughter, Deborah (who married Richard Vanderford) is sufficient proof that Thomas Bonner of Chowan County, North Carolina is the same Thomas Bonner who died in Clarke County, Georgia in 1804. Additionally, Thomas's son, Josiah, named a son, Thomas Jones Bonner (born 8 June 1818 - died 30 April 1843).

The Bible page produced earlier is proof that Nathan and Elizabeth Slaughter Jones were not the parents of Margaret Jones Bonner.

From a Deed of Gift dated in July 1766 from his father, Henry Bonner, is proof that Thomas Bonner was born between July 1745 and May 1746.

@ Records of Wilkes County Georgia show that Henry Duke was a member of the Revolutionary War and was captured in Augusta, Georgia in September 1780 at a place called "The White House" (a local meeting place). Henry was hanged by the British in the stair well of the house.

In, "Some Georgia County Records, Volume 2, page 233, as copied from Greene County records in the Original Deed book D, pages 708 and 709."

"15 October 1789. Robert Flournoy of Wilkes County to Thomas Bonner of Greene County for 500 pounds. 200 acres in Washington County now Greene on the south fork of Powell's Creek bounded south by Benjamin Gilbert & said Flournoy, west by Hardwick, north by said Bonner and partially by Robert Flournoy. Signed: R. Flournoy. Witness: Leavin Maddux, Zadock Bonner, Juedan Bonner. Proved by Jurdan Bonner 18 March 1791 before Michael Rogers, J. P.

(Plat drawn at end of Deed) Registered: 20 July 1792."

CHAPTER III

JORDAN BONNER

(1767 - 1841)

Relatively little is known by this writer about Jordan Bonner. The name Jordan is seldom found among the descendants of his father's other sons and daughters. It is probably a family name belonging originally to a Quaker family which frequently occurs in the Colonial records of Chowan County, North Carolina and other communities in the region around Albemarle Sound in the Northeastern part of North Carolina.

Old Carolina records reveal the fact that the Bonners and Jordan were intermarried. There were close personal and economic relations among the families of Bonner, Jordan, Luten, Standing, Jones and Blount of eastern North Carolina. Jacob Jordan who died in Chowan County in 1795 had sons named; Jacob, Joseph and Jonathan, and daughters named, Rachel, Leah, Patience and Sarah. Quaker church records of the Perquimans County monthly meeting in 1783 show that # Leah Jordan, because she had married one Bonner who was not a Quaker, was excommunicated from the brotherhood. However a later record, 1798, concerning a land sale by Jordan Bonner in Georgia gives his wife's name as Rachel.

On 14 February 1748, William Bonner was witness to a marriage in Chowan between Thomas Luten, Jr., and Catherine Jones. On 14 February 1752, one Thomas Bonner married Mary Standing which was witnessed by William Luten. On 21 August 1744, one William Bonner married Sarah Luten in Chowan County. In 1775, Joseph Blount, Jr married # # # Lydia Bonner at which time Thomas Jones provided his surety. On 25 August 1792, William Bonner witnessed the marriage of John Hall and Hannah Jones. The will of William Jones of Chowan County was probated on 16 March 1774 and his legatees were; Charity Walker, Esther Johnson; Rachel Luten and James Jones. Thomas Bonner was one of the executors of his estate.

The relationship of the Bonner family to the Quaker community is further evidence in the records of Greene County, Georgia. There on 20 June 1792, Jordan Bonner and his father, Thomas, witnessed the will of Ezekiel Slaughter, a Quaker, who had left Halifax County, Virginia in 1788 and had arrived in the

Powell's Creek Community of Greene County (later Taliferro) along with the Bonners.

About the time that Jordan Bonner appeared first as a taxpayer (in 1793) he acquired "for 100 pounds Sterling" one hundred acres on Shoulderbone Creek in Hancock County just south of his father's place on Powell's Creek below the Hancock-Greene County lines. On 18 January 1798, he sold this tract to Suzanna Moon for $500.00. It was this deed of transfer to which his wife also attested (by making her mark) as "Rachel Bonner." # #

Jordan moved to Clarke (then Jackson) County with his father and brothers and was joint administrator of his father's estate in 1805. In 1800 he bought of Hugh Ector and his wife, Eleanor, of Oglethorpe County 700 acres on the middle fork of the Oconee which was Barber's Creek, which is a few miles north of Dove's Creek Community. At about the same time he acquired additional land from John Cobb. His wife Rachel apparently died sometime before 1810, for Jordan married % Mary Adams in October of the following year. At this time he owned 1,700 acres of land and one family of slaves. He began disposing of his land in 1809 during which year a total of 1,519 acres was sold for $4,538 in seven different sales. The largest of these was 865 acres which lay between Barber's Creek and the Appalachee River which was sold for just $4.00. No record of Jordan's activities in Georgia has been found subsequent to this period. It is highly probable that he joined the early tide of migration to Alabama and Mississippi whose public lands were first opened for sale in 1803. A search of the early records of those and other states in the Southwest might prove rewarding to one seeking more data on this family.

The below information is part of the 1995 update of this work.

In the original work of James C. Bonner, Jordan was listed as the second oldest son of Thomas and Zadock as the eldest son.

Leah Jordan married Henry Bonner, who is thought to be a brother of Thomas (born ca 1744). Henry died in 1797 in Chowan County.

Jordan's first wife was __?___ Martin by whom he had a child. They were killed in a house fire while living in Clarke County. He then married Rachel Moon, daughter of Suzanna Moon.

Lydia Bonner was a daughter of Thomas and Mary Bonner of Chowan. This Thomas was an uncle to Thomas and was known as Thomas Bonner, Sr. in the records of Chowan.

% Jordan Bonner married Polly (Mary) Adams on 3 October 1811.

Jordan Bonner was the eldest son of Thomas and Margaret Jones Bonner. He was born at the family plantation in the section of Chowan County known as Green Hall which is approximately four miles north of the present town of Edenton, North Carolina. Jordan probably married almost immediately after the family's arrival in Georgia at which time he was about 18 years of age.

The below information was furnished by Mr. Darrell Harrington, a descendant of Jordan Bonner.

It was about the year 1793 that Jordan Bonner lost his first wife and child in a house fire. In 1796, he married Rachel Moon and had the following children:

1. Hiram Bonner (born 1798 -

2. Onnie Bonner (born 1801 - died 1867) married Jonathan Brown.

Based on the above information, the following was found to be important to this work.

Rachel Moon was a daughter of Richard and Susannah Moon. Richard Moon died in Hancock County, Georgia in 1795. His Last Will and Testament reads:

"Will of Richard Moon of Hancock of Hancock Co., Planter. Beq to my son Simon, one shilling; to my son Richard, one shilling; to my oldest daughter, Mary, one shilling; to my daughter Lowry, one shilling; to my daughter Susey, one shilling; to my daughter, Hannor, one shilling; to my daughter, Narget, one shilling; to my daughter, Rachel, one bay horse, one speckled cow and yearling, a bed and furniture, pot, plates, dish and basin which I give to well beloved daughter Rachel. I beq to my beloved wife, Susan Moon, my plantation I now live on, 125 acres of land in Guilford County, North Carolina. Appoint my wife Susannah, Extrxx. Dated 15 January 1795. Probated 27 February 1795."

For anyone wishing further research on this family, the records of Guilford County, North Carolina may shed more light.

Back to information furnished by Darrell Harrington.

Rachel Moon Bonner died in 1809 and after she died, Jordan went to the Mississippi territory for a short period of time. After arriving back in Clarke County, Georgia, he married, on 3 October 1811, Mary (Polly) Adams (born 19 October 1791 - died 24 March 1869). When Jordan and Polly married he was 44 years of age and she 20 years of age. Shortly after the marriage they went back to the Mississippi territory and settled on a plantation in what is now the western edge of Alabama near Toxey in Choctaw County.

Their Children:

1. Mahaly Bonner (born 1813 - died 1879) married John Parker (born 1803 - died 1850's.)

2. Wilmoth Almira Bonner (born 1826 - died 1924). It was a letter that Wilmoth wrote about her father in 1900 that identified Deborah as the girl that married Richard Vanderford.

Jordan and Polly settled at Boiling Springs about 2-1/2 miles west of the present town of Toxey, Alabama. At that time it was Washington County. Jordan died on 8 May 1841. He and some members of his family are buried in the "Bonner Family Cemetery." I am told that tombstones mark their final resting place.

An interesting side note about Bonner family. (Sheriff) Thomas Bonner of Beaufort County, North Carolina had a son, Thomas, who had a son, Benjamin. Benjamin moved to South Carolina near the present town of Gaffney. When Thomas Bonner (died 1804) went to South Carolina he also lived in Upper South Carolina and when he received bounty land it was located just north of Gaffney. Question - Did Thomas Bonner (died 1804) go to South Carolina to be near Benjamin because they were kin? Or was it just coincidence? When Jordan moved to Washington County, Alabama, grandsons of Benjamin Bonner of Gaffney, South Carolina also settled near Jordan Bonner near the town of Gilbertown, about three miles north of Toxey. Question - Did the two Bonner families settle near each other because they were kin or was it just coincidence?

Jordan Bonner published his will on 2 February 1841. It was recorded in Orphans Court, Washington County, Alabama on 31 May 1841. In the will are the following names:

Sons: Henry, James, William, Allen, Josiah, Thomas, George W., Seaborne. Daughters: Auene, Elizabeth, Mahala, Mary, Emila, Wilmouth Almyra, Rebecca Ann, Amelia, Arrena.

The Will of Jordan Bonner

I, Jordan Bonner, of the County of Washington and State of Alabama, do make and publish this my Last Will and Testament, forever revoking and marking void all former wills by me at any time heretofore made, and first -- I direct that my Body be decently interred in the burying at or near where my son Henry lives and that funeral be conducted in a manner corresponding with my estate and situation in Life, and as to such worldly estate as it hath pleased God to intrust me with I dispose of the same as follows:

First - I direct that all my debts and funeral expenses be paid as soon after my decease as possible out of the sale of my horses, cattle and stock of every description together with my present crop of cotton. And I direct that my dwelling together with the Eighty acres of land attached remain the property of my wife, together with the household and kitchen furniture and a Negro woman named Sarah and six cows and calves during her life provided that she does not marry, and then to be equally divided with the increase between my two sons James and William and my daughter Arrena. But in case she does not marry I direct that my Executors take Possession of the said property immediately after the fact and divide it as above directed between the said James, William and Arrena.

And I further direct that my daughter Elizabeth have her part of my property a Negro girl named Silvia with other property of Horses and hogs given her several years since.

And I further direct that my daughter Mahala have as her part of my property a Negro girl named Hannah, to together with stock and other property given her years since.

And I further direct that my son Allen have as his part of my property a Negro boy named Jeff and a Negro girl named Patience, which I gave him a bill of sale for a few years since, together with some stock and other property given about the same time.

And I further direct that my daughter, Mary, have as her part of my property a Negro girl name Cloandda together with stock and other property given several years since.

And I further direct that my son Josiah have as his part of my property a Negro boy named Jerry and a Negro girl named Sarah Ann, which I give a bill of sale for together with a tract of land which I gave him a deed to stock and other property.

And I further direct that my son Thomas have as his part of my property a Negro boy named Dick and a Negro girl named Esther, which I gave him a bill of sale for together with a tract of land which I gave him a deed to stock and other property.

And I further direct that my daughter Emily have as her part of my property a Negro girl named Sellah together with one fourth the proceeds of the sale of Real estate.

And I further direct that my son George W., have as his part of my property have as his part of my property, not to have possession of it until he is twenty one years old, a Negro boy named Frank and a Negro girl named Malissa and one fourth of the sale of Real estate together with stock and other property previously given him.

And I further direct that my daughter Wilmoth Almyra have as her part of my property a Negro girl named Jane and one fourth of the sale of Real Estate.

I further direct that my daughter Rebecca have as her part of my property a Negro girl named Caroline and one fourth of the proceeds of sale of Real Estate.

And I further direct that my sons James and William and my daughter Amelia have as their part of my property to share and share alike (besides what has before been mentioned) two Negro boys named Harry and Will and two Negro girls named Harriet and Peggy and their increase and I further direct that my Executors sell to the best advantage all my Estate except the tract on which my house is situated which is above mentioned and divide the net proceeds thereof between my four children as before stated viz; my daughter Emily, my son George W., and my two daughters, Wilmoth Almyra, and Rebecca Ann to share and share alike.

And I further direct that all of my named children to remain with and under the Guardianship of their mother during their minority and they be as well educated as their means will permit.

And I do hereby make and ordain my sons Seaborne and Allen Executors of my Last Will and Testament.

In witness whereof I, Jordan Bonner, the testator, have to this my Will written on one sheet of Paper, set my hand and seal this the Second day of February, A.D., one thousand Eight hundred and forty one.

Signed, sealed and delivered in the presence of us who have subscribed in the presence of each other.

H. J. Y. Moss
Josiah Rogers
His
Richard C. (X) Doggett
Mark

Jordan Bonner (Seal)

State of Alabama
Washington County

Orphans Court
3rd Monday of May 1841

This day came into open Court the within named Henry J. Y. Moss, one of the Subscribing witnesses to the foregoing will who being duly sworn upon his oath saith that he saw Jordan Bonner sign said Will and he also declared in the presence of the other subscribing witnesses this to be his Last Will and Testament and that each witness signed the name in the presence of the Testator ---and this witness further saith the Testator was of sound disposing mind at the time of signing the same.

Sworn in Open Court. Attest: Wm Grimes, Clerk
Recorded - 31 May 1841.

Note - The above will is recorded in the *Records of Wills, Book B,* Probate Court Office of Washington County, in Chatom, Alabama.

CHAPTER IV

ZADOCK BONNER

(1769 - 1848)

Zadock Bonner was listed with his brother, Jordan, as a chain bearer in the survey of Thomas Bonner's original plat in Greene County in 1788. Zadock paid a poll tax of four shillings in Greene County in 1789 at which time he was 20 years old, having been born on 17 June 1769. In August 1794, he appeared on the rolls of Captain Whitfield's Militia Company of Hancock County as an Ensign. It was probably while he lived at the Bonner farm on Powell's Creek that he married Susan Johnson (daughter of Colonel Bigby Johnson) for his oldest son, Smith Bonner was born there on 13 April 1798.

Like many Georgians of that day, Zadock was a speculator in wild lands lying in the southern and western parts of the state. In 1811 for example, he owned nearly 2,000 acres in Clarke, Wilkinson and Wayne Counties. By 1820 his holdings consisted of more than 3,500 acres. His home place in Clarke County consisted of 248 acres and there were holdings of 490 acres each in Wayne and Irwin Counties, 980 acres in Appling, 500 acres in Early, 202 acres in Pulaski and 606 acres in Wilkinson County. While his sons and most of his brothers became relatively large slave owners, Zadock invested his money almost entirely in land. In 1825 he was married to Lucy Jackson of Clarke County. He died in Carroll County in 1848 and was among the first to be buried in the Church yard of Old Camp Methodist Church a few miles west of Carrollton, Georgia.

At least five of Zadock's children moved to Carroll County with him in 1829 shortly after that county was opened for settlement. In all likelihood, this was his entire family. Zadock's name does not appear on the Clarke County records after 1825. This family appears to have sojourned for a few years in Henry and Fayette Counties before moving to Carroll, for it was in Henry County that his oldest son, Smith Bonner, was married and where his wife, Frances, and their four children returned from Carroll after Smith's death in 1832. Smith's children were; John, Susan, Thomas and Zadock. Some of these are buried in the cemetery near the White House in Henry County.

The first Bonner settlement in Carroll County was made near the Chattahochee River a half dozen miles from Acorn Bluff, the home of the Creek Chief William McIntosh. The Bonner occupied lots 106, 143 and 148 in District Four. They were among the original settlers of Carroll County, arriving in the County while the Creek Indians still hunted on the banks of the Chattahochee River.

Carroll County was organized in 1826. Two years later, on 28 June 1828, Smith Bonner was given the contract to build the first county jail at Carrollton. One of the oldest monuments in the county is the monolith near the later site of Liberty Church erected by Zadock Bonner to mark Smith's grave. It bears the date of 1832. According to tradition Smith was killed in a scuffle with one of his brothers who struck him a blow in the groin from which he never recovered.

Abigail Bonner (born 1809 - died 1890), apparently the oldest daughter of the elder Zadock was married in 1826 to James Freeborn Garrison (born 1802 - died 1860) whose family had moved from North Carolina by way of Clarke and Fayette Counties, Georgia. They settled in Carroll County on land just south of what later became the campus of West Georgia College Campus. The house, located on a bluff overlooking Buffalo Creek, was still standing in 1963 and known locally as the Hay's Mill Place. During the time that the Garrisons occupied this house, the place was known as "The Fullwood Springs." The Garrisons moved to Texas immediately after the Civil War settling north of Nacodoches, near the site of what later became the town of Garrison. The children of Abigail and James F. Garrison were; Zadock B (born 20 April 1829); Sarah Ann (born 27 May 1831); Susan Mandeville (born 8 June 1833); John H. (Born 14 July 1835); Thomas Smith (born 17 May 1837); James Freeborn (born 25 July 1839); Margaret Maria (born 4 October 1841); Ruth Eliza (born 15 February 1844) and William Barnett Moss (born 8 May 1847). The *Carroll County Times* of 14 June 1878 noted that James Garrison "whose family moved to Henderson, Texas" came by Carrollton on his way home from the University of Virginia where he had studied law.

By 1840, Zadock Bonner, Sr and his three surviving sons; Zadock, Jr, Thomas and John as well as his daughter, Abigail Garrison, had moved to that part of Carroll County just west of Carrollton where they reared their families. The younger Zadock, like his father, had a penchant for speculation in land. He became perhaps the wealthiest citizen of the county in the decade following his father's death in 1848. In 1847 he returned for taxes a total of 4,730 acres of land of which only 1,500 acres was in Carroll

County. The latter consisted of lots 93,94,95,98,99,100,122,126 and 127 in the eleventh district. It was his proud boast that no man could settle within two miles of his house on lot 99 without his consent. His additional land was held for speculation in various sections of Georgia including Appling, Irwing, Wilkinson, Wayne, Floyd, Dade, Murray and Cherokee Counties. Being the third largest slave owner in the county, he grew extensive cotton crops on his Carroll County plantations. Near his homesite was found valuable gold deposits the working of which yielded him approximately #three-quarters of a million dollars before the Civil War. Known as "*Bonner's Bonanza,*" the mine was worked simply with unskilled plantation labor. After the Civil War the land was leased and stamp wills were erected on the site.

Zadock, Jr (born 1804) was married on 28 December 1825 to Lucy Ridgeway Jackson (1806-1872), a widow and the daughter of Drury Ridgeway, an old settler who came to Georgia from South Carolina who subsequently moved to Columbus. She was born in Elbert County on 1 June 1806 and moved to Clarke County settling at Bald Springs Church. According to the census enumeration for 1850, the children of Zadock and Lucy Bonner were; Emily C. (Born 1829) who married Dr. George Gamble; Octavia (born 1834) who married John B. Gamble; Caroline (born 1837) who married Captain James Tumlin; Martha (born 1839) who married Mr. Whitmel Sterling; Susan (ca 1841) who married William Freeman Bonner; Georgia (born 1843) who married Captain John A. Terrell and George A. (Born 1845) who married in 1872, Martha McGuire. Zadock Alexander (born 1842) died in infancy. The old residence at the Bonner's Mine remained in the family until about 1940. It was still standing as late as 1963.

On the census records for 1860 appears the name of William F. Bonner, age 38, the husband of Susan who was listed as 29 years of age. Being a descendant of Whitmal Bonner, William Freeman Bonner was his wife's cousin. Their children in 1860 were; Eliza, Lucy and Carrie, ages eight, five and four, respectively. Later additions to the family were: Zadock, Charles and Georgia. The family lived in the Laurel Hill Community near the Bonner mine. Freeman Bonner enlisted in Company "C." 26th Battalion of Georgia Volunteers during the Civil War and was promoted to Lieutenant. In 1860 he owned 250 acres of land and 14 slaves. He moved to Texas in the 1870's.

Thomas Bonner (born 1807 - died 1881) the third son of the elder Zadock, built his house on lot no. 99 in district ten, probably in 1840. This house, as well as much of his 700 acres plantation became part of the campus of West Georgia College. The house which is a two-story structure with a Greek revival facade, has been moved some 200 yards from its original location in front of the new women's dormitory. In 1963, it was being used as a faculty resident in a wooded area east of the college buildings. In its original location it sat on a slight elevation on thre north side of the Carrollton-Bowden road. On the south side of the road opposite the dwelling was a plantation, gin, and other farm buildings, all signs of which have long since disappeared. The burial ground for Negro slaves was the plot on which the west wing of Melson Hall was constructed. This plantation was raided by Federal soldiers under General Stoneman in 1864.

Thomas Bonner (born 1807) married Lucinda Ridgeway (born 1808), Their children were; Susan (born 1830) who married Alex Steed; Thomas (born 1832) who married Mattie Underwood and who became a Captain of Calvary in the Confederate Army. Harriet (born 1833); Sarah Jane (born 1835) who never married; William Smith (born 1836) who married Francis Rosens Gamble and who became a Captain commanding a wagon train in the Confederate Army; Sanders (born 1838) who died as a result of a knife wound incurred in a fight with Pat Mandeville in 1865; Larkin (born 1842) who died unmarried in Alabama in 1879; Carolyn who married Mike Sanders and Ann who married Dr. B. S. Smott of Alabama on 2 October 1860.

In May 1836, Thomas Bonner (born 1807) raised a volunteer company to participate in the Creek War of that year of which he was a Captain and his brother, Zadock was First Lieutenant. In offering the services of the company to Governor William Schley, he requested that they be sent to the Alabama line, just west of Carroll County. Ironically enough, the Creek uprising had begun with the murder by the Indians, in Alabama, of George Bonner, the Sheriff of Macon County who was a first cousin of Thomas and Zadock.

Thomas (born 1807) was an early sheriff of Carroll County. In 1847, he returned 1,900 acres for taxes in the county, which included lots 68,94 and 99 in the tenth district; lots 36,115, and 133 in the ninth district; lots 209 and 310 in the eighth district; lot 47 in the seventh district, in addition to two 160 acre lots in Murray County. The 1860 census lists him as owning 24 slaves, being the fourth largest slave holder in the county. Soon after the Civil War, ###Thomas Bonner removed with his family to Alabama settling near Ashland in Clay County, where he is buried and in which vicinity many of his descendants were living in 1963. Among his descendants were Pete and Herbert Bonner who were football players at Auburn University.

The youngest of the elder Zadock's sons was John, born in

Fayette County, Georgia on 17 February 1817. He was married on 13 November 1835 to Martha M. Gillispie who died about 1857. On 3 September 1857 he married Martha Ann Upchurch who is listed on the 1860 census as the same age as himself. She was the daughter of Gay and Pathie Upchurch and was born in May 1833. She died on 13 January 1881 of pneumonia. Finall, on 7 August 1881, he married Lucy J. Wood who survived him. He had a total of twenty-three children, seventeen of whom survived him. His death occurred on 25 August 1893 and he is buried at Old Camp Cemetery, West of Carrollton along with many other members of his family.

John Bonner (born 1817) was regarded after the Civil War as one of Carroll County's most successful farmers. In 1880 he owned 1,200 acres of land, a mill and ginnery some two miles east of Bonner's Mine. His farm was highly diversified. He was frequently elected to the Board of County Commissioners as he represented the county in the legislature in 1882-83. He was also a Methodist minister with which church most of the Carroll County Bonners were affiliated. His residence, built before the Civil War, was standing in 1963, though unoccupied.

The census of 1860 lists his children living with him at that time as; Frances M. (Born 1837); Susan (born 1840); Martha J. (Born 1844); Thomas (born 1855); Margaret (born 1845); James S. (Born 1953); John Milton (born 1841); Jacob (born 1859); William, Fayette, Zadock, Charles, Love, Robert, Jerusha, Josephine, Georgia, Ella, Mellie and Allie. John Milton Bonner, the oldest of these sons, was among the ex-confederate calvary men who fought in the Union Army against the Indians on the western frontier during the Civil War. He enlisted in Company "E," First Georgia Calvary Regiment on 21 March 1862. Captured in Tennessee and exchanged, he was later recaptured and sent to Rock Island, Illinois where he joined the Union Army on 6 October 1864. He was a member of Company "E," Second Regiment, U. S. Volunteers which served on the western frontier. He was discharged at Fort Leavenworth, Kansas on 7 November 1865. He married in January 1867 Nancy Miles (born 1847). Their oldest son, Charles A., was born in 1869.

In addition to his four sons described above, the elder Zadock had six daughters. Abigail, the oldest of these has already been discussed. Others were; Jerusha who married Jesse Clements; Betsy who married a McCarthy; Pauline who married a Bloodworth; Mahala who married Lovic P. Clements and Susan who married Jesse Robertson. Not much is known of these families. The records of Jesse and Lovis P. Clements have been located in the 1860 census of Cass County, Texas where they were living at the beginning of the Civil War, not far distant from where the family of Abigail Garrison later settled. These records show that Mahala was then 40 years old and her husband fifty-three. Of their ten children, the oldest, a son was born in Alabama in 1840, as were the next five children. Thomas, age 10, and three of ther remaining younger children were born in Texas. This pattern indicates that Mahala and Lovic P. Clements were married about 1838 soon after which they moved to Alabama and migrated to Texas about 1850.

Jesse Clements who married Jerusha Bonner was a brother of Lovic. They were sons of Judson Clements who died in Georgia. The Cass County, Texas census for 1860 indicates that Jerusha was 36 years old at that time and her husband was forty-eight. They apparently were the first of three Bonner girls to migrate to Texas, for their oldest child, a daughter, was born there in 1839. All eleven of the younger children were born in the Lone Star State.

JUDGE ZADOCK BONNER

(1804 - 1891)

from
The Carroll County Times
23 May 1873

The eleventh district in this county is considered one of the best farming districts in it. Here are also located the well known Bonner Gold Mines and Bonner's Store, both owned by Judge Zadock Bonner. These mines are situated nine miles southeast of Carrollton on the road to Franklin. The country between here and there is better than ordinary and is dotted with some of the neatest and smuggest farms and farm houses we have seen in the county. Those of Mr. John Bonner and W. G. Marchman are especially worthy of note.

The editor of this paper made a visit on last Friday to Judge Bonner, at his home. The liberality and hospitality of Judge Bonner in entertaining his friends and visitors has become so well known throughout this county, that we deem it unnecessary to state that we were treated in the most magnificent style. The judge is one of those hosts who can never do enough for his guests. His hospitality is that of the old time kind and is indeed the judge is a fine specimen of the gentleman of the old school. Judge Bonner is, we assume, one of the oldest settlers of Carroll County. He has ben living at his present place residence some thirty odd years. It is here that he has accumulated, and that principally by mining too, the valuable property which he is still the possessor of, not withstanding that he had over two hundred Negroes freed by the late war. He owns altogether some fourteen hundred acres of land here, of course immensely valuable, on account of the gold mines on it. It was made for the purpose of looking at these mines that our visit was principally made. Not much is being done at present in them, there being only three or four miners on the place who are principally engaged at this time in "Sluicing." In company with several gentlemen and one of these miners, we were shown around the "diggings." Through the courtesy of the younger miner, Mr. Hilton, who acted as chaperon for the party, we were shown the modus operandi of "panning," the simplest of all processes for getting the precious dust, the filthy lucre, out of old mother earth. The first pan full panned out by Mr. Hilton yielded about 14 grams of the "pure stuff," the second only about four ---making about 75 cents worth. The panning was done in about 15 minutes. The dust was got at different places, where heretofore a deal of mining has been done. The mere fact that Judge Bonner, by the simplest of processes had made a great deal of money out of them, is sufficient evidence that a fortune is in store for someone who will work them with improved methods. Judge Bonner, it is true, is able to work his mining with improved methods, but he is now getting old, and does not care to undertake such a job in his old age.

The below data was a 1995 updated from the original work.

In 1994 dollars, the gold extracted from the mine would sell for approximately $380,000,000.

The records show that Drury Jackson was Lucy's first husband, not her father. On 2 August 1821, Lucy B. Ridgeway was married to Drury W. Jackson in Clarke County. On 28 December 1825, she married Zadock Bonner in Clark County.

The Clay County, Alabama Cemetery Book does not list Thomas Bonner. However his daughter Jane Bonner (3 February 1835 - 25 September 1925) is shown as buried in the Sardis Cemetery.

In order to better understand the families of the above Bonners, the following has been listed to make understanding the various families easier to read.

Zadock Bonner, Sr.
(1769 - 1848)

Wife:
Children:

1. Zadock Bonner, Jr (1804 - 1891)
2. Thomas Bonner (1807 - 1881)
3. Abigail Bonner (1809 - 1890)
4. John Bonner (1817 - 1893)
5. Jerusha Bonner (1820 -
6. Mahala Bonner (1824 -
7. Betsy Bonner
8. Susan Bonner

Zadock Bonner, Jr
(1804 - 1891)

Wife:
Lucy Ridgeway Jackson

Children:

1. Emily C. Bonner (born 1829 -
2. Octavia Bonner (born 1834 -
3. Caroline Bonner (born 1837 -
4. Martha Bonner (born 1839 -
5. Susan Bonner
6. Zadock Alexander Bonner (Born 1842
7. Georgia Bonner (born 1843 -
8. George A. Bonner (born 1845 -

Thomas Bonner
(1807 - 1881)

Wife: Lucinda Ridgeway (born 1808 -
Children:

1. Susan Bonner (born 1830 -
2. Thomas Bonner (born 1832 -
3. Harriet Bonner (born 1833 -
4. William Smith Bonner (born 1836 -
5. Sanders Bonner (born 1838 -
6. Larkin Bonner (born 1842 -
7. Carolyn Bonner
8. Ann Bonner

Abigail Bonner
(1809 - 1890)

Husband: James Freeborn Garrison (1802 - 1860)
Children:

1. Zadock B. Garrison (born 20 April 1829 -
2. Sarah Ann Garrison (27 May 1831 -
3. Susan Mandeville Garrison (born 8 June 1833 -
4. John H. Garrison (born 14 July 1835 -
5. Thomas Smith Garrison (born 17 May 1837 -
6. James Freeborn Garrison (born 25 July 1839 -
7. Margaret Maria Garrison (born 4 October 1841 -
8. Ruth Eliza Garrison (born 15 February 1844 -
9. William Barnett Moss Garrison (born 8 May 1847 -

John Bonner
(1817 - 1893)

Wife: (1st) Martha M. Gillispie (ca 1820 - 1837)
Married: 13 November 1835

(2nd) Martha Ann Upchurch (1833 - 1881)

Married: 3 September 1857

(3d) Lucy J. Wood

Married: 7 August 1881

Children:

1. Frances M. Bonner (born 1837 -
2. Susan Bonner (born 1840 -
3. John Milton Bonner (born 1841 -
4. Martha J. Bonner (born 1844 -
5. Margaret Bonner (born 1845 -
6. James S. Bonner (born 1853 -
7. Thomas J. Bonner (born 1855 -
8. Jacob Bonner (born 1859 -
9. William Bonner
10. Fayette Bonner
11. Zadock Bonner
12. Charles Bonner
13. Love Bonner
14. Robert Bonner
15. Jerusha Bonner
16. Josephine Bonner
17. Georgia Bonner
18. Ella Bonner
19. Mellie Bonner
20. Allie Bonner

There are three more children whose names are unknown. There were twenty three children in all. Also, there is confusion in the numbers of the marriage and deaths of the first two wives. The dates do not match the births of the children.

CHAPTER V

Deborah (Nancy) Bonner

(1772 - after 1860)

Deborah Bonner was the eldest daughter of Thomas and Margaret Bonner. According to the Georgia census of 1850, she stated that she was born in North Carolina. Probably she was born at the family plantation at Green Hall in Chowan County.

This chapter was not part of the original work of James C. Bonner. In 1964, he did not know the name of the Bonner girl who had married Richard Vanderford and consequently she was left out of the family history. Therefore this entire chapter is part of the 1995 update information.

Just before the Thomas Bonner family left North Carolina for South Carolina Thomas purchased a slave girl in Deborah's name. The Deed of Sale can be found in the Chowan County Courthouse in Edenton, North Carolina at the Register of Deed's Office in *Deed Book Q*, page 243.

John Lewis
to　　　　　　　　　　　　Deed of Sale
Deborah Bonner

North Carolina - Known all men by these presents that I John Lewis of Chowan County and province aforesaid, Planter, for and in consideration of the sum of Thirty Pounds proclamation money to me in hand paid by Deborah Bonner, daughter of Thomas Bonner, junior of the county and province aforesaid, Planter, whereof I do hereby acknowledge the receipt and myself therewith satisfied, have bargained and sold and delivered unto the said Deborah Bonner, she, her heirs, executors, administrators, or assigns, One Negroe girl, called Rose, and I the said John Lewis for myself, my heirs, executors, administrators, and assigns against all and all manner of persons shall warrant and forever defend by these presents.

In witness whereof, I have hereunto set my Hand & Seal this 20th day of March 1776.

Signed, sealed and delivered in presence of, (No names listed)

John Lewis (seal)

Received the day and date within mentioned the sum of Thirty Pounds proclamation money in full for a Negroe girl called Rose, witness my hand.

John Lewis

North Carolina

Chowan County March Inferior Court of Pleas and Quarter Session 1776.

Present: His Majestys Justices

Deed of Sale of a Negroe girl from John Lewis to Deborah Bonner daughter of Thomas Bonner, Junior, was acknowledged in open court according to law.

Test: Thomas Jones, Clerk Current

Registered (by) Alexander Gellalty. Regr.

The above document was the last found for Thomas and Margaret prior to their move to South Carolina. Sometime between 1776 and 1779 they made South Carolina their home until after the end of the Revolutionary War.

It should be remembered that the administrators of the estate of Thomas Bonner (died 1804) petitioned to sell at public auction land and a grist mill to settle the accounts left by Thomas. The records show that Deborah's husband, Richard Vanderford, purchased the 50 acres of Land with the grist mill for $1,000.00 on 12 months credit on 5 January 1807.

In January 1995, I received the below information from Mrs. Louise Vanderford McDonald of Texas. She is a descendant of Richard and Deborah Vanderford. She furnished interesting information. Her family records show that Deborah went by the name of "Nancy" in her adulthood. This bit of information is interesting because the name Deborah is not in the Bonner family line until Deborah Whedbee married Henry Bonner in 1705. After this generation of this Bonner family, the name Deborah disappears from this branch of the Bonner family line. Deborah's brother, Thomas, named one of his daughters Nancy. She was born 1809.

Lineal Line of Louise Vanderford McDonald

1. Thomas Bonner (born ca 1744 - 30 December 1804)
Married: Margaret Jones
When: 6 May 1766 in Edenton, North Carolina

2. Richard Vanderford (born ca 1768 - 1845)
Married: Nancy (Deborah) Bonner (1772 - after 1860)
When: About 1789 in Greene County, Georgia

3. Barzillai Vanderford (1799/1800 - 24 July 1876)
Married: Milbery Taylor (1802/1804 -
When: 22 February 1826

4. John Daniel Vanderford (27 September 1828 - 17 July 1893)
Married: Mary Holland Jobe (28 July 1838 - 24 November 1912)
When: 22 February 1855

5. John Fletcher Vanderford (21 February 1866 - 23 October 1925)
Married: Melissa Elizabeth Byrum (31 March 1872 - 22 April 1951)
When: 1 December 1889

6. John Daniel Vanderford (8 October 1897 - 25 February 1991)
Married: Jessie Grace Goodman (9 November 1896 - 18 August 1991)
When: 12 November 1921

7. Artie Louise Vanderford (31 December 1924 -
Married: Frank G. McDonald (9 April 1916 -
When: 22 December 1948

8. LuAnn Leonese McDonald (15 January 1957 -
Married: Dalbert Ray Thiele (13 May 1957 -
When: 22 March 1979

9. Lindsay Leonese Thiele (25 March 1991 -

Lineal List from Deborah (Nancy) Bonner

Married: Richard Vanderford (Ca 1768 - 1845)
When: About 1789 in Greene County, Georgia
Children:

1. Minta Vanderford
2. John Vanderford (ca 1796 - ca 1875 in Mississippi)

Married: (1) Mary _____.
(2) Mary Catherine Weaver

3. Thomas Vanderford (ca 1798 -
4. Barzillai Vanderford (ca 1800 - 24 July 1876 in Alcorn County, Miss)
5. William Vanderford (22 July 1801 in Jackson County, Georgia -
6. Charlotte Vanderford

Married: Noah Strickland

7. Josiah Vanderford
8. Augustus Vanderford
9.. Allen Vanderford

Undoubtedly, Josiah and Allen were named after Deborah's brothers.

1797 - Richard Vanderford was living in Greene County, Georgia
1799 - Richard was in Jackson County, now Clarke County, Georgia
1800 - 3 February - Richard purchased 200 acres of land on Beaverdam Creek in Greene County, Georgia from William Reddock, Sr.
1801 - Richard was in Lloyd district, Jackson County, now Clarke.
1802 - 25 October - Richard's son, Howard, signed an affidavit in Clark County, Georgia backing Jordan Bonner's claim that in 1801 Creek Indians stole two horses valued at $200.00 total.
1802 and 1805 - Richard was in Greer district, Clarke County, Georgia.
1805 - Richard drew two blanks in the 1805 Georgia Land Lottery.
1809 - Richard was in Funderburke district, Clarke County, Georgia.

1813 - 7 August - Richard received 37-1/2 acres of land inheritance (worth $46.07) on Cedar Creek, Chatham County, North Carolina.

1815 - Richard was in Funderburke district, Clarke County, Georgia.

1820 - Richard was in Athens Township, Clarke County, Georgia with his wife, 5 sons and 2 daughters.

1830 - Richard was in Clarke County, Georgia with his wife, 2 sons and a daughter.

1837 - 8 July - Richard Vanderford and Lewis Arthur sold to Allen C. Vanderford land on the Appalachee River adjoining the lands of Vanderford and Brooks for $1000.

1847 - Clarke County, Georgia. Richard Vanderford at the approximate age of 79 years passed away, probably in Clarke County, Georgia at Dove's Creek Community.

1850 - Richard's widow, Nancy, was living with her daughter, Charlotte Strickland and family , in Jackson County, Georgia.

1860 - Richard's widow, Nancy, was living with her son, William Vanderford and his family, in Walton County, Georgia.

CHAPTER VI

WHITMAL BONNER

(ca 1775 - before March 1819)

Whitmal Bonner appears first on the tax books of Greene County in 1796 at which time he owned 65 acres on Shoulderbone Creek and one slave. He was enrolled in "Captain Kimbrough's district, Lower Battalion of Greene County" which was near his father's place on Powell's Creek. He remained in this community three or four years after which time his taxable property had increased to approximately 300 acres and four slaves. He appeared on the Appalachee River in 1803 where he returned land for taxes in Clarke County. In 1808, he appears in Morgan County where he began to purchase land in the adjacent county of Jasper. In 1817, he bought from Isaac Newton, lot number 97, in the sixteenth district. This lot of 200 acres lies on Shoal Creek within six miles of the Courthouse in Monticello, on the road leading to Shady Dale, Georgia. Since this apparently was a highly developed farm, it is believed that it became his place of residence. A two-story house of hewn logs probably dating to this period was standing in 1963 on this lot. A less likely location of Whitmal's residence is on lot number 224 in the thirteenth district, acquired from William Keener in 1815. This lot lies south of Monticello on Wolf Creek. (Earlier, he had bought a fractional part of this lot from Phoebe Gibbs.) Still a third location might be lot number 15 lying also on Wolf Creek in the fourteenth district which had been drawn by John Pearce in the land lottery of 1806. Apparently this purchase of John Pearce in 1808 for $550 was the first land purchase by Whitmal in Jasper County.

Whitmal died intestate in 1821, by which time he had acquired a relatively large estate. The records of the administration of this estate indicates that his wife at this time was Alice (Allie) Selman, daughter of Colonel John Selman who lived on Freeman's Creek, in Clarke County. Whitmal was the father of fifteen children ten of whom were minors. In the division of his property each legatee received from one to three Negroe slaves.

His oldest son, Jonathan, had married Elizabeth Freeman on 23 May 1815. It was their son, William Freeman Bonner, who has already been referred to as marrying his second cousin, Susan Bonner, of Carroll County. Jonathan was living in Pike County in

1823 from whence he later removed to Chambers County, Alabama. His oldest daughter, Edna, was married in 1852 to William J. Scott, a Methodist Minister, author and editor of *Scott's Magazine* which he published in Atlanta after the Civil War. In writing of his wife's father (Jonathan Bonner) he referred to him as "a large and prosperous planter --- who was related by consanguinity to many of the best and foremost people of Georgia, Alabama, Mississippi and Texas and was by descent the great-great grandson of One of the Signers of the Meckleburg Declaration."

George W. Bonner, the second son of Whitmal, also removed to Macon County, Alabama, where as Sheriff of that County he was among the first victims of the Creek Indian uprising of 1836. This Indian uprising, the last to occur East of the Mississippi, was the prelude to the final disappearance of the Creek Indians from Alabama.

About Josiah M. Bonner, the third son, and Whitmal Jones Bonner, Bedford Bonner and William S. Bonner, the three minor sons, nothing is known by this writer. Some information exists concerning Whitmel's ten daughters however. Lorena (sometimes spelled Laurania) was born 4 July 1807. Sometime after her father's death she married Thomas Butrill and moved to that part of Western Georgia which later became Heard County where they raised a family. One of their sons, James Butrill (born 1831), moved to Hogansville, Georgia in 1893. One of the older daughters of Whitmal, Bethany (sometimes spelled Bethene), was married to Wiley J. Sterling on 28 January 1816. This family moved to Troup County where they had several children. One of these, Dr. Whitmal Sterling, married his cousin, Martha Bonner, of Carroll County, Georgia, a daughter of Zadock Bonner, Jr (1804- 1891). Caroline Bonner, another daughter of Whitmal about 1828, met and married Henry Faver of Wilkes County While visiting her sister, Bethany, in LaGrange, Georgia. The Favers moved to Meriwether County where the following children were born: John Randolph; Henry; James; Whitmal; Belle; Mary; Frances and Josephine. When their oldest child, John Randolph Faver, was eighteen about 1839, the family moved with a large contingent of slaves to Northeast Texas where they cleared land, planted cotton, and built a large white-columned house in the traditional fashion of middle Georgia.

One of Whitmal's oldest daughters, whose name is unknown, married James M. Hubbard. Hubbard together with Wiley J. Sterling was listed as one of the legatees in 1820. Colonel John Selman was made guardian of Mary J. Bonner, Carolina Bonner,

Matilda Bonner, Lorena Bonner, Mattie Mae Bonner and Polly Bonner. (A younger daughter, Betsy Bonner, was also listed in the Selman guardianship). Since Selman their grandfather lived in Clarke County it is likely that these girls reached maturity and married in eastern Georgia. There are admittedly some contradictions in the records of the administration of Whitmal's estate. One item mentions the sale of 20 slaves totaling $6,700 and each legatee's share of the estate was $564.80. According to this there would be only twelve legatees instead of sixteen, including his wife and children.

None of Whitmal's children can be identified on the census records of Jasper County in 1830, a fact which suggests that the older children had migrated to western Georgia or to the newer states west of the Chattahoochee by that time. Since the name "Whitmal" an is unusual one and likely to be repeated in succeeding generation, to should be relatively easy for descendants to identify to this family.

In the March Term Court 1819. Letters of Administration and warrant of appraisal granted to Ally Bonner and Jonathan Bonner on estate of Whitmal Bonner. Christopher Hobson and Alsea Holefield entered themselves security for $20,000.

The above is in the book, *Some Georgia County Records, Volume* 2.

Also in the same book is, "In court on 6 September 1819, Whitmel Bonner, Late of this County, etc."

In Court in January Term 1821, "On application of Bedford Bonner, Lemorah Bonner, Matilda Bonner, William S. Bonner, Mary J. Bonner and Whitmel J. Bonner to have guardians appointed for them. Ordered that Colonel John Selman be appointed. Court Adjourned."

The above is proof that Whitmal Bonner was dead before March 1819.

Stated above is the fact that Jonathan Bonner was a direct descendant of a signer of the Mecklenburg Address. Below are the signers of that document and one of which is related to the descendants of Allen Bonner, probably through one of the wives.

SIGNERS OF THE MECKLEBURG ADDRESS
20 May 1775

Officers

Abraham Alexander
John McKnight Alexander

Delegates

Colonel Thomas Polk
Ephriam Brevard
Hezekiah J. Balch
John Phifer
James Harris
William Kennon
John Ford
Richard Barry
Henry Down
Ezra Alexander
William Graham
John Quarry
Hezekiah Alexander
Adam Alexander
Charles Alexander
Senator Zacheus Wilson
Waightsill Avery
Benjamin Patton
Matthew McClure
Neil Morrison
Robert Irwin
John Flennikan
Senator Richard Harris

CHAPTER VII

THOMAS BONNER

(1779 - 1862)

Thomas Bonner was one of the younger sons of the elder Thomas Bonner (ca 1744 - 1804) and about whom there is considerable information in the country archives of Georgia. Fortunately for this study, the census enumerator visited his house in August 1860, shortly before his death, and these records reveal the information that he was born in South Carolina in 1779. His wife, Elizabeth Duke, who survived him, was born in Georgia in 1786. She was probably was the sister of Edmund Duke, Jr and the daughter of William Duke, Sr.

In 1860, Thomas Bonner (born 1779) was living on the Little River in Morgan County, within a few hundred yards of Sewell's Methodist Church. This is in the southwest corner of the county near where it joins both Walton and Newton Counties. Living with him at this time was one family of slaves and an overseer, Robert Crowley, age 25. The census enumerator recorded the fact of his being blind which condition dated back to 1848. It was in that year that he began to divide his land among his children. His will is recorded in this chapter and it mentions six sons, seven daughters and ten grandchildren. Of his thirteen children, only Sarah Ann (born 7 January 1823) had died. She had married William Winfrey who survived her. The executor of the will, which was proved on 20 August 1860, was his "trusty friend, Alexander Pharr of Newton County." Pharr died before the administration was completed and he was replaced by William T. Elliott in 1867. At the time of his death in 1860 his real estate was valued at $1,000 and his personal property at $8,000. In addition to slaves his personal property included such items as: 9 heads of cattle, 2 horses, an ox-cart, "old buggy and harness," a wheat fan, fodder, corn, bacon and miscellaneous household goods which were to remain in possession of his wife. Thomas Bonner (born 1779) appeared on the Clarke County tax books in 1802 in Captains Lloyd's district on the Appalachee River. His tax of 31 cents was the minimum figure and it indicates that he owned no land and no slaves at this time. In 1830, the census enumerator of Morgan County listed a total of ten children and seven slaves. Nine years later a record of his land holdings reveals the same pattern of land speculation as that of his brothers, although his land deals were on a smaller scale. His home place on Little River where he died contained 433-1/2 acres and in addition there were 233-1/2 acres in the nineteenth district of Morgan County and lots of 202-1/2 acres in Heard County, 202-1/2 acres in Harris County, 202-1/2 acres in Lee County and 202-1/2 acres in Henry County, making a total of approximately 1,500 acres.

Deed records of Morgan and surrounding counties suggest liberal gifts of land to his sons and daughters most of whom lived on neighboring farms. In 1848, for example, he granted to his son, Bennett W. Bonner, lot number 67 and parts of lot number 66 in the nineteenth district of Morgan County, containing 202-1/2 acres "worth $1,000" but retained the right of himself and wife to continue living on the place. In August of 1849, Bennett conveyed the same tract back to his father for $1,000. In July 1855, his son, Josiah, sold Henry Henderson, a brother-in-law living in Jasper County, the northeast portion of number 92, "said lot adjoining Thomas Bonner, Senior. William R. Hawkins, Henry Cooper (sons-in-law) and Thomas Bonner, Jr." Josiah died at Oakland, Mississippi on 28 March 1892. His Bible is in possession of Gordan Josiah Bonner of Tallahatchee County where many of his descendants were living in 1965.

The last will and testament of Thomas Bonner (born 1779) reflects further evidence of liberal dowries to his daughters as well as gifts to his sons. Apparently he had lived most of his adult life at the house where he died. On lot number 67, which in 1860 was in the Adsborough district and his Post Office was Ebinezer. The house disappeared about 1940. This write visited it in 1931 and found it to be story-and-a-half frame structure fronted by two rows of elm trees. The road in front of his house was closed about 1935. Thomas Bonner was buried at Sewell's Church about a quarter of a mile distant from his house. In 1965, the base of the chimney and the old spring were the only signs remaining of his home-site.

The family Bible of Thomas and Elizabeth Duke Bonner is in the Possession of Judge James William Bonner of Blakely, Georgia, a great grandson. The Bible lists his children as follows: William Bonner (born 13 September 1803); James Bonner (born 16 May 1806) who married Nancy Applewhite on 7 August 1828; Bidda Bonner (born 31 January 1808) who married James Green on 15 June 1827; Nancy Bonner (born 16 December 1809) married James Spence on 15 January 1827; Thomas Bonner (born 12 March 1812) married Nancy P. Davis; Mary Bonner (born 4 February 1814) married William R. Hawkins in April 1830; Elizabeth Bonner (9

November 1816) married Noah Cooper on 28 August 1833; Allen Bonner (born 11 February 1818) whose second marriage was to Elizabeth Ann Ivey of Walton County occurred on 29 December 1846 - his third wife was Elizabeth Prince; Susan Bonner (born 9 November 1819) married Henry W. Henderson of Jasper County; Josiah Bonner (born 24 February 1821) married Sinah Burks on 23 September 1841; Sarah Ann Bonner (born 7 January 1823) married William Winfrey; Bennett W. Bonner (born 16 November 1824); Carolina Bonner (born 28 July 1826) married James Welborn.

The descendants of Thomas Bonner (born 1779) became widely scattered. The oldest son, William, was in Henry County in 1830 but his subsequent career is unknown. His sons-in-law, Noah Cooper and James Welborn apparently were in Sewell's Church Community until well after the Civil War since a number of these two families and one member of the Hawkins family are buried there. Henry Cooper, who died in 1886, is among these. In the same lot are: Reuben Hill Cooper (1847 - 1931); Sim Cooper (1884 - 1939); Sarah M. Cooper (1838 - 1924); Janie D. Cooper (1850 - 1908); Josiah T. Welborn; Lubie E. Welborn (1881 - 1883) son of Josiah T. Welborn and Mrs. E. A. Hawkins (nee Harper) born 1879 - died 1907.

Of Thomas Bonner's thirteen children only the history of the four youngest sons, Josiah, Allen, Thomas and Bennett are known. Thomas went to Alabama where he died sometime after the Civil War. His oldest son, James Thomas Bonner, died at Rock Island, Illinois during the Civil War as a Confederate prisoner. He had enlisted from Fayette County, Alabama.

Josiah began to dispose of his land in Morgan County as early as 1849 when he sold his brother, Allen, the last half of lot number 66. Six years later he sold to his brother-in-law, Henry M. Henderson of Jasper County, part of lot 92. After the Civil War, in 1869, he started with his family to Texas. Arriving at the Mississippi River he found that stream swollen and was forced to stop in Mississippi where he remained, settling near his double cousin, Thomas Duke, who had arrived earlier from Middle Georgia. Josiah Bonner died at Oakland, Mississippi on 28 March 1892. His Bible is in possession of Gordan Josiah Bonner of Tallahatchee County, Mississippi where many of his descendants are living in 1965. Josiah's ten children were: Sarah Elizabeth (11 July 1842 - 20 November 1936); Susan Ann (1 December 1844 - 29 May 1908); Caroline F. (1 July 1846 - 6 April 1852); Allen Thomas (born 24 September 1847 and died in Confederate Service at Andersonville, Georgia on 20 June 1864; Elisha Henry (8 February 1848 - 28 March 1932) who married Mattie Shores; Josiah Trust (4

June 1850 - 29 June 1927); James W. (17 February 1852 - 19 June 1907) who married Ida Andrew Thomas; Alexander R. (25 May 1853 - 5 January 1927) who married Lucy Hudson; Sophronia Abigail (18 May 1856 - 20 November 1936); William Bennett (14 December 1857 - 6 December 1929) who married Mattie Adams; John F. (15 May 1859 - June 1943) who married Elizabeth Rushing; Samuel Jesse (18 September 1863 - 12 November 1909) who married ___?___ Fowler.

Allen Bonner (born 1818) moved from Morgan County to Henry County and finally to Clayton County where at the beginning of the Civil War he was operating a modest farm and a grist mill near Jonesboro, Georgia on lot 44 in the twelfth district. Being exempt from military service under the Confederate draft law, he became a Captain in Governor Joe Brown's militia where acquired a reputation as an effective drill-master. Being in the direct path of Sherman's invading Army in 1864, Allen Bonner left Jonesboro before the end of the war and moved to Carroll County. He settled near Roopville on lot 36 in the eleventh district. Sometime later he moved to another farm on the Upper Bowden - Carrolton Road a few miles west of the Little Tallapoosa River. Here he died on 23 July 1901 and is buried in the Bonner lot along with four generations of his family at Old Camp Cemetery. His wife, Elizabeth, died on 17 May 1907.

Allen Bonner had eleven children. Sarah Euphemia, the only child of his first marriage, was born 3 August 1842. Sarah's first husband was killed in the Civil War and she later married Thomas Burkes. They moved to Cherokee County, Alabama and died there. Four sons were born to Allen and Elizabeth Ivey Bonner. They were: Francis Marion (born 25 September 1847); George Thomas (1 May 1849 - 17 October 1933); Jasper Andrew (born 14 September 1850) and John Iverson (21 January 1852 - September 1925). The children of his third marriage were: Florida Jane (born 21 January 1857); James Allen (born 18 February 1860); William Luther (born 6 October 1861); Mary Ann (born 29 July 1863) and Martha Elivira (or Ella) (born 8 September 1865) who married Watt Copeland. They moved to Texas and died there. As already related, James Allen and William Luther moved to Tennessee where they founded the Community of Bonnertown and died there during the first third of the twentieth century.

Bennett William (born 1824) was a close associate of his brother, Allen. The two lived as neighbors in Henry and Clayton Counties and removed together to Carroll County where they continued a close relationship. Bennett became a surveyor and once served as the official surveyor of Carroll County. He died on

November 1898 and is buried with his brother a the Old Camp Methodist Church. (Probably the same Church where John Bonner, Son of Zadock Bonner, Sr is buried.) Bennett's wife, Frances, born 27 June 1827, died on 23 October 1916.

LAST WILL AND TESTAMENT
of
THOMAS BONNER
(1779 - 1862)

GEORGIA
Morgan County

In the name of God, Amen. I, Thomas Bonner, Sr of the County and State aforesaid being advanced in life but sound of mind and memory do make this my last will and testament.

Item 1st. It is my desire that my body be buried in a decent Christian-like manner and my soul to God, who gave it.

Item 2. It is my wish that my just debts be paid.

Item 3. It is my will that what property, lands, Negroes and every species of property I may be possessed of shall be held and enjoyed by my wife for and during her lifetime, with the exception of my household goods which goods and furniture I give to my wife in fee simple for her to do with as she pleases and after her death the property thus willed to her for life to be sold and the proceeds from the sale to be distributed among each of my children and grandchildren as hereinafter directed.

Item 4. Having heretofore given **my son, William Bonner,** money and property which I consider to be an equal portion of my estate I give him forty dollars more in addition to what he has had;

and to **my son, James Bonner,** in addition to what he had heretofore received from me, eighty dollars;

Having heretofore given to **my son-in-law, James Green,** money and property I will him nothing more from my estate.

I give to my nine grandchildren and the children of **my daughter, Biddy Green,** to wit: Joe, Tabitha, Martha, James, Nancy, Sarah A., Mary, Noah and Pleasant Green, each one hundred dollars.

Having heretofore given to **my son-in-law, James Spence,** land and other property which I consider to be his full share of my estate, I give him nothing more from my estate.

Having heretofore given to **my son, Thomas Bonner, Jr.,** land and stock, I further will him four hundred dollars more.

Having heretofore given to my **son-in-law, William K. (Kemp) Hawkins,** lands and other property I will and desire that nothing more from my estate shall go into his hands.

Item 5. It is my will and desire that my Executor hereinafter named when he shall have sold and collected the proceeds of my estate that he pay into the hands of **my daughter, Mary Hawkins,** four hundred dollars for her sole and separate use of herself and her daughters, free from the debts or control of her husband.

Having heretofore given to **my son-in-law, Noah Cooper,** and other property I further will him eighty dollars.

Having heretofore given to **my son, Allen Bonner,** lands and other property, I further give him eighty dollars.

Having heretofore given to **my son, Bennett Bonner,** property and money to an amount which I consider to be more than equal share of my estate, it is my will that he have nothing more from my estate.

Having heretofore given to **my son-in-law, William Winfrey,** lands and other property as much as I desire to give him, I will him nothing more.

Item 6. I will and bequeath to **my grandson, Allen H. Winfrey, son of my daughter, Sarah Winfrey, deceased,** one hundred dollars.

Having heretofore given to **my son-in-law, Henry W. Henderson,** property to an amount which I consider his full share, I give him nothing more.

Having given to **my son, Josiah Bonner,** heretofore lands and other property, I further Will him the sum of four hundred dollars more.

Having heretofore given to **my son-in-law, James Wellborne,** Negroes and other property as much as I wish him to control, I give him nothing more.

Item 7. It is my will and desire that my Executor when the proceeds of my estate shall have been collected that he pay into the hands of **my daughter, Caroline, wife of James Wellborne,** the sum of four hundred dollars for her sole and separate use of herself and her children free from debts and control of her present or any future husband.

Item 8. It is my will in case of death of Negroes or depreciation in the value of property that my legatees under this will shall receive a deficit in proportion to the respective amounts --- or in case of an increase in the value of the property --- a surplus.

Item 9. My trusty friend, Alexander Pharr of the County of Newton, Executor.

Thomas Bonner

20 August 1860.

Thomas Bonner's will was probated at court 12 January 1863. The above will is on file in the Archives in Atlanta, Georgia.

The below information is part of the 1995 update of this work.

When I read that Judge James William Bonner had the Bible of Thomas and Elizabeth Duke Bonner in Blakely, in 1993, I went on a search to locate it. I eventually received information that the Judge had passed away and is buried in Blakely, Georgia. I found his daughter, Jane, and she was ever so gracious to furnish the below certified copy of the Bible.

"I HEREBY CERTIFY THAT THE BELOW INFORMATION WAS TAKEN FROM THE BIBLE OF THOMAS BONNER AND HIS WIFE, ELIZABETH DUKE BONNER."

The Bible, being too fragile to machine copy, the following is hereby furnished.

HOLY BIBLE
CONTAINING
OLD AND NEW TESTAMENTS
TRANSLATED OUT OF THE ORIGINAL TONGUES
AND WITH THE FORMER
TRANSLATIONS DILIGENTLY COMPARED AND REVISED
WITH CANNES MARGINAL REFERENCES
By
Hervey Wilbur, A. M.
The Bible was Published by White, Gallaher & White, 1829, New York
FAMILY REGISTER

William Bonner was born
September 13th, 1803

James Bonner was born
May 16th, 1806

Bidda Bonner was born
January 31st, 1808

Nancy Bonner was born
December 16th, 1809

Mary Bonner was born
February 4th, 1814

Elizabeth Bonner was born
November 9th, 1816

Allen Bonner was born
February 11th, 1818

Susan Bonner was born
November 9th, 1819

Thomas Bonner was born
March 12th 1812

Sarah Ann Bonner was born
January 7th, 1823

Caroline Bonner was born
July 28th, 1826

Josiah Bonner was born
February 24th, 1821

Bennett W. Bonner was born
November 16th, 1824

I hereby certify that I have correctly reproduced the Family Register pages, spelling and spacing, and that other information concerning the Bible in my possession is correct. The Bible came into my possession through my father, Judge William Bonner, who is buried in Blakely, Georgia.

(Signed) Jane Bonner Peacock

November 13, 1993.

The above copy of the Bible page is part of the Revision of 1995 by John Wesley Curry.

CHAPTER VIII

MARY ELIZABETH BONNER

(1779 - after 1870)

Mary Elizabeth Bonner was a twin to her brother, Thomas. It appears that she and her brother, Thomas, married brother and sister, Elizabeth and Edmund Duke, Jr. This assumption is supported by the fact that Thomas' son, Josiah, moved to Mississippi and settled near his double first cousin, Thomas Duke (see previous chapter on Thomas Bonner.)

The entire chapter is new to this work, being part of the 1995 revision.

Mary's full name came to light from correspondence with various Bonner descendants in Mississippi and Texas. Additional support is evidenced by the fact that many of Mary's siblings had daughters named, Mary and Elizabeth.

Mary's husband, Edmund's family is unknown, according to the records located so far about the Dukes. Nowhere in the available Georgia records are records that state exactly who Edmund and Elizabeth's parents were. One family that fits a profile is that of John Taylor Duke, Sr., who had a son, Thomas Duke, who died in Morgan County, Georgia in 1828.

The following information has been furnished to this writer by Mr. Joseph William Lineberger of Georgia who has spent many years researching the Duke family. He suggests that the following best fits the profile to be the family of Edmund Duke, Jr and his sister, Elizabeth Duke.

DUKE FAMILY

Father: Captain Henry Duke, a veteran of the Revolution, Probably in Virginia. He was a member of a Battalion of Minute Men.

Wife: Elizabeth Taylor

Their children:

1. Robert Duke (Revolution Service) born in Lunenburg County, Virginia. Married before 1757 in Lunenburg County. He died about 1784 in Kershaw County, South Carolina.

2. Henry Duke (Revolution Service). He was born about 1750 and died in September 1780 during the Battle of Augusta, Georgia.

He was captured and hanged by the British at a meeting place called the "White House," in the stairwell.

3. James Duke (Revolution Service), born in Lunenburg County, Virginia. He died before 1787 in Wilkes County, Georgia.

4. Edmund Duke. (Note - It was this man that caused the son of Thomas Duke, Edmund Duke, to be called "Junior." This was the normal practice of the time.

5. John Taylor Duke, Jr., whose wife was Lydia __?__. He was born in Lunenburg County, Virginia and died in 1803 in Orange County, North Carolina.

6. Thomas Duke (Sr), whose wife was Elizabeth __?__.

Their children:

a. John T. Duke (born 1771 - died 1849). He was born in Virginia and died in Newton County, Georgia. He married on 17 April 1792 in Wilkes County, Georgia, Mary Wooten.

b. Jane (Jenncy) Duke. She was born in 1772 in Virginia and married Matthew Stone.

c. Charles Duke, born 1779 in Georgia. He married Nancy Ann __?__. He died about 1862 in Cleburne County, Alabama.

d. Henry Duke, born 1780 in Georgia.

e. Edmund Duke (Jr), born 1781 in Georgia. He died in Carroll County, Georgia about 1866. He married Mary (Elizabeth) Bonner, born 1779) about 1800 in Greene County, Georgia.

f. Elizabeth Duke, born 1786 in Georgia. She married Thomas Bonner (born 1779) in Greene County, Georgia about 1802. She died in Morgan County, Georgia after 1860. She is probably buried at Sewell's Church along with her husband.

It is believed by this author that the above Thomas Duke was the same man who was living in Morgan County, Georgia in 1830. It is a fact that Thomas and Elizabeth Duke Bonner lived their entire adult lives in Morgan County and, therefore, it stands to reason that Thomas Duke was the father of Elizabeth. The following is noted in the records of Morgan County, Georgia: Thomas Duke was born about 1755, probably in Lunenburg County, Virginia and died in 1830 in Morgan County. He served as a private in the Wilkes County, Georgia Militia during the American Revolution and later drew land in the 1827 Georgia Land Lottery based on that service. His grave site is not known.

This entire chapter and the information contained therein is part of the revision of 1995.

CHAPTER IX

ALLEN BONNER

(1781 - 1827)

The fourth son of Thomas Bonner (born ca 1744) was Allen, whose birth year was approximately 1781. His name appeared first on the tax books of Clarke County in 1802 at which time he returned 247 acres adjacent to land owned by his father and brothers "on the waters of the Appalachee," in the Dove's Creek settlement. Since he appeared first as a landowner at this time it is possible that the year of this birth may have been earlier than 1781. All records concerning him indicate an early and persistent talent for acquiring property in both land and slaves, and the ownership of land at the age of twenty-one was the rule rather than the exception among his family associates. By 1808, he had acquired a total of 800 acres, mostly in Wilkerson and Baldwin Counties, and he had begun to invest in slave labor. Six years later, in 1814, he acquired land in Randolph (now Jasper) and Jackson Counties, and had increased his holdings in the Dove's Creek settlement to 400 acres. He also owned nine slaves. In 1820 his tax return included twenty slaves, approximately 2,000 acres of land and on a "four wheel carriage," the latter being the object of one of Georgia's earliest form of a luxury tax. In 1825, which is the last year in which his name appears on the Clarke County tax books, he listed what appeared to have been his home place of 243 acres at Dove's Creek, approximately 1,200 additional acres "on the Appalachee" (probably also in Clarke County), one 202-1/2 acres lot in Baldwin and Jasper Counties and Approximately 1,000 acres west of the Appalachee in Walton County. His personal property alone consisted largely of slaves, amounted in value to $9,000. He died in 1827 at the approximately age of forty-six years. A total of twenty-one slaves were sold in the settlement of the estate, ranging in price from $150 to $400 each. Sold in a period of depression in Middle Georgia, they bought only $5,150. The names of these slaves are listed in the records.

It appears that Allen Bonner still lived at Dove's Creek on the Appalachee River at the time of his death, and he was the last of the Bonners to reside in this settlement. James Meriwether was the administrator of his estate, the records of which are numerous and scattered, being found in the archives of various Middle Georgia

Counties. These records not only help to substantiate his birth as 1781 but also identify his wife and children.

Allen Bonner married Lucy Awtrey, the second daughter of Absalom and Mary Lucy Awtrey of Clarke County. Absalom Awtrey was born in 1751 in Lincoln County, North Carolina and served in the Revolutionary War. He and his descendants followed the same path of migration across the middle of Georgia, as did the family of Thomas Bonner (born ca 1744). Like the Bonners, the Awtreys intermarried with such well-known Middle Georgia families as the Treadwells, Hills, and Strawns.

Several minor children of Allen and Lucy Bonner are known to have survived their father. William A. Drake, in 1837, married Allen's daughter, Mahala, who ten years earlier had been the wife of Colonel Hill of Walton County. William Drake became the guardian of Allen, Jr and Frances Emily, described as "orphans of Allen Bonner, deceased." Among the older surviving children of Allen, Sr were: Lucy Ann and Jerusha. The former married John T. Marrow of Heard County and Jerusha married Richard Simms of Newton County. Henry L. Reese was also listed as one of the legatees in 1828, indicating that Allen Bonner, Sr., was the father of a still sixth child whose name is unknown.

Allen Bonner's wife, Lucy, survived him. She is known to have been living in Walton County in the 1830's. Since that county lies immediately west of the Appalachee River, it is quite possible that her residence was near, if not actually, at the site of the old Bonner homestead at Dove's Creek. Lucy apparently died shortly before 1837, for in that year the six heirs sold to Richard Vanderford and Lewis Arthur for $1,500 a tract of "331 acres known as the dower of Mrs. Lucy Ann Bonner late widow and relict and relict of ther said Allen Bonner, deceased." Each of the heirs was entitled to a sixth part of a dower which was sold at auction. It is not known what became of the two minor children surviving their mother in 1837, whose names were: Allen, Jr and Frances E. Bonner.

The below is part of the 1995 update information.

Lucy Awtrey Bonner (relict of Allen) married Henry Green before 1835.

Note - There is a possibility that Lucy lived many years after 1835 and that the sale of her dower was a settlement of the estate of her husband, Allen, because she had remarried.

If Allen's birth year is correct, then he was born in South Carolina, according to the information about a bounty land grant, dated in 1784, to his father that proves that in 1784 the family was still residents of South Carolina.

CHAPTER X

JOSIAH BONNER

(1787 - 1851)

Josiah Bonner was born, probably in Georgia, on 5 May 1787, and he was one of his father's three minor children at the time of the latter's death in 1804. His name appeared first on the Clarke County tax books in 1809, being listed in Funderburg's (Funderburke's) district along with his brothers. He was married, 2 February 1810, to Nancy Williams Hubert (born 1791), the daughter of Gabriel Hubert and Elizabeth Bonner Hubert.

Gabriel Hubert was born in North Carolina in 1769, the son of Benjamin Hubert. He moved to Greene County, Georgia in 1786 and settled near Powell's Creek where, in 1790, he married Elizabeth Bonner # who was born in North Carolina in 1767. The exact relationship between Josiah Bonner and his mother-in-law is unknown, but all indications point to a double kinship between the two families. This point is further emphasized by the fact that a son of Gabriel Hubert, James Nevel Hubert (born 1793) was married to Anne Bonner, whose parentage is unknown to this writer. Hubert moved with his family from Greene to Clarke County along with the Bonners. On 4 June 1804, he proved his headright to 600 acres of land and was granted that amount in the general area of the Dove's Creek settlement. In addition to Nancy, Gabriel Hubert had five other children, all of whom were sons. One of these, John Rutherford Hubert (born 1801), went with Mirabeau B. Lamar to Texas where he practiced law, held the office of District Attorney at Houston and later served as Associate Land Commissioner at Nacogdoces.

Gabriel Hubert must have died in Clarke County in 1812, for in that year Josiah Bonner was appointed guardian for "James Hubert, orphan of Gabriel Hubert, deceased." By this time Josiah had acquired 85 acres of land on the Appalachee River and one slave. It was soon after this that he moved away from Dove's Creek and his name is not included on the Clarke County tax books after 1813. He appears next in Pike County, Mississippi near his brother, Willis, had a land claim in 1818. From there he later moved to Madison County and finally to Carroll (later West Carroll) Parish, Louisiana, where he died near Forest, Louisiana on 9 December 1851.

Josiah and Nancy Hubert Bonner were the parents of eleven children. Gabriel H., the oldest, was born 20 December 1810 and died on 4 November 1861. The Others were: James Lucien (27 August 1812 - 13 September 1853); Elizabeth Ann (6 June 1816 - 14 January 1852); Thomas Jones (8 June 1818 - 30 April 1843); Hiram Runnels (22 October 1820 - 13 November 1853); Seleta Caroline (4 May 1823 - 7 May 1849); Cecilia Catherine and Lavenia Emmeline (each born 14 November 1825 - the former died 12 May 1904 and the latter on 17 July 1849); Mary Latham (14 January 1829 - 30 September 1835); Josiah Fletcher (28 November 1829 - 20 September 1857) and Martha Ann (2 January 1833 - 18 April 1851.)

All of Josiah eleven children, with one exception, were relatively short-lived. For over fifty years Cecilia Catherine, remained the only surviving child of her father. The others had died between the ages of nine years and fifty-one, the average age at the time of their death was just under thirty years. Since Longevity is a fairly consistent trait of the descendants of Thomas Bonner (born ca 1744), the death record of Josiah's family is a matter for interesting speculation. Eli H. Baxter of Hancock County noted in 1845 that the lands of the Southwest were "but painted sepulchers," full of disease and death. "Their children that survive infancy," he affirmed, "are delicate, sickly and rickety from the cradle to the grave." About the same time another Middle Georgian wrote: "Within the last fifteen years between forty and fifty families have moved from this county and settled in --- New Alabama. More than half of these have died. None have improved their estates."

While these statements were made largely to discourage the heavy-migration of Georgia and then westward in a belt some seventy miles wide which stretched along the fall line from Augusta to appoint near or just south of Dallas, Texas. This was the most common route of family migration in early Southern history. This pattern was followed by the ancestors of President Lyndon Johnson whose forebears are found in Georgia, Alabama and Texas, in the same communities where the Bonners sojourned.

This region along the fall line is sometimes known as the Old Piedmont cotton belt. It was in this belt of mixed farms and great plantations that the history of the Bonner family was made. Here they were born, reared their children and were buried. Some reached that affluence characteristic of the plantation master, others were small farmers, and a few were less noteworthy in their economic achievement. Hard work was the common lot of all of them. Those who became affluent were often blessed by gifts of perseverance and better luck than most. Zadock Bonner once reminisced about his youth in Middle Georgia. He told how often he waited between his plow handles early on a spring morning for enough daylight to enable him to plow a straight furrow. Hard work, good management and a little luck placed him among the foremost men of his county in the two decades preceding the Civil War.

The following is part of the 1995 update of this work.

From what this writer understands about the Bonners of North Carolina, Elizabeth Bonner, wife of Hubert Gabriel, may have been a descendant of William Thomas Bonner of Bertie County, North Carolina. If someone wishes to research this branch Hubert family, the families of the sons of the above William Thomas Bonner should be checked.

In the book, *Some Georgia Records, Volume 2,* Page 21, by Silas Lucas, Jr, the following is found:

"Administration bond dated 25 June 1811. Elizabeth Hubert and James Meriwether. Administrators of Gabriel Hubert. Sureties: David Meriwether and Josiah Bonner."

The following data was published in Texas about the Landfair family. It was mailed to me with the title sheet missing. My apologies!

Eliza (Ann) Bonner, consort of Robert Landfair, born 6 June 1816 and died 14 January 1852. She is buried in the Old Forest Cemetery, Forest, Louisiana. Her father was Josiah Bonner, born 5 May 1787 and died 9 December 1851.

On page 287 of the same book the following is found:

Loiusiana Tombstone Inscriptions of East and West Carrol Parishes. Copied and published by the Louisiana Society, Daughters of the American Revolution, Volume 6, pages 112 and 135.

Nicholas D. Ingram married Lavinia Emaline Bonner, sister of Eliza Bonner Landfair, on December 1839 in Madison County, Mississippi. Book F, page 84.

1850 Census. Carroll Parish, 115, 115.
Josiah Bonner, born 1790 in Georgia. (Note - this is Josiah born 5 May 1787)
Elizabeth M. Bonner, born in 1816 Mississippi.

Sample Bonner, born in 1849 in Louisiana.

1860 Census, Carroll Parish, Ward 5, Oak Grove 764, 734.
Gabriel H. Bonner, born 1811 in Georgia.
Margaret E. Bonner, born in 1812 in South Carolina.
Wilbur F. Bonner, born in 1842 in Mississippi.
James J. Bonner, born in 1848 in Mississippi.
Mary E. Bonner, born in 1850 in Mississippi.

Nancy Williams Hubert, mother of Eliza Ann Bonner, was a first cousin of the Honorable Hiram G. Runnels who was elected Governor of Mississippi in 1833 and of his brother, Hardin Dudley Runnels, whose son, Hardin Richard Runnels, served as Speaker, Texas House of Representatives in 1853 and 1855. Governor Runnels of Mississippi and Hardin Dudley Runnels were the sons of Colonel Harmon Runnels who served in the Mississippi Constitutional Convention of 1817 and his wife, Hester Hubert born in 1762 in North Carolina, the sister of Gabriel Hubert and the aunt of his daughter, Nancy Williams Hubert. Gabriel and Hester Hubert were two of the children of Benjamin B. Hubert, a French Huguenot, who married Mrs. Mary Williams, widow of Paul Williams of Frederick County, Virginia in 1748. From Virginia, the Huberts moved to Caswell County, North Carolina and in 1785 or 1786, they moved to Warren County, Georgia (then part of Wilkes). The will of Benjamin B. Hubert was signed 26 July 1793 and was the first recorded in Warren County, Georgia.

Genealogy of *The Family of Benjamin B. Hubert, A Huguenot* by Miss Sarah Donelson Hubert of Barnett, Warren County, Georgia. Published in 1897 by the Franklin Printing and Publishing Company of Atlanta, Georgia. This booklet was loaned to the author (Sarah Hubert) by Mr. Robert Lamar Landfair of Jackson, Mississippi.

Mr. Robert Lamar Landfair sent this list of the children of Thomas Bonner and Margaret Jones:

1. Jourdan Bonner who married Polly Adams on 3 October 1811.
2. Zadock Bonner who married Lucy Ridgeway.
3. Thomas Bonner.
4. Whitmal Bonner.
5. William Bonner born in 1775. (Note - This is the only document that states that Thomas had a son named William. If true, he died before December 1804.)

6. Willis Bonner.
7. Josiah Bonner, born 5 May 1787 and married Nancy Williams Hubert. He died on 9 December 1851.
8. **Deborah Bonner who married Richard Vanderford.**
9. Elizabeth Bonner. (Note - This was "Mary" Bonner who married Edmund Duke, Jr.)

Mr. Robert Lamar Landfair also sent this information on Josiah and Nancy Williams Hubert.

Josiah Bonner was born 5 May 1787 in Greene County, Georgia and died on 9 December 1851 in Carroll Parish, Louisiana. He married Nancy Williams Hubert on 2 February 1810 in Clarke County, Georgia. Nancy was born 20 October 1791 and died in Madison County, Mississippi, in 1834 or 1835.

Josiah Bonner and Nancy Williams Hubert were the parents of the following children:

1. Gabriel Hubert Bonner (born 20 December 1810 in Clarke County, Georgia and died 4 November 1861), married Margaret E. Brown on 28 May 1831.

2. James Lucien Bonner (born 29 August 1812 in Clarke County, Georgia and died on 13 September 1858 in West Carroll Parish, Louisiana), married Sarah Ann L. Reid on 30 October 1851.

3. Eliza Ann Bonner (born 6 June 1816 in Clarke County, Georgia and died on 14 January 1852 in West Carroll Parish, Louisiana) married Robert C. Landfair in 1830/31.

4. **Thomas Jones Bonner** (born 8 June 1818 in Clarke County, Georgia and died on 30 April 1843.) Note - This man's name poses an interesting set of questions. (A). Was the "Thomas" of his name taken from his grandfather, Thomas Bonner? (B). Was the Jones of his name taken from his grandmother's maiden name? Or (C). Was he named after his grandmother's, (Margaret Jones's), father?

5. Hiram Runnels Bonner (born 22 October 1820 in Lawrence County, Mississippi and died on 13 November 1853 in West Carroll Parish, Louisiana.)

6. Seleta Caroline Bonner (born 4 May 1823 in Lawrence County, Mississippi and died on 7 May 1849 in West Carroll Parish Louisiana), married John Wayne Eppes on 9 February 1837.

7. Lavinia Emaline Bonner (born 14 November 1825 - died 17 July 1842 in Carroll Parish, Louisiana), married Nicholas D. Ingram on 23 December 1839.

8. Cecelia Catherine Bonner (born 14 November 1825 - died 12 May 1904) married Benjamin C. Sample on 10 November 1841.

9. Mary Latham Bonner (born 14 January 1828 in Madison County, Mississippi and died there on 30 September 1835.)

10. Josiah Fletcher Bonner (born 28 November 1829 in Madison County, Mississippi and died on 20 September 1852.)

11. Mary Ann Norwood Bonner (born 2 January 1833 in Madison County, Mississippi and died on 18 March 1851 in West Carroll Parish, Louisiana) married John M. Key on 7 March 1850.

After the death of Nancy Williams Hubert, Bonner, Josiah Bonner married:

Second - Sarah K. Eppes.

Third - Mrs. Elizabeth M. Scanland on 24 August 1848.

Children:

12. Sample Bonner (born 2 November 1849 in Carroll Parish, Louisiana and died there on 4 August 1852.)

13. Josiah Bonner (born 27 September 1851 in Carroll Parish, Louisiana and died there on 27 January 1852.)

Mr. Robert Lamar Landfair, a descendant of Robert Landfair and Eliza Ann Bonner sent the Bonner Revolutionary Record, which he reports, has been established with the Daughters of the American Revolution. The father of Eliza Ann Bonner (Mrs. Robert Landfair) was Josiah Bonner. His father, Thomas Bonner, junior was born about 1744 in Chowan County, North Carolina. He enlisted in Roebuck's Regiment at Spartanburg, South Carolina and fought in the American Revolution. Thomas and his wife died in Clarke County, Georgia.

Part Three

FOREWORD

This section of this work is about the kin people of Nancy Applewhite, wife of James Bonner. I came upon her ancestors by accident and thought it would be a real waste not to include them here. As an artist once say, "It's now or never!"

What I found surprising was that her Barnes ancestors lived near the Bonners in Chowan County in the early 1700's and the records show that her Blanchard ancestors were friends with the Bonners of Chowan County, as noted in the text.

Nancy Applewhite was also descended from the Isle of Wight County, Virginia, Applewhites and that information is also included here. Nancy's daughter, Martha Caroline Bonner, married into the McConniell family and that family is also noted herein. The interesting part of that is Martha's husband, James Allen McConniell was a great grandson of William Tate, Sr., who purchased two plots of land that Martha's great grandfather, Thomas Bonner, sold to William Tate, Sr., in 1787.

Nancy Applewhite and James Bonner's descendants are also included in this work because knowing who they are and not including them would be a disservice of the worst kind. Some members of our vast family never furnished me the information that I needed. I included what information I have.

John Wesley Curry

CHAPTER I

The Barnes Family

The ancestors of Nancy Telitha Applewhite are as follows:

1. Robert Barnes (ca 1670 - ca 1740)
   Wife: Elizabeth
   Children: (1) Joseph Barnes (ca 1690 - 1751)
   (2) Mary Barnes

2. Joseph Barnes (ca 1690 - 1751)
   Wife: Elizabeth
   Children: (1) Jacob Barnes
   (2) Mycha Barnes
   (3) Dempsey Barnes (ca 1730 - 1807)
   (4) Jetho Barnes
   (5) James Barnes

3. Dempsey Barnes (ca 1730 - 1807)
   Wife: Sarah
   Children: (1) Joseph Barnes
   (2) Jesse Barnes
   (3) Thomas Barnes
   (4) John Barnes
   (5) James Barnes
   (6) Susanne Barnes Daniel
   (7) Elizabeth Barnes (16 August 1782 - 31 August 1842)
   (8) Sarah Barnes Blackburn
   (9) Polly Barnes

4. Elizabeth Barnes (16 August 1782 - 31 August 1842)
   Husband: Robert Applewhite (12 February 1771 - 18 September 1839)

Nancy Telitha Applewhite, wife of James Bonner, (son of Thomas and Elizabeth Duke Bonner) was descended from Robert Barnes of Perquimans County, North Carolina, who is the Progenitor of this branch of the family. It is not known whom his father was, although it may have been Richard Barnes of Nansemond County, Virginia.

Robert Barnes

(Ca 1670 - ca 1740)

Robert Barnes was in Perquimans County prior to January 1715, as evidenced by the following Deed of Sale.

"21 March 1736. Thomas Speight, Esq., of Perq. And Mary his wife sold to Lott Sterling (Stallings) of afore' for 30 pounds, 235 acres a plan' called 'Sandy Ridge' adj 'Middle Swamp' that issueth out of Carerene (Katherine) Creek Swamp to a diving line of Charles Wilkes & **Robert Barnes** on line of Kitchens & Snooks. A survey made for Thomas Blitchenden as by **Pattent to Robert Barnes 19 January 1715** & sold by him to said Speight. Test: Elias Stallings, Lewis Skinner."

(Ref: *History of Perquimans County,* page 111, by Mrs. Watson Winslow.)

"9 July 1713. Lott Sterling of Perq., Planter, for 10 pounds 22 barrels of Tarr p'd the 25 December next by Richard Harrel of afore', Planter - sold 170 acres adj John Harrel, 'Now in possession of said Richard.' formerly William Kitchens, as by Deed 15 July 1719, **Sold by Robert Barnes** to Lewis Skinner & by him to Lott Sterling. Test: Gilbert Scot, James Scot." (Ref: Idem, page 113.)

"**Robert Barnes** of Perq Prec't for a Con' pd by Charles Wilkes of ye said place - sold a parcel of land on Thomas Brooks a patent from the Lorde Pro.' 19 February 1715/16. **Elizabeth Barnes her dower of right.** Test: Francis Toms, Peter Denmans. Seal 7 January 1716/17." (Ref: Idem, page 69.)

The proof of the children of Robert and Elizabeth Barnes is as follows:

"Robert Barnes of Perq., Planter - for love I do bear **for my son, Joseph and my Daughter, Mary Barnes** do give a bed & furniture, Pot & Pot Hooks, small pewter dish, 1 Pewter Bason, 3 Pewter Plates, 6 new pewter spoons, & 1 pewter Tankard & all the rest of my goods & chattels, Hogs, Cattle, Sheep & house hold goods now in my dwelling on Plan' known by name of 'Anthony Whary's plan.' 16 April 1733. Test: Thomas Callaway, Aba'm Warren. (Ref:

The History of Perquimans County, page 104, by Mrs. Watson Winslow, originally published in Raleigh, North Carolina in 1931.)

The Last Will and Testament

of

Joseph Barnes

(Ca 1690 - 1751)

In the name of God, Amen. I, Joseph Barnes of Northampton County in the province of North Carolina being sick and weak in body but in perfect sense and memory do make this writing my last will and testament in manner and form following; Viz, Imprimis. I give my body to the Earth Decently to be buried and my soul along to Almighty God who gave it and as for the Worldly goods which I hath received God to bestow on one I give and bequeath in manner following, Viz;

I devised to my son Jacob one hundred acres of land to him and his heirs forever. I likewise give to sd son Jacob two cows and calves and one small gun.

Item. It is my will that **my three oldest son, Viz; Jacob, Mycha, & Dempsey** each of them eight pounds to **my two youngest sons Jethro and James** to be equally divided between them the sd Jethro & James.

Item. I also devise to my said son Mycha one hundred and forty acres of land to him & his heirs forever. I also give and bequeath to my son Mycha two cows and calves and one gun.

Item. I devise to **my son Dempsey** two hundred acres of land to him and his heirs forever. I likewise give and bequeath to my son Dempsey two cows and calves.

Item. It is also my will that my son Jacob, Mycha & Dempsey have an equal share in the orchards that are on the land afore devised to them.

Item. I give and bequeath to **my beloved wife, Elizabeth Barnes** the remainder of all my estate.

Item. I so make this my last will and testament. In witness whereof I have this seventeenth day of April signed and sealed the same and in the year of our Lord one thousand seven hundred and fifty one.

Signed sealed & delivered The mark of

James __?__ Joseph B Barnes

The mark of
Henry h g Gay, Jurat
Charles Skinner
The mark of
Julian Whitley

Northampton County SS August 1751

The within written will was exhibited into court by Elizabeth Barnes Relict widow of the Testator & was proved by the oath of Henry Gay one of the subscribers witness thereto and there being no executor nominated in sd will administration is granted to sd Elizabeth Barnes with the will annexed which was proved to be certified.

Test: __?___. Clerk Current

The above will is on file at the Archives in Raleigh, N. C.

The last will and testament of Dempsey Barnes is on file in the archives in Raleigh, N. C.

THE LAST WILL AND TESTAMENT

of

DEMPSEY BARNES

(Ca 1730 - 1807)

In the name of God, Amen. I Dempsey Barnes of the county of Edgecombe and the State of North Carolina being of sound and perfect memory Blessed be God for his mercies this Twenty Fifth day of March in the year of our Lord one thousand eight hundred and seven make and publish this my last will and testament in manner following that is to say -

First, I recommend my Soul to God who gave it and my body to be decently buried at the discretion of my executors.

First (sic), my desire is that all my just debts be paid -

Item. I give unto **my son, Joseph Barnes,** all the property that he hath received.

Item. I give and bequeath unto **my son, Jesse Barnes** the property that he hath already received.

Item. I give and bequeath unto **my beloved son, Thomas Barnes,** all the property that he hath already received.

Item. I give and bequeath **unto my beloved son, James Barnes,** all the land on the North side of a Branch that runs through my plantation into Tosnot Swamp up the prong of said Branch to a path leading from or near the Head of said Branch to Robert Coleman's to the back line also all the property that he hath already received.

___?___ **unto my beloved wife, Sarah Barnes,** one half of the balance of my land, one half of my Brandy __?__, one half of my Cyder Casks, one half of my orchards to her during her natural life then it is my will and desire that the above property that I have __?__ unto my wife should decease **unto my beloved son, John Barnes,** and the other half of my land not before given away lying on the South side of above mentioned Branch I give to my son, John Barnes immediately after my death to him and his heirs forever also one half of the __?__ and casks and all the property that he hath already received.

Item. I give and bequeath **unto my beloved daughter, Susanne Daniel,** forty dollars in cash also all the property that she hath already received.

Item. I give and bequeath **unto my daughter, Polly Barnes,** three hundred dollars, one hundred of said money to be paid months after my death and the other two hundred at the death of my wife, also two cows and calves, one feather bed and furniture, one calf named 'Blaze' and a __?__ saddle.

Item. I give and bequeath **unto my beloved daughter, ELIZABETH APPLEWHITE,** seventy five silver dollars in cash also all the property that she hath already received.

Item. I give **unto my beloved wife, Sarah Barnes,** three beds and furniture, one flax wheel & haskel also one cow and calf and all the rest and residue of my estate not before given away __?__ unto my wife during her natural life and after her death my will and desire is that all the property that I have __?__ unto my wife should be sold after her death by my Executor at twelve months credit.

Item. My will and desire is that Nathan Barnes, my grandson, **son of Sarah Blackburn,** should have three hundred dollars out of the money arriving from the sale of the property I __?__ to my wife during her life and one horse worth forty dollars also one good bridle and saddle two cows and calves one bed and furniture. If the said Nathan Barnes should die without lawful heir it is my will and desire for the said property to be equally divided between all my children except my son John and James or should there be more of __?__ residue of my property besides discharging the Legacy to Nathan Barnes to be equally divided between all my children except my son John and James Barnes --- And I hereby made and ordain sons Joseph Barnes and Jesse Barnes executors to this my last will and testament.

IN WITNESS whereof I the said Dempsey Barnes have to this my last will and testament set my Hand and Seal the year and date above written signed, sealed, published and declared by the said Dempsey Barnes the testator as his last will and testament in presence at the time of signing and sealing thereof.

His
Dempsey db Barnes (Seal)
Mark

Test: L. W. Baker
William ww White
Edgecombe County August Court 1807

The within last will & testament of Dempsey Barnes was duly proved in open court by the oath of William White one of the subscribers and witness thereto -- And the executors therein named were at the same time qualified thereto in due form of __?__ Ordered that the same be certified and the will received.

Test: E. Hall, Clerk Current

The above Elizabeth Applewhite was married to Robert Applewhite, and they were the parents of Nancy Telitha Applewhite who married James Bonner in 1828.

THE BLANCHARD FAMILY

The earliest record of a member of the Blanchard family was that of Benjamin Blanchard, who was granted a tract of land containing 455 acres "upon Wareck (Warrick) Swamp, at the mouth of Beaver Dam", dated 16 October 1701. The area is now in Gates County which, in 1701, was part of Chowan County.

This same Benjamin Blanchard passed away in Nansemond County, Virginia in 1719. "Benjamin Blanchard, Nansemond County, Virginia. 5 June 1719. Sons: Robert, **Benjamin,** Absalom. Daughter, Catherine and her husband William Weston. Wife, Catherine and son Robert named executors. Test: Aaron Blanchard, Will Hill, Joseph Grifing (Griffin), Thomas Rountree." (Source: Hathaway, Volume 1, Number 2, page 185).

Benjamin Blanchard, son of Benjamin Blanchard, was the father of Elizabeth who married Joseph Barnes, son of Robert Barnes. Benjamin Blanchard died in 1763 in Chowan County, North Carolina.

"Benjamin Blanchard, 1763 Division of Estates, Chowan County. Wife: Sarah. Sons: Uriah, Robert, Reuben, Absalom. Daughters: Christian Hinton, Judeth Hinton, **Elizabeth Barnes,** Bethany Bond, Milleson Blanchard, Absole Blanchard." (Source: Hathaway, Volume 2, Number 2, page 256.)

The above Elizabeth Barnes was married to Joseph Barnes and were the parents of Dempsey Barnes.

CHAPTER II

THE APPLEWHITE FAMILY

(APPLEWAITE)

The Applewhite family associated with the Isle of Wight County, Virginia Applewhite family probably originated in Suffolk, England in the Parish of Stoke-on-Ashe. The Pedigree of Applewhite of Stoke - Ashe, is contained in a manuscript in the British museum. The Applewhites of Isle of Wight probably came to Virginia after settling in Barbados for a short period of time. It is noted in the records that in 1679, Mrs. Applewhite, widow, was the owner of 169 acres in Barbados and on 6 May 1679, two servants of Mr. Henry Applewhite, Luke Rainy and Dennis Burne, embarked at Barbados in the ketch *Prosperous*, for Virginia which was commanded by David Fogg.

The records strongly suggest that Henry Applewhite (2) was the first of the family to settle in Isle of Wight County, Virginia for it was there in 1668 that he, Joseph Bridger, Sr., and Colonel Robert Pitt were involved in a lawsuit with Major Daniel Parke. This is the earliest appearance of Henry Applewhite. He listed himself as a merchant when he purchased 100 acres of land that had formerly belonged to Edmond Palmer from Roger Davis on 20 March 1674/75. Henry Applewhite was a Justice in 1680, a Burgess in 1688 and in 1702-04 he was a Captain of Militia in Isle of Wight County. His will was probated there in 1704. He gave his son, Henry, his great Bible and signet ring, his son William his silver rapier and his son John his silver headed cane. (Source: Seventeenth Century Isle of Wight County, Virginia, page 205, John Bennett Boddie, Wilmette, IL, 1938. 1993., also Wills and Administrations of Isle of Wight County, Virginia, 1764 - 1800, page 42, Blanche Adams Chapman, Smithfield, Virginia, 1938.1994.)

William Applewaite (Applewhite) (born ca 1536 in Stoke-on-Ashe County, Suffolk, England - died 1566/67 at the same place). He married Katherine Rout (born ca 1540 in Stoke-on-Ashe County - died between 1566 and 1634 at the same place). (Source: *World Family Tree, Volume 2*, chart 2910.)

Their children:

1. William Applewhite (born about 1561 in Stoke-on-Ashe and died between 1589 and 1652 at the same place. He married but his wife's name is unknown.

2. John Applewhite (born about 1585 in Stoke-on-Ashe County and died about 1634 at the same place). He married, at the same place, Lydia __?__ who was born about 1594.

3. **Henry Applewhite (1)** (was born about 1610 in Stoke-on-Ashe. He died about 1679 in Barbados). The name of his wife is unknown.

Their children:

1. **Henry Applewhite (2)** (born about 1643 either in Barbados or England - died after 26 August 1703 in Isle of Wight County, Virginia.) He married about 1699 in Isle of Wight County, Ann ___?__. This Henry Applewhite was a Captain of Militia in Isle of Wight County.

Their children:

1. **Henry Applewhite (3)** (born about 1664 - died 27 April 1741 in Isle of Wight County.)

2. Thomas Applewhite (born about 1673 probably in Isle of Wight, Virginia and died in 1732 at the same place).

3. William Applewhite (born about 1675 in Isle of Wight County).

4. John Applewhite (born about 1676 in Isle of Wight County - died in 1735 at the same place). He was married to Sarah Copeland. (Source: Wills and Administrations of Isle of Wight County, Virginia, 1647 - 1800, page 125, Blanche Adams Chapman, Smithfield, Virginia. 1938. 1994.)

5. Anne Applewhite (born about 1677 in Isle of Wight).

Henry Applewhite (3) (born about 1664 probably in Isle of Wight County - died 27 April 1741 at the same place). About 1700 he married Ann "Nancy" Marshall, (born about 1677 in Isle of Wight County - died 1747 at the same place) daughter of Humphrey Marshall and Priscilla Thomas. Henry Applewhite (3) first appears in Isle of Wight County in 1692. He was Sheriff of Isle of Wight County in 1709. He married Ann Marshall before 1711 when he is mentioned in the will of Humphrey Marshall. He was a Member of Burgess, in Isle of Wight County, during 1723 - 1726 and a Captain of the Isle of Wight County Militia. He was a

County Justice in 1702. (Source: *Wills and Aministrations of the Isle of Wight County, Virginia, 1647 - 1800.* pages 141 and 158, Blanche Adams Chapman, Smithfield, Virginia. 1938. 1994. Also: *Seventeenth Century Isle of Wight County, Virginia,* pages 205 and 205, John Bennett Boddie, Wilmette, IL, 1938. 1993.)

Their children:

1. Priscilla Applewhite (born about 1702 in Isle of Wight County). She married Nathaniel Ridley. He died about 1753 in Southampton County, Virginia.

2. Amy Applewhite (born about 1703). She married in 1738 in Isle of Wight County, Samuel Davis, Gentleman, son of John Davis, Sr., and Mary Green. Samuel was born about 1672 and died in 1738 in Isle of Wight County.

3. Anne Applewhite (born about 1704 in Isle of Wight County). She married Edmund Godwin.

4. Thomas Applewhite (born about 1708 in Isle of Wight County.)

5. **Henry Applewhite (4)** (born ca 1695 in Isle of Wight County - died before 22 September 1739 in Isle of Wight County). He married Mary Council.

6. John Applewhite (born before 1716 in Isle of Wight County.)

7. Arthur Applewhite (born before 1716 in Isle of Wight County.)

8. Sarah Applewhite (born before 1723 in Isle of Wight County) She married William Lawrence.

9. Mary Applewhite

The above information was furnished by Mr. Richard R. Dietz of El Monte, California, confirmed by data from Mrs. Helen N. Battleson of Urbanna, Virginia and passed to me by Mrs. Carol Martoccia of East Carolina University, Greeenville, North Carolina. Their generosity is very much appreciated.

A Thomas Applewhite was a merchant in London, England who shipped merchandise to the New World from about 1649 to about 1677. The following is found in *Complete Book of Emigrants,* page 288 for the year 1677: "20 July - 17 August. Shippers by the *Crown Mallago,* Mr. Thomas Applewaite. Bound from London for Virginia, etc. (PRO: E190/72/1, 80/1)."

In the Book, *Cavaliers and Pioneers, Volume Three, 1695 - 1732,* page 17, the following is found: "Bartholomew Fowler, (granted)

1260 acres. Lower parish of Isle of Wight Co; on Blackwater Branches; 28 October 1697. Beginning at Geo. Peirce (Pearce); to Col. Joseph Bridger; on head of Burgh's Swamp; by John Williams &c. **Granted Captain Henry Applewaight, 20 April 1682 and deserted and now granted by order."** Also page 24. **"Henry Applewaight (Applewaite). (Granted) 600 acres Isle of Wight County near Kinsale Swamp adjoining James Bryan down run of the main Black Water Swamp. 15 October 1698. Granted Bridgeman Joyner 29 April 1692, deserted and now granted by order &c transportation of 12 persons."** (See page 102) Henry Applewhite was also granted, on 15 October 1696, 600 acres in the same general location and deserted it. (See page 137) On 2 November 1705 this same tract was reassigned to William West. On 13 November 1713 Richard Drake was assigned 200 acres in the Blackwater Swamp area for transportation of 4 persons, Henry Applewhite being one of them (See page 320). **"Henry Applewhite, Gentleman, 320 acres (New land) Isle of Wight County on North side of Nottoway River between the Cyprus and Cedar Swamps. 31 October 1726. 30 shillings and importation of Edward Matravers."**

In Broddie's 17th Century Isle of Wight, Virginia - "Humphrey Marshall died in Isle of Wight County, Virginia in 1711, leaving a will in which no sons were named but daughters are mentioned. Ann Marshall who married Captain Henry Applewhite (born ca 1695 - died 1739) and Mary Marshall who married Thomas Hill." (Note - In the book, *Marriages of Some Virginia Residents,* by Dorothy Ford Wulfeck, page 29, the following is found: "Captain Henry Applewhite, Sheriff in 1709, son of Henry Applewhite, married Ann Marshall, daughter of Humphrey Marshall as noted in his will of 18 December <u>1771</u>" in Isle of Wight County, Virginia"). Obviously 1771 should be 1711.

Henry Applewhite (4) (ca 1695 - before 22 September 1739)

Wife: Mary Council

Children:

1. Henry Applewhite (5) (born 1730 in Isle of Wight County - died 11 May 1783 in Southampton, Virginia). Married Ann Harris (born about 1738 in Isle of Wight County - died 3 February 1795 in Southampton, Virginia.)

2. Thomas Applewhite (born ca 1733 - died about 1803)

Thomas Applewhite (ca 1733 Isle of Wight County - 1803 in Halifax County, N. C.)

Wife: Unknown

Children:

1. Thomas Applewhite (ca 1768 - 11 April 1828 in Halifax County, N. C.)

NOTE - In 1790 Thomas was living in Wayne County, N. C., where he purchased 200 acres of land on South side of Cabin Branch from Henry Pope for 40 pounds current money. Witnesses included: John Applewhite, "Senyer", and John Applewhite Jr.

2. **Robert Applewhite** (12 February 1771 in Halifax County, N. C. - 18 September 1839 in Stewart County, Georgia. Will probated 9 January 1840). He married **Elizabeth Barnes.**

3. Henry Applewhite

4. John Applewhite (Note - on 25 September 1787, John Applewhite, Jr., of Wayne County, North Carolina, "Planter" purchased from Benjamin Alford, Planter, of Wayne County 150 acres of land for 80 pounds lying on south side of Acock's Swamp.

5. Mary Applewhite

The following birth records are a copy from a family Bible that was owned by Jesse Applewhite, which is now in the hands of Jesse's descendants who live in Thomasville, Georgia. It was furnished to me by Mrs. Ann Miller Greer of Columbus, Georgia. Mrs. Greer informed me that many of the Applewhites are buried on the U. S. Army Base at Fort Benning, Georgia which suggests that the Applewhites owned the land that became Fort Benning.

---

1. Thomas B. Applewhite (born 1799 in Halifax County, North Carolina - died 25 March 1857 in Webster County, Georgia) married Nancy Davis.

2. Sarah Applewhite (born 1803) married 12 October 1826 in Stewart County, Georgia to Job Glover.

3. John Applewhite (born 1804 in Morgan County, Georgia) married 3 December 1824, in Morgan County, Georgia, to Hannah Jones.

4. Robert Applewhite, Jr (born 1806 in Morgan County, Georgia.)

5. **Nancy Applewhite** (born 1810 in Morgan County, Georgia - died after 1870 in Stewart County, Georgia) married **James Bonner** in Morgan County, Georgia on 7 August 1828.

6. Elizabeth Applewhite (born 1812 in Morgan County,

Georgia) married 12 October 1836, to Bray Warren in Stewart County, Georgia.

7. Jesse Applewhite (born 1814 in Morgan County, Georgia - died 27 October 1872 in Thomas County, Georgia) married Mary Magdalene Hill on 2 February 1837 in Stewart County, Georgia. (Note - This man's descendants now live in Thomasville, Georgia).

8. Susannah Applewhite (born 1816 in Morgan County, Georgia) married 6 December 1839 in Stewart County, Georgia, to Lewis A. Britt.

9. General Washington Applewhite (born 1818 in Morgan County, Georgia). Married, on 30 November 1836, in Stewart County, Georgia, to Rachel R. Bruson. On 19 August 1862, he enlisted in the 29th Georgia Infantry Volunteers of Thomas County, Georgia.

10. Martha Ann Applewhite (born 16 October 1819 in Morgan County, Georgia - died May 1880 in Coffee County, Alabama) married 4 December 1836 in Stewart County, Georgia, to John William Harper.

11. James J. Applewhite (born 1821 - died 4 March 1844 in Stewart County, Georgia.)

12. Louisa (Eliza) Applewhite (born 1824) married 30 December 1847 in Stewart County, Georgia, to Bright Holland.

13. Clementine Applewhite (born 1827) married: 1st - on 25 May 1845 to C. W. Allen. 2nd - on 28 January 1847 to Benjamin Jackson.

As noted above, Nancy Applewhite married James Bonner on 7 August 1828. Nancy's full name was Nancy Telitha Applewhite. This information was as passed to my family by Nancy's daughter, Martha Caroline Bonner. The following is on file in the records of Morgan County, Georgia.

"Georgia - Morgan County

To any minister of the Gospel, Judge, Justice of the Inferior Court or Justice of the Peace, you are hereby authorized to join **James Bonner and Miss Nancy Applewhite** in the Holy State of Matrimony according to the Constitution and Laws of this State and for so doing, this shall be your sufficient license.

Given under my Hand and Seal this 7th day of August 1828.

John W. Porter, CCO"

The remaining part of this work is about the descendants of

James and Nancy Applewhite Bonner.

As noted above, James and Nancy were married in Morgan County, Georgia in 1828. It is not known as of this writing where they moved to after they left Morgan County, but in 1860, it is believed that they were in Heard County, Georgia since it was in Heard County that Martha Caroline married James Allen McConniell in 1866. Names of the children of James and Nancy as passed down the family line were:

1. Josiah A. Bonner. (Born 1850)

2. Benjamin Bonner. He went to the Civil War and never cam home.

3. Sarah Bonner.

4. Mary Bonner (born 1834)

5. Harry Bonner.

6. Susannah Bonner (born 7 January 1838 - died 17 April 1923). She married William Houze (House) about 1862 and had a son, William Houze, Jr. William House, Sr., died in service of the Confederacy. He joined the 14th Alabama Regiment in Auburn, Alabama, according to a pension granted to Susannah. # William Jr is listed in the 1870 census as being eight years old.

7. **Martha Caroline Bonner** (born 20 September 1846 - probably in Stewart County, Georgia - died in Clay County, Alabama on 19 January 1933.) She called herself "MC" in many of her letters. She married, on 2 August 1866, in Heard County, Georgia, James Allen McConniell (born 12 November 1838 in the Anderson District, South Carolina - died on 31 July 1917 in Clay County, Alabama). James Allen McConniell, in 1860, worked on a farm in Heard County, Georgia as a mechanic. In July 1861, he went to Auburn, Alabama and enlisted in the 14th Alabama Regiment and was assigned to Company F. According to his pension application, in 1910, he was wounded at the Battle of Seven Pines on 1 June 1862. On 9 April 1865, while serving under General Robert E. Lee, was at the surrender at Appomattox, Virginia while a member of the 14th Alabama. There he took the Oath of Allegiance, was released and paroled to go home to Georgia. Martha and James are buried in the Cragford Cemetery, Clay County, Alabama.

8. Emily Bonner, also known as E.S. A. (Born 1832), according to Martha Carolina, she married and moved to Arkansas and never came home.

However, the 1850 census of Stewart County, Georgia has the following children for James and Nancy Bonner:

1. E. S. A Bonner (believed to be Emily) born 1832.

2. Mary Bonner (born 1834)

3. Susannah Bonner (born 1838)

4. James B. Bonner (born 1843)

5. M. C. (Martha Caroline) Bonner born 1846

6. J. A. (Josiah) Bonner born 1850

7. Nancy E. Bonner (Note - Nancy is listed in the 1860 census in Heard County and probably was born there.)

By 1860, the family had moved to Heard County, Georgia and there Nancy Applewhite lists her age as 41. (Author's note - It has come to my attention the full name of of James Bonner was James Thomas Bonner; that he joined the Confederate Army in Fayette County, Alabama, and died in 1864 while a prisoner of war in Illinois.)

In the 1870 census of Heard County, Nancy Bonner is listed as head of household which denotes that her husband, James, had died since the last census. Also listed in the census are: Josiah A. Bonner, age 21, whose occupation is farming; Nancy E. Bonner, age 19; Susannah Houze, age 31 who is listed as farm laborer and her son, William Houze, age 8.

In the 1880 census of Heard County only Nancy Applewhite Bonner and her daughter, Nancy E. Bonner are in the household.

Children of James Allen McConniell and Martha Carolina Bonner:

1. Julie Anne Frances (born ca 1867 - died 12 December 1921). Married Asa LaCurtis Kirkland on 12 May 1881. Their children: James Benjamin Kirkland (born 1885); Rena Kirkland (born 1887); Mattie Elizabeth Kirkland. (Note - This writer has in his possession a photograph and written on the back is, "The Kirkland Kids, Rolf, Francis and Rosie". The is no date but appears to have been taken in the 1920's.

2. Nancie Telitha (born 25 August 1869 - died 22 December 1951). She married Richard (Hent) Jones (born 22 June 1869 - died 6 June 1952) on 7 September 1893. Their children: Minnie Jones; Lona or Lonnie Jones; Andrew Jones; Bertha Jones; Vodie Jones; Francis Jones; James William Jones. Nancie and Hent are buried in the Cragford Cemetery, Clay County, Alabama.

3. John Melton (born 1871 - died 9 July 1933) He married Lizzie L. Waldrop on 22 January 1896. Their children: Arizona who was burned to death as a small child and is buried in the Cragford Cemetery; Myrtle (born 15 February 1898 - died 11 March 1901). Myrtle is buried in the Cragford Cemetery and her tombstone is marked, "Myrtle, daughter of J.M. & L. L. McConniell"; Rosie Mae, who died in 1914 of typhoid fever and is buried in Heard County, Georgia; Marshall was still living in the 1980's in Heard County, Georgia; Gulema; Floyd; Rastus are buried in Heard County, Georgia; Margaret was still living in the 1980's in the State of Virginia.

4. Emma Ardamisa (born ca 1873 - died 11 July 1903). She died of cancer. She married William Henry Burdette on 28 January 1895. They had a child, Ludia Burdette.

5. Susannah Victoria (born 5 April 1875 - died 19 April 1941). There is confusion about where she is buried. Her sister, Mattie, claimed that she is buried beside her parents in Cragford Cemetery. Another story is that she is buried beside her son, William Arthur McConniell, near Oxford, Alabama. Susannah never married but as family legend goes, "she was taken advantage of by one of her brothers-in-law" about 1892. From that union, Victoria had a son, William Arthur McConniell, who became a preacher in his adult life. Arthur married Madessia (Dessie) Geneva Butler on 23 August 1912. This writer, with his mother, visited Arthur and Dessie when they lived in Oxford, Alabama in 1956. We were made very comfortable during our visit. (Author's note - Recent information has brought to light that James Alenn MCConnell's grandfather was William McConnell and it is apparent that William Arthur was named after the senior William).

6. Tullula (Denia) Sadenia (born 14 April 1877 - died 4 May 1971). She married Daniel Jackson Cotney (born 24 April 1875 - died 16 March 1966.) Their children: Eulas James William (born 14 July 1899 - died 9 September 1925) who married Vera Bolt (born 3 January 1901 - died 9 September 1960) who are buried in the Cragford Cemetery; Isaac Huston (born 7 August 1901 - died July 1955) and is buried at Fort Valley, Georgia; Oliver Odell (born 28 November 1903 - died 7 November 1983) and is buried at Opp, Alabama; Lula Vasti (born 6 February 1905) married __?__ Clark; Daniel Zero (born 16 April 1908 - died 8 November 1982) and is buried Bessemer, Alabama; Roxie Bell (born 4 January 1912) who married __?__; Artford Genatious (born 17 July 1916 - died 1 November 1974) and is buried in Montgomery, Alabama.

7. Josiah Franklin (born 7 January 1880 - died 29 January 1957).

(In letters written by his mother, Martha, to Nannie Mae Mathis Curry, his name is noted as "Josiah" but on his tombstone, his name is Joseph. He was a Master Mason and has a Masonic Square and Compass on his tombstone. He married Lenora Jane Robertson (born 14 June 1882 - died 13 May 1968) on 28 December 1899 at the home of her father, P. Y. Robertson (born Oct 1843 - died 30 March 1913) by the Reverend John Leake Joiner. The best man was Sims Childs (W. S. Childs born 10 August 1881 - died 9 July 1965) and the bridesmaid was Sim's fiance, Tempa Carter (Martha Tempie Carter (born 19 July 1883 - died 24 October 1960). Josiah and Lenora Jane are buried in the Corinth Baptist Church Cemetery in Clay County, Alabama. Josiah and Lenora had the following children: Zulu Alza (born 6 January 1902 - died 7 March 1959) who never married and is buried besides her parents; Emory Gordon (born 27 April 1904 - died 7 June 1933) who married Lucille Smith (born 24 February 1904) on 23 December 1929. They had no children. Emory was a foreman on a road construction job near Chattanooga, Tennessee and in the process of moving a tractor left that was unattended by a co-worker, the tractor overturned and caught fire. Emory was penned underneath the machine and was burned to death. Emory is buried in the Shiloh Cemetery near Lineville, Clay County, Alabama. In 1987, there was a tombstone that shows Emory's name and that of his wife, Lucille. It is not known if Lucille remarried; Verdis Ruth (born 17 November 1907) and was still living in 1987. She married James Homer Walker (born 2 October 1901 - died 26 October 1972 and is buried in Lineville City Cemetery) on 25 February 1923 at the home of Reverend Lee Jordan in the Corinth Community of Clay County. Verdis Ruth and James Homer had children: Gordan (born 6 January 1924 - died 9 June 1950) and is buried in Lineville City Cemetery. Gordan fought in World War II, held the rank of Sergeant. He was seriously wounded and died of those wounds in 1950. Nolan; Clyde; Opal; Docia (Dot) who married Rudy Nelson who, in 1995, lives in Childersburg, Alabama. Dot and her husband had a son, Ben Nelson who lives in Childersburg, Alabama near his distant Curry cousins; Annie Beatrice (born 29 November 1910 - died 6 January 1980) who married John Willis Denny at the home of her parents in September 1936, by Reverend Tom Preston. They had children: James W.; Wilda Sue; and Nelda R.; Zodus Edward (born 22 October 1916) married Pauline Pitts in June 1939. Their children: Jane; Joe; Ricky; and Carol (in the mid 1980's Zodus and Pauline were living in LaGrange, Georgia; Georgia Ree (born 19 September 1918) married Durward Henry Hines on 17 June 1939 in LaGrange, Georgia by Reverend T. W. Flowers. In the late 1980's, Georgia and Durward were living in

Deltona, Florida. They had two children: Frank and Edmond.

8. Lewis Monroe (born 1881 - died 22 December 1884.)

9. "Little Buddy" (stillborn 20 April 1882.)

10. Lola Lee (born 31 January 1884 - died 2 February 1884) She bled to death from her navel.

11. James Asbury (born 27 April 1885 - died 15 May 1954) married Emily Jane Moncus (born 10 September 1887 - died 28 April 1945) on 4 October 1903. They are buried in the Corinth Baptist Church Cemetery in Clay County, Alabama. Their children: Allen Winchester (born 3 August 1904 - died 23 September 1975); Maggie Vestula (born 3 October 1906 - died August 1908); Frankie Joeanna (born 27 February 1910) married ___?___ Smith; Henry Jackson (born 9 November 1911 - 28 June 1973 who is buried beside his parents); Price Durell (born 2 July 1916 - died 26 November 1964); James Gary (born 15 August 1919); Stanley Owens (born 19 July 1921).

12. Mattie Eula (born 15 April 1888 - died 21 October 1979). She was born in Cleburne County, Alabama and died in a rest home in Sylacauga, Talladega County, Alabama. She married William Wesley Mathis (born 4 February 1845 - died 4 January 1928) on 2 September 1909 at the home her parents in Clay County, Alabama by the Reverend A. C. Johnston. Family tradition is that William Wesley was the youngest of ten children and was born in Abanda, Chambers County, Alabama. Also in tradition, is the fact that he worked in a shipyard during the Civil War. It is a family legend that he did not trust banks and buried his money somewhere around his home near Cooley Crossroads in Clay County. His money has never been found. About the year 1927, he started to have lapses of memory, and later that year was committed to the Veteran's Asylum. On 3 January 1928, while at the institution, he found a door open and wandered outside in a cold rain. When found, he was soaking wet and contacted pneumonia during the night. He passed away the next day. He died in the Veteran's Asylum in Tuscaloosa, Alabama and is buried there. She next married a Mr. Helms and later a Mr. Bass. Nothing is known of these men.

Children of Mattie Eula McConniell and William Wesley Mathis:

1. Nannie Mae (born 12 July 1910 - died 3 February 1988).

2. Elsie Ava Lee (born 21 October 1916 - died 27 November 1993), born in Clay County Alabama, probably in the old family home near Cooley Crossroads.

3. John Allen (born 11 December 1922 - still living in March 1996), also probably born near Cooley Crossroads.

While living in Renfroe, Talladega County, Alabama, Nannie Mae Mathis married Leo Dewey Curry (born 11 December 1908 - died 13 December 1993). Although they were divorced in 1955, the children had his body flown from North Carolina, where he was living at his death, and placed beside his first wife, the mother of his children, in the Curry family cemetery in Childersburg, Alabama. Nannie Mae Mathis Curry died in Waycross, Georgia while visiting her youngest daughters, Linda and Louise.

Children of Nannie Mae and Leo:

1. John Wesley Curry, born 2 June 1934, in the Miller's Creek Community between Talladega and Mumford, Talladega County, Alabama.

2. Loyace Dean Curry, born 14 March 1936, at the home of her great uncle Andrew Jackson Curry in Pitt County, North Carolina between Marlboro and Joyner's Crossroads.

3. Nannie Sue Curry, born 31 July 1937 at the home of her grandmother, Mattie Mathis, between Childersburg and Sylacauga, Talladega County, Alabama, at the house we affectionally called, "The house at the foot of the mountain".

4. Charles Michael Curry, stillborn in March 1939, at the "house at the foot of the mountain."

5. Roderick Selton Curry, born 20 September 1940 at Rural Route 1, Snow Hill, Greene County, North Carolina.

6. Leo Wayne Curry, born 9 October 1942, at 808 Cypress Street, Hopewell, Prince George County, Virginia.

7. Mary Louise Curry, born 8 May 1944, at above address.

8. Robert Allen, born 19 July 1945, at above address - died 25 November 1975 while living in West Palm, Beach, Florida, and is buried there.

9. Linda Dianne Curry, born 27 October 1947, at 808 Cypress Street, Hopewell, Virginia.

CHAPTER III

THE DUKE FAMILY OF SUSANNAH BONNER HOUZE

An interesting side story that came to light, as furnished by Mr. Joseph William Lineberger of Georgia, was about the family that Susannah Bonner married into.

THE DUKE FAMILY

The progenitor of this branch of the Duke family was Robert Duke, whose wife is unknown.

Children:

1. Stephen Duke (born 1766 in Craven District, South Carolina - died about 1844 in Upson County, Georgia. He is buried on a farm east of Thomaston, Georgia. He married Mary Granger about 1786 in Camden/Lancaster, South Carolina.

Their children were:

1. Elizabeth Duke, born about 1787 in Camden/Kershaw, South Carolina and married Andrew Howze.

2. Nancy Agnes Duke, born about 1788 in Camden/Kershaw, South Carolina - died before 3 September 1849 in Monroe County, Georgia. She married __?__ McKee.

3. Joel Duke, born about 1789 in Camden/Kershaw, South Carolina - died after 1860 in Talladega County, Alabama. He married, about 1820, in Conecuh, Alabama, Elizabeth Watson.

4. Green Duke, born 29 November 1790 in Camden/Kershaw, South Carolina - died 16 February 1873 in Pike County, Georgia. He married Nancy Jane McKee, about 1815.

5. Margaret "Peggy" Duke, born about 1794 in Camden/Kershaw, South Carolina - died before 1879 in Monroe County, Georgia.

6. Thomas G. Duke, born 19 January 1795 in Camden/Kershaw, South Carolina - died about 1864 in Lineville, Clay

County, Alabama. He married Louisa Webb on 23 June 1820 in Fairfield District, South Carolina. They were divorced on 29 November 1825 in Jasper County, Georgia. Elizabeth Duke married Anderson Howze, son of James Houze and Milla __?__.

Their children:

1. James M. Howze who was born in South Carolina.

Other children, if any, are unknown.

James M. Howze married, on 7 January 1831, Condarell Burt, in Monroe County, Georgia.

Their children:

1. Nancy A. E. House, born 1834.

2. Martha A. C. House, born 1836.

3. Samantha J. House, born 1838.

4. William Houze, born 1840, married Susannah Bonner.

5. Narissa House, born 1842.

6. John Morrow house, born 14 February 1844 - died 9 July 1900 in Heard County, Georgia. He married Josephine Bennett on 25 January 1872.

7. Hibernia House, born 1845.

8. Antoinette C. House, born 1846.

9. Henry G. House, born 1848 in Georgia. Married Martha J. __?__.

10. Georgia A. House, born 1853.

11. Mary E. House, born 1856.

William Houze, born 1840 - died October 1862 of measles. He married Susannah Bonner about 1861 (My note -probably in Heard County, Georgia.)

Their children:

1. William Houze, born 1862. (My note - nothing else is known of this William Houze, the son.) Did he live to adulthood?

William Houze, Sr., was a member of Company "F", 14th Alabama Regiment, C.S.A. Question - Did he enlist with James Allen McConniell, who was also a member of the 14th and in 1866 and married William Houze's sister-in-law, Martha Carolina Bonner?

CHAPTER IV

THE McCONNIELL FAMILY

There was one thing that my mother told me about James Allen McConniell. He always insisted that his last name was spelled with an "i" and the estate records show that in most cases the name was spelled with an "i."

Family Status:

William McConniell (ca 1780 - 1864)
Wife: Anne Tate
Children:
1. Newton McConnell (ca 1808 -
2. Sarah (Sally) McConnell
3. David McConnell (ca 1806 -
4. Genlon McConnell (ca 1804 -
5. Allen McConnell (ca 1810 - after 1869)
6. Charles McConnell
7. William McConnell, Jr.
8. Margaret McConnell
9. Davis McConnell
10. Mary McConnell

I was always led to believe that James Allen's father, Allen McConnell, was born in Scotland and that he came to America by himself. I had long ago given up that I would ever find his parents. But in my search for anything about Allen, I came across the name of "William McConiel" in South Carolina in the Anderson District (where James Allen McConniell was born, according to his pension request for service during the War between the States). The name of William was listed many times and I was hoping that Allen's full name was William Allen McConnell, I wrote for the estate papers of William McConnell. There are 119 pages outlining his estate and the settlement of it after his death (It took almost 20 years to finally settle it). About three pages into the reading I came across the names William and Allen and realized that I had two people, not one, and I entertained the thought that I not only wasted my money but was probably wasting my time by reading the document. I had nothing else to do so I continued to read. At about page 60 I found a power of attorney made by Allen to his brother, William, who was living in Heard County, Georgia, stating that William, Senior, was their father. In 1869, Allen was alive and well and living in Randolph County, Alabama. He did not die in South Carolina as I had always believed. Finding the estate papers of William McConniell led to this chapter about my McConniell family.

In 1783, William McConnell lived in that area of South Carolina where General Francis Marion fought the British; which was in and around the present city of Florence, South Carolina. Francis Marion was known as "The Swamp Fox" because of his tactics of fighting the British and disappearing into the swamps of the Great Pee Dee River. In 1783, William McConnell was a resident of the Georgetown District as noted in the jury lists for Georgetown in that year. William was qualified to serve on a petit jury. Other McConnells included: In 1777, James McConnell (place of resident not noted); 1783, George McConnell of Georgetown, grand jury; 1783, James McConnell of Georgetown, grand jury and petit jury; 1783, Robert McConnell of Georgetown, grand and petit jury; 1783, Thomas McConnell of Georgetown, grand and petit jury.(Source: *South Carolina Jury Lists, 1728 through 1783,* page 85. Warren. 1977.)

The following McConnells served in the American Revolution from South Carolina;

1. George McConnel served under General Marion in 1780, 1781 and 1782. He was at the Fall of Charleston;

2. James McConnel served under Captain Pickens in the Militia. Other times he served under Colonal McDonald and General Marion;

3. John McConnel (1) served as a private from 1780 to 1783 under Captain Pickens;

4. Robert McConnel served 150 days as a private from 1780 to 1782;

5. Thomas McConnel served in the Militia in 1780 under General Marion;

6. Ferrence McConnell enlisted in the First Regiment on 29 December 1776 for the duration and deserted on 15 March 1779;

7. John McConnell (2) served, in 1778, 48 days as a privates under Colonal Bratton. He served 64 days as a Lieutenant of horse and 38 days as a Captain of horse during 1780. Also in 1780 he served 92 days as Captain of foot. In 1781, he served 40 days as a private and during 1782, he served as a private on foot;

8. Manuel McConnell was born in Charles County, Maryland - died 9 September 1842. In May 1780 while residing in Abbeville District, South Carolina he enlisted under Lieutenant Benjamin Lawrence and Colonel Pickens. In the fall of 1780 he was under Captains James McCall, Moses Liddell and Colonels Washington and Lee. He was in the Battle at Hammond's Store, Cowpens and the seige of 96. In May 1782 he was under Captain Richard Hurd and Colonel James Jackson of Georgia;

9. Reuben McConnell served 104 days in the militia in 1778, 1780, 1781 and 1782.;

10. Robert McConnell served 31 days in the militia under General Marion in 1782;

11. **William McConnell**. "He served sixty-three days in the militia under General Marion during 1782. In addition, he supplied beef for Continental use during 1781." (Source of all the above: *Roster of South Carolina Patriots in the American Revolution,* page 606. Moss. 1983.)

The above John McConnell (2) was born in 1752 and died on 2 September 1822. Where he was born is unknown but he died in White County, Georgia. (Source: *Georgia Revolutionary War Soldier's Graves,* page 702. Arnold and Burham. 1993.)

It can be noted from the above that George, James, Thomas, Robert and William served under General Francis Marion which might denote that the five men were related and lived in proximity to each other. Additionally, these same men were adults in 1783 when they were qualified to served on the various juries in Georgetown.

"Issued the 18th July 1784 to Mr. William McConnell for twenty one pounds sixteen shillings and eleven pence Sterling for 63 days militia duty done in General Marion's brigade in 1782 And for 1375 lb in beef supplied for Continental use in 1781. Two accounts audited &c. Principal £21.16.11; Interest £1.10.7. Amount duty £4.4.0. Supplies £17.12.11. Total £21.16.11. (Source:*Stub Entries to Idents Issued in Payment of Claims Against South Carolina Growing out of the Revolution. Book G-H.* Edited by Wylma Anne Wates. Page 91. 1955. Printed by Columbia South Carolina Archives Department.)"

It is not known when William McConnell brought his family to South Carolina but he was in the state before 1781.

The estate papers provided many valuable clues about the William McConnell family. After reading the papers, I read the book, *Pendleton District and Anderson County, South Carolina - Wills , Estates, and Legal Records,* complied by Virginia Alexander, Colleen Morse Elliott and Betty Willie and published by the Southern Historical Press, Inc. and found the following will on page 39.

WILL OF JAMES TATE

To wife Anne; Negroes Jack, Venus and Prince, Thomas, Biley, Buck and Ned. Son, Samuel. If ever my son William should come into this country and be in majority, wife and son Samuel to give him comfortable way of living during his lifetime. **If any of the heirs of my sister Ann who was married to *William McConnell*** should appear son Samuel is to give them 2£ Sterling. Executors: Wife and son Samuel. I have made over also their shares to wit of my two daughters Margret and Elizabeth by deeds of gift. I allow my son-in-law Farler Thompson to pay executors the sum of $300.00, that is $100.00 to my grandson George Camble, Tate Burton, and $100.00 to Richard Speak to help relieve my Negro Tamer who is mortgaged in his account and $100.00 to my son Samuel Tate the same Farley Thompson is indebted to me on account of sale of my Negro Isaac which helped him obtain his land.

Dated: 4 June 1807. (Signed) James Tate
Witness: Thomas Sherrar
George Burton
William Tate Speak
Proven: 13 April 1808.

Note - A William Tate was in Greene County, Georgia on 10 November 1797, where he was a witness to the Will of John Heard. This could be the son of James Tate. (Source: *Some Georgia County Records,* Volume 2, page 316. Lucus. 1977 & 1994.) Also, a Samuel Tate was in Olgethorpe County, Georgia on 18 May 1797, where he was a witness of the Will of John Morgan. (Source: Idem, page 148.)

Using the Will of James Tate as a guide, it can be surmised that all of William McConnell's children had been born by 1807. It is estimated that he was about 60 years old at the time.

It would be interesting to know why the McConnell's chose South Carolina to immigrate to from Scotland, which, according to his son, Allen, who stated to his son, James Allen, is where they came from. It would also be interesting to know why Upper South Carolina was chosen to be their home. William McConnell died in January 1864 and the court decided that he died intestate, even though a will was published in 1861. It may have been because both executors of the will had passed away or the court found something not to its liking. William McConnell published his will on 12 October 1861. In it he names a son, Genlon, who is not found in the records in later years. He is not listed as an heir to his father's estate in 1864 which suggests he had died earlier and without heirs

---

South Carolina
Anderson District

Know all men by these presents that I William McConell of said State and District do make and declare this my last will and testament in manner and form following. First that my worldly estate shall be sold at my death and all my just debts paid also I give and bequeath unto **my son, Newton,** the sum of one hundred dollars also give and bequeath unto **my daughter Salley** the sum of fifty dollars and one good bed and then they are to have an equal share of the balance of my estate and I do hereby constitute and appoint **my son David & Genlon McConnel** sole executors of this my last will and testament.

In witness whereof I do hereunto set my hand and seal this the 12 day of October in the year of our Lord Eighteen hundred and sixty one.

Witness: His
T. W. West William McConniel
___?___ Mark

The location of the McConnell plantation was found to be "on waters of Generostee Creek" in Anderson District consisting of 425 acres of land. Generostee Creek and Little Generostee Creek were located between the Savannah River and the town of Anderson. When a dam was constructed to create Lake Hartwell the McConnell plantation and both creeks were flooded. (Source: *The Official Military Maps of the Civil War,* by Major George B. Davis, U. S. Army and others. Complied by Captain Calvin D. Cowless, 23d U. S. Infantry. Government Printing Office. 1891 - 1895. Plate CXLIII).

James Allen McConniell once stated that the community of McConnells, South Carolina, located in present York County between York and Chester on U. S. Highway 321 was named after his family.

In a "petition for Settlement" of the personal estate of William McConniel filed on 27th October 1865, the following are listed as "heirs of William McConniel."

1. Charles McConnell
2. William McConnell
3. Allen McConnell
4. Margaret Harris
5. Heirs of Daniel McConnell - unknown
6. Heirs of John McConnell - out of state
7. Newton McConnell
8. Mary McCarly
9. Sarah (Sally) McConnell
10. Heirs of David McConnell

Judging from the above it can be surmised that Allen McConnell and others who are listed as "not being out of state" were, in fact, still in South Carolina in October 1865. It is noted that the above were the children of William McConnell, Senior, and that his sons, David, Daniel and John were dead. Notice that Genlon McConnell is not listed as an heir so it is safe to assume that he also is dead. On 5 February 1866 payments were made to the following and in the amounts shown for their portion of the estate of William McConnell, deceased, by the administrator of the estate, Reuben Burriss.

1. Newton	$550.00	2. Allen	$985.00
3. David	985.00	4. John	575.00
5. William	525.00	6. Daniel	525.00
7. Charles	575.00	8. Margaret Harris	225.00
9. Sarah	300.00	10. Mary McCarly	300.00

On 26 December 1871, in Mississippi, Rachel Dunn, daughter of John McConnell and grand daughter of William McConnell, Sr., gave a power of attorney to settle her portion of the estate of William McConnell.

On 23 April 1872, Elizabeth Elliott and her husband, Henry M. Elliott, of Lowndes County, Mississippi, gave a power of attorney to settle their portion of the estate of William McConnell.

On 6th May 1872, a declaration was made in Anderson County in court that Rachel Dunn and Elizabeth Elliott were the only "luminary" heirs of John McConnell, deceased, son of William McConnell, deceased.

Also found in the estate papers of William McConnell is proof that his sons, Allen and William, Jr., were alive and well in 1869. Allen was in Randolph County, Alabama and William was in Heard County, Georgia, which might explain why Jame Allen McConnell was living in Heard County when he married Martha Caroline Bonner in 1866. James Allen may have been living near his uncle, William McConnell, Jr.

The State of Alabama
Randolph County §

To whom these presents shall come greetings. Now all men by these presents that I **Allen McConnel** of the said County and state having full confidence in the competence and integrity of **William McConnel** of the COUNTY OF HEARD IN THE STATE OF GEORGIA have appointed and do by these presents constitute and appoint said William my true & lawful attorney in fact, for me and in my name to receive and receipt for any and all personal property of any and all kinds in deciding chosen in action and money's that may due or coming to me as ONE OF THE HEIRS OF WILLIAM McCONNELL, SENIOR, LATE OF SOUTH CAROLINA in the District of Anderson in said State of South Carolina and FATHER OF THE MAKER OF THIS DEED of power of attorney as also to make any deed or deeds receipt or receipts acquitances and discharges that may be required or proper to enable the said first mentioned William to receive into his poseon (possession - my word) or under his control and to reduce to money all and every description of property both real and personal that may be due or coming to me as HEIR OF MY SAID FATHER and to sell and dispose of for me and in my name all and any property real or personal choses in action & money and to give all deeds clearances receipts and acquitances that I ought or could do were I personally present in and about the receipt as sale of any thing that may be due or coming to me as heir of my said father. __?__ confer money & validfying all and ___act makes and ___my said attorney may do for me and in my name in and about the receipts sale discharge receipts and deeds my said attorney may do and make for me in discharge of the power herein conferred.

In testimony whereof I have hereunto set my hand and affixed my seal this the nineth day of February AD 1869.

In the presence of Allen McConnel (Seal)

(witness)
S. R. Johnson
Circero D. Hudson

The State of Alabama
Randolph County

I, Robert H. Bolt Clerk of the Circuit Court in County and State aforesaid hereby certify that C. D. Hudson a subscribing witness to the foregoing conveyance known to me appeared before me this day and being sworn stated that ALLEN McCONNELL the grantor in the conveyance voluntarily executed the same in his presence and in the presence of the other subscribing witness on the day the same bears date that he attested the same in the presence of this grantor and of the other witness and that such other witnesses subscribed his name as a witness in his presence.

Given under my hand and seal of Office at **WEDOWEE** and that said court is a Court of Records this 18 day of January AD 1869.

(Seal) R. H. Bolt
Clerk C.

On 25 November 1868 a list of payments to the heirs of William McConnell, deceased, included the following: Newton; Mary McCarly; Malinda; Sarah; William (1); William (2); Margaret Harris; Charles (1); Charles (2); **Allen;** David (heirs); John (heirs);. There is another document that shows a R. M. McConnell receiving payment.

On 16 January 1870, a power of attorney was made to Reuben Burriss of Anderson District by Margaret Harris, Sarah A. McConnell, and Hester J. McConnell of Walker County, Georgia. The exact nature of the document is unclear but it had to do with the settlement of the estate of William McConnell, Sr., deceased.

On 24 July 1876 in Walker County, Georgia, a statement is made by Mary Ann McConnell that her daughter, Mary Jane McConnell was the only child of Richmond McConnell.

On 17 June 1878 in the 953 district of Walker County, Georgia, Mary Harris stated that Daniel McConnell, deceased, was a son of William McConnell who died in the State of South Carolina in Anderson County and that **David McConnell** left seven children, viz:

1. William McConnell who died about 1865 in the State of Arkansas without heirs.

2. Sarah Ann McConnell who was still living in Georgia and is unmarried.

3. Margreh (Margaret) McConnell who died about the year 1866 in the West without heirs

4. Richmond McConnell who died during the late war between the states leaving one heir, Mary Jane McConnell, who is a minor and the only living child of the said Richmond McConnell.

5. Thompson McConnell who never married and went to the war in 1861 and who has not since been heard of, only that he was dead and who deponent believed to be dead.

6. Mary Hester McConnell who is still living in the State of Georgia and is unmarried.

7. Pinkney McConnell who died during late war between the states without heirs.

Mary stated further that she was a sister of the deceased David McConnell. (Note - She is also listed as "Margaret" in the records.)

On 28 June 1878 in Walker County, Georgia, F. W. Copeland was appointed guardian of Mary Jane McConnell by the Court of Ordinary.

On 7 September 1878 in Walker County, Georgia, Mary Ann Cape on oath stated that she was the wife of Richmond McConnell, late of Walker County, Georgia who was the son of David McConnell, deceased and grandson of William McConnell, deceased, of Anderson County, South Carolina and that Richmond died before his grandfather.

In other affidavits statements were made that Richmond died after his grandfather. The was much correspondence between the two jurisdictions trying to establish the death years of William and Richmond. Exact dates were required to help settle Richmond's portion of his grandfather's estate. The records show that Mary Jane McConnell was accepted as an heir, so the matter was settled.

The following names are contained in Judge of Probate records as receiving monies from the estate of William McConnell, deceased.

9 Dec 1869 - Charles McConnell
" William McConnell
" **Allen McConnell**

17 Dec 1869 - MeLinda McConnell
3 Jan 1870 - W. C. Gentry & M. C. McConnell Gentry
28 Feb 1870 - Newton McConnell
" Margaret McConnell
" Mary H. McConnell

22 Oct 1870 - B. A. McConnell
Dec 1870 - Mary McCarly
" Elizabeth Elliott
" Rachel Dunn
" Mattie A. McConnell
" F. W. Copeland guardian for Mary Jane McConnell
" Mary Ann Cape

The estate records of William McConnell are on file at the Archives in Columbia, South Carolina.

Allen McConnell, son of Willia McConnell, married Telitha Gentry (probably a daughter of John and Elizabeth Gentry of the Anderson District of South Carolina. John's will was accepted in probate court on 6 June 1840).

According to family tradition, as passed by Martha Caroline Bonner McConnell, the following were children of Allen and Telitha McConnell.

1. Lewis McConnell

2. Mark McConnell

3. Marizzle McConnell (born 1832 - died 1892)

4. Frankie Muhulda McConnell (born 1842 - died 11 January 1932). She married into the Nutt family and had a daughter, Neely.

5. Elizabeth McConnell (Elizabeth died in 1868 in Stewart County, Georgia) who married Jarvis Rountree Fillingham who died before 1870.

6. Jane McConnell married Jason Harry (born 20 March 1823 - died 8 September 1902). Jason Harry is buried at the Cragford Cemetery in Clay County, Alabama. They had two daughters, (1) Mary Burdette Harry. Mary is buried at the Cragford Cemetery. (2) Claudia Harry born 4 September 1885 - died 7 February 1907). Claudia is buried next to her father. (Claudia was a beautiful young woman according to her photograph.)

7. James Allen McConniell (born 12 November 1838 in Anderson District, South Carolina - died 31 July 1917 while living at Postal address at Almond, Alabama. He married Martha Caroline Bonner on 2 August 1866 in Heard County, Georgia. They are buried in the Cragford Cemetery. James Allen served in the 14th Alabama Regiment during the Civil War. He joined in July 1861 in Auburn, Alabama, and was assigned to Company "F." He was wounded at the Battle of Seven Pines, Virginia, on 1 June 1862. He continued to serve and was present for the Surrender at Appomattox on 9 April 1865 where he surrendered, was paroled at the same time and place. In Alabama in 1907 he was allowed a pension for his war service. It was reported to be $25.00 per month. The family of James and Martha are listed elsewhere in this work.

On 9 September 1847, Lewis McConnell was a buyer in the estate sale of William S. Hunt.

On 1 October 1866, Lewis McConnell was a witness to the will of Stephen Liverett on the waters of the Rocky River in Anderson District.

Taxpayers in Anderson District: In 1835, Thomas McConnell; In 1836, Thomas, William and Daniel; In 1842, Thomas, William and L. (Lewis?) H. McConnell; In 1853, Davis, William and James H. McConnell; In 1854, Samuel F., James, David and William; In 1856, David, William, Jr., James H., and Samuel F. McConnell.

THE TATE FAMILY

As noted previously, the wife of William McConnell was Anne Tate who was a daughter of William Tate, Sr., as noted in the will of her brother, James Tate, dated 4 June 1807.

Family Status:
William Tate, Sr. (ca 1730 - before 8 May 1798)
Wife: Elizabeth (ca 1735 - after 1807)
Known children:1. Jesse Tate, married Mary ____.
2. William Tate, Jr.
3. Ann Tate, married William McConnell
4. James Tate, married (1st) Sally ____ (2nd) Anne ____.

The exact date that William Tate, Sr., came to South Carolina is not known but he was in South Carolina before 1777 and he was a veteran of the American Revolution from South Carolina.

"William Tate - BLWt 2229-200-Lt

Before resigning on 22 December 1777, he was a Captain - Lieutenant in the Fifth Regiment. He was appointed Lieutenant in the Fourth Regiment on 8 October 1779. After being taken prisoner at Charleston (South Carolina), he was exchanged during October 1780. *Yearbook, 1893;* Heitman, page 533; A.A. 7628; C226; C.C." (Source: *Roster of South Carolina Patriots in the American Revolution,* page 916, by Moss. 1983.)

"Officers South Carolina Regiment - Continental Establishment" - William Tate, Captain/Lieutenant in the 5th Regimen.". (Source: *South Carolinians in the Revolution,* page 62, by Ervin. 1949).

(From the Diary of Josiah Smith, Jr.)

"Provisional Articles of Peace between Great Britain and the United States were signed in Paris, France on 15 November 1782 but was not legally terminated until 1783. Under an Act ratified on 12 March 1783 the Governor of South Carolina was authorized to appoint an auditor for each judicial district to adjust all claims arising out of the Revolution. For Camden District - **William Tate**." (Source: *Roster of South Carolinians in the Revolution,* page 115, by Ervin. 1949). (Author's Note - Camden district included what later would became Spartanburg District).

Sometime later William Tate, Sr., was in that part of Camden district that would become Spartanburg District/County for it was there in 1787 that he purchased two plats of land from Thomas Bonner (died 1804 in Clarke County, Georgia.).

"16 June 1787. Thomas Bonner (formerly South Carolina now Georgia) to William Tate, Sr., Esquire (Spartanburg); for 100L sterling sold 150 acres on both sides of Cherokee Creek, waters of Broad River; granted 1 May 1786. Witness Ola Trimmer and J. Thomson. Signed Thomas Bonner by Attorney Vardry McBee."

"16 June 1787. Thomas Bonner (formerly South Carolina now Georgia) to William Tate, Sr., Esquire (Spartanburg); for 60L sterling sold 143 acres on both sides of Cherokee Creek, waters of Broad River; granted 1 May 1786. Witness Ola Trimmer and J. Thomson. Signed Thomas Bonner by attorney Vardry McBee." (Source: *Spartanburg County/District South Carolina, Deed Abstracts, Books A-T; 1785 - 1827*, page 13).

"29 November 1791. William Tate, Sr., (Spartanburg County) to Andrew Hopkins; for 60L sterling sold 143 acres on both sides of "main" Cherokee Creek of Broad River; granted 1 May 1786. Witness Joseph Dill and James Clarke. Signed William Tate. Witness oath 11 March 1797 Joseph to Henry McCray. Recorded 25 September 1797." (Source: Idem, page 132)."

"17 May 1798. James Tate (Spartanburg) to John Ross (Same) for 10L sold 23 acres on West side Broad River including Tate's Ferry; part of grant 26 October 1767 by North Carolina Governor to Francis Batey and eventually sold to William Tate (LATE OF SPARTANBURG) and by his will to his son James Tate. Witness, James Smith and William Gibson. Signed James Tate. Witness oath 18 May 1798 James Smith to H. McCray. (Source: Idem, page 133)."

"22 December 1803. James Tate and wife Sally and mother Elizabeth (York District) to Thomas Dear (Spartanburg); for $3,000 sold (1) 318 acres where William Tate lived and died on west side of Broad River; at upper end of small part excepted; willed to James Tate and his mother Elizabeth; (2) two tracts (a) 46 acres sold by John Ross, deceased, to James Tate on west side Broad River; part of 200 acres granted 23 December 1768 by Governor William Tryon of North Carolina to John Tygret and part of grant 2 April 1792 from South Carolina Governor to John Ross; and (b) 200 acres; borders Tate's Mill tract and John Ross. Witness, Peter Quin, John Trimmer, Abraham Green and James Wight. Signed James Tate and Sally and Elizabeth's mark. Witness oath 19 May 1804 Abraham Green to John Rickman. Recorded 4 June 1804. (Source: Idem, page 269 & 270)."

"8 August 1803. Elizabeth Tate (Spartanburg) to son-in-law Abner McAfee (Lincoln County, North Carolina); for love and affection give "all goods and chattels"; Hugh, Eudy, Bet, Willis and their increase. Witness Arthur Graham "Jucatsonz," William Martan and William Collins. Signed Elizabeth Tate's mark. Witness oath 20 August 1805 Elizabeth Tate to John Rukman. Recorded 13 November 1805. (Source: Idem, page 307)."

"30 March 1807. James Laurence and William Tate (Union District), executors of will of William Tate, Deceased, (Spartanburg) to George Walker (Spartanburg); for $500 sold 150 acres on both side Cherokee Creek of Broad River; granted 1 May 1786 **to Thomas Bonner** and sold by William Tate in his lifetime to George Walker ---see a bond given by William Tate to George Walker, "assenee" to Jesse Tate, deceased. Witness, Samuel Tate to Francis Laurence. Signed James Laurence and William Tate. Witness oath 6 April 1807. Samuel Tate to Daniel Wilbanks. Recorded 7 April 1807. (Source: Idem page 337)."

"12 September 1807. George Walker (SC) to son, William Walker, a son of Clara Miraman (or Mireman) (sic); for love and affection give 150 acres on both sides of Cherokee Creek of Broad River; granted 1 May 1786. Witness Clara Mireman and Daniel McClaren. Signed, George Walker. Witness oath 2 April 1808, Daniel McClaren to A. Benson. Recored 2 April 1808. (Source: Idem, page 363)."

"2 September 1808. Gabriel Benson, Sheriff (Spartanburg) to William Walker Meremon; for $12.50 sold 150 acres on both sides Cherokee Creek of Broad River; granted 1 May 1786 to Thomas Bonner; sale due to writ from Spartanburg Common Pleas Court Susanna Walker vs George Walker; sale 7 March 1808; sold to Susanna Walker but she doesn't want "titles to be made to her only" so titles made to William W. Meremon. Witness: Vincent Bennett and George Walker. Signed, Gab Benson. Witness oath 2 September 1808 Georger Walker to Abner Benson. Recorded: 2 September 1808. (Idem, page 376)."

It would be of interest to the reader, that the land Thomas Bonner sold to William Tate, Sr., is located in present day, Cherokee County, South Carolina, just north of present day Gaffney, South Carolina. Benjamin Bonner, grandson of Sheriff Thomas Bonner, and many members of his family are buried near Gaffney, South Carolina.

In a previous chapter it was noted that a kinship must have existed between Sheriff Thomas Bonner of Beaufort County, North Carolina and the Bonner family of Chowan County, North Carolina. It was also noted that Thomas Bonner (died in Clarke County, Georgia) must have lived in Upper South Carolina when he fought in the South Carolina militia near Benjamin Bonner, a grandson of Sheriff Thomas Bonner. Additional proof to support that premise is found in the following paragraph. Notice the description of the land and the mention of the Tate family and Bonner family.

"7 December 1820. Thomas Dare (previously spelled Dear) (Spartanburg) to Abner Benson (Spartanburg); for $5,000 sold (1) 318 acres on South side of Broad River where Thomas Dare lives; border: Michael Gaffney; except 23 acres now owned by William Ross; granted to Francis Beatis (previously spelled Batey) who sold to William Tate and willed to James Tate and Elizabeth Tate (now Roberts) who sold to Thomas Dare; (2) 46 acres in two parts (a) sold by John Ross, now deceased, to James Tate and sold to Thomas Dare; part of 200 acres granted to John Tygert; and (b) 200 acres part of grant 2 April 1792 from North Carolina Governor (sic) to John Ross who sold to "said" Tate; border: McGowen, Tate's Mill tract, John Ross and James Tate: (3) 57 acres in Union District on Pepleses Creek of Broad River; and (4) 140 acres in Union District on Cherokee Creek; border: Levi Pennington, John Leek, William Cumberland and Cherokee Road. Witness William Rickman, **Briant (Bryant) Bonner** and Daniel White, Esquire. Signed Thomas Dare. Witness oath 19 May 1821 Daniel White to E. Bomar. Recorded 19 May 1821. (Source: Idem, page 648)." (Note - Bryant Bonner was a son of Benjamin Bonner. Benjamin was a son of Thomas Bonner and Thomas was a son Sheriff Thomas Bonner of Beaufort County, North Carolina).

As noted above Thomas Bonner, who died in Clarke County, Georgia in 1804, sold his South Carolina bounty land to William Tate, Sr. In 1866, in Heard County, Georgia, William Tate, Sr.'s great-grandson, James Allen McConniell, would marry Thomas Bonner's great-granddaughter, Martha Caroline Bonner.

There has been so much published about the Beaufort County, North Carolina Bonners that it will not be covered in detail here. However, to continue the point about a relationship between the Beaufort County and Chowan County, North Carolina Bonners the following needs to be noted:

Sheriff Thomas Bonner (of Beaufort County, N. C.), had a son, Thomas, who had a son Benjamin who moved to the Spartanburg District of South Carolina (now Cherokee County) with his wife, Frances. Their children: Dempsey (Sr), born 4 February 1771; Bryant, born 14 October 1774; Delithia, born 16 January 1773. Bryant was a Baptist preacher who founded the Grassy Pond

Baptist Church, in Gaffney, South Carolina. Dempsey Bonner, Jr., moved his family to Alabama "near Tuscaloosa," where Dempsey DeKalb Bonner was born on 15 April 1832. Members of his family later moved to near Houston, Mississippi. The "near Tuscaloosa" place was actually Gilbertown, Alabama located in present day Choctaw County. Note that this time frame is the same as when Jordan Bonner was living in now Choctaw County, Alabama.

It would also be interesting to know if/how the above William Tate is related to the "Tates of De La Pre Abby" as mentioned in the work of James C. Bonner as mentioned in part two of this work. Since that Tate family had male children named "William," it seems natural that William Tate of South Carolina is descended from that illustrious family. Note that Sir Bartholomew Tate was Knighted by King Henry VIII and Bartholmew has a grandson, Sir William Tate, who had the Bonner Coat-of-Arms created on his tombstone.

For those of us who are descended from the family of William McConniell, the following is copied from part two of this work, written by James C. Bonner, showing the likely bloodline to Sir Bartholomew Tate who was knighted by King Henry VIII.

"Sir Bartholomew Tate who received the honor of Knighthood from King Henry VIII, was the original purchaser of the Monastery lands of De La Pre Abby in the County of Northampton. His grandson, Sir William Tate, married, in 1597, Elizabeth, the eldest daughter and Heiress of Edward, the Eleventh and last Baron Zouche of Haryngworth. The Zouche family was descended in the whole line from the Soverign Princes of Brittany, a fact which gives the American House of Bonner, a Royal descent. On the south side of the Chancel at Hardingstone, there today, is an Altar tomb probably in memory of the late Sir William Tate, who is known to have left fifty pounds for the creation of such a structure. The arms are now almost obliterated, but are unmistakably that of Bonner."

"Returning again to the main stem of the (Bonner) family, we find that Reverend Anthony Bonner, the elder, had a bother, William Bonner, who married Elizabeth Tate of the illustrious Tates of De La Pre Abby family. Elizabeth was born in 1671 at this historic Northamptonshire Mansion."

It appears, because of the same name theory, that William Tate, Sr., of South Carolina was a direct descendant of the famous house of Tate. For the descendants of William McConniell who are also descended from the Bonner family, it may be easier to establish a bloodline to Sir Bartholomew Tate through William McConniell than through the Bonner family. The are many gaps in the Bonner family that has frustrated researcher for years. Further research will probably prove this theory to be true.

CHAPTER V

THE LAST WORD

By

John Wesley Curry

I thought that since this is a family history and it is written primarily for my descendants, I would add the highlights of my military career for their information. And since I was involved in a very unpopular war that tore this nation to shreds I thought they might be interested about what I did in that war.

I enlisted in the United States Marine Corps on 10 February 1953 while living at 525 32nd Street, Newport News, Virginia. I was sworn in at the Recruiting Station in Richmond, Virginia. I was assigned to Platoon 62, Item Company, 2nd Recruit Training Battalion, Parris Island, South Carolina. (Promoted to Private First Class in 1 May 1953.) upon graduation about the 10th of May, I was assigned to Fuel Platoon, Supply Company, 2d Service Battalion, 2d Marine Division, FMFLANT, Camp Lejeune, North Carolina. Where on 1 June 1954, I was promoted to Corporal and on 1 May 1955, I was promoted to Sergeant. In November 1955, I was assigned to Marine Corps Supply Center, Albany, Georgia; In March 1957, to the Inspector-Instructor Staff, 3d Special Infantry Company, U. S. Marine Corps Reserve, New London, Connecticut; where on 1 May 1957, I was promoted to Staff Sergeant (E-5), In October 1957 my billet was phased out and I was assigned to Headquarters and Service Company, 3d Force Service Regiment, 3d Marine Division, FMFPAC, Okinawa; In August 1958 I was assigned to Material Battalion, Marine Corps Base, Camp Lejeune, North Carolina; In July 1959 to Headquarters and Service Company, Marine Barracks, 8th & "I" Streets, SE, Washington 3, D. C; In March 1962 to the Naval Air Technical Training Center, Naval Air Station, Memphis, Tennessee for duty as a student in basic aircraft electronics (Avionics) school and on 1 May 1962, I was promoted to Staff Sergeant (E-6); In May 1963 I was transferred to 2d Marine Aircraft Wing, FMFLant, Cherry Point, North Carolina and Marine Aircraft Group - 24, where I was assigned to Headquarters and Maintenance Squadron - 24 & in

July 1963 to VMFA - 531(a F-4B Fighter Squadron) where I was assigned as an aircraft electronics technician in the Communication, Navigation and Identification Shop; In June 1964 I was transferred with VMFA - 531 to Naval Air Station, Atsugi, Japan for duty with Marine Aircraft Group - 11, 1st Marine Aircraft Wing, FMFPac, and in April was transferred with VMFA - 531 to DaNang Air Base, South Vietnam, for duty in a combat zone. In July 1965, I was assigned to Naval Air Technical Training Center, Memphis, Tennessee as a student in advanced Avionics (AVIB) school; In May 1966, I was assigned to 2d Marine Aircraft Wing, Cherry Point, North Carolina with Marine Aircraft Group - 14 and with VMA (AW) 225, (an A-6A Bomber Squadron) for duty as an Avionics Chief in charge of about 125 men in all three avionics shops, (Communication, Electric and Fire Control (Radar)), where on 1 May 1966 I was promoted to Gunnery Sergeant; In September 1967 I was transferred back to Danang Air Base, South Vietnam to VMA (AW) 242, (an A-6A Bomber Squadron) for duty with Marine Aircraft Group - 11, 1st Marine Aircraft Wing, FMFPac, for duty as an Avionics Chief for my second tour in a combat zone. On 13 November 1968, I was assigned to Marine Air Control Squadron - 6, Marine Aircraft Control Group - 28, 2d Marine Aircraft Wing, Cherry point, North Carolina, where I was commissioned a Second Lieutenant and where in 13 February 1970, I was promoted to First Lieutenant. On 1 March 1971, I was "decommissioned," and was reverted to Master Sergeant and assigned to VMAT (AW) 202, Marine Aircraft Group -24 at Cherry Point, N. C., and on 15 April 1971, I was promoted to Master Gunnery Sergeant with a date of rank of 1 March 1971. Upon my request on 1 September 1972, I transferred to the Fleet Marine Corps Reserve with the rank of Master Gunnery Sergeant. On 1 March 1983, I was transferred to the Retired List and promoted to First Lieutenant.

In all I was promoted eleven times in 18 years and it took me nine years to go from pay grade E-5 to E-7.

While serving in Vietnam as an Avionics Chief in the A-6 program, I was the youngest in age (33), and the most junior in rank (GySgt) and had the least experience (only 17 months) of the Avionics Chiefs of the other two A-6A bomber squadrons (who were both manned by Master Sergeants). Those other two squadrons were VMA (AW) 225 stationed at Cherry Point, and VMA (AW) 533 stationed at Chu Lai, South Vietnam. In my fitness report covering the period from 13 November 1967 to 31 January 1968, the following was written in the section, "that would further classify the noncommissioned officer's performance and qualifications." It was written by 2dLt Lloyd Y. Salmons, USMC, my reporting officer, who was a "Mustang." (Author's note - Lloyd and I retired the same day. Less than a year later he passed away. I've often wondered if his death was because of what we went through in Vietnam. A lot of men could not adjust to the uncaring attitude and animosity displayed by the American people toward the Vietnam veterans).

"While serving in a combat zone as Avionics Chief of this A6A squadron, a position normally held by a Master Sergeant, Gunnery Sergeant Curry has proven himself a true professional. He is a mature, enthusiastic, aggressive individual with a definite "can-do" attitude which enables him to obtain outstanding results quickly and accurately. GySgt Curry is an alert, frank, earnest, dedicated, determined person with an accomplished informed knowledge of the Avionics field. Working with limited resources of trained supervisory personnel and old airplanes, many of which are on the third extension of service tour, he has thorough tireless effort, professional competence and sound judgement been instrumental in more than doubling the number of operationally ready aircraft. During this period GySgt Curry personally designed and built to my complete satisfaction a status board showing the daily running totals of the numbers of various weapons systems in the A6A aircraft which have been in an "up status" during the previous 24 hours. This procedure takes but a few minutes daily to update and saves as many as 50 man-hours of research at the end of the month in order to complete the avionics portion of the squadron's Sitrep (Sitrep - Situation Report - a report that was classified Secret and went to the Department of Defense). GySgt Curry has shown unlimited growth potential and is of outstanding general value to the Marine Corps. As a means of self improvement, he is currently enrolled in Electronics Engineering Technology by Capitol Radio Institute.

GySgt Curry is imminently qualified for selection to Master Sergeant. Based on my fifteen years in the Marine Corps Aviation, GySgt Curry is the most outstanding Avionics Chief I have ever seen.

This period of observation has been under combat conditions."

A few months later it was decided that I should be recommended for a commission to Second Lieutenant as a reward for the accomplishments I had done. The following is a copy of that recommendation.

MARINE ALL WEATHER ATTACK SQUADRON - 242

Marine Aircraft Group - 11

1st Marine Aircraft Wing, FMF, Pacific

FPO San Francisco, California 96602

01:JRP:chl

1421

5 June 1968

From: Commanding Officer
To: Commandant of the Marine Corps (Code DPB)
Via: (1) Commanding Officer, Marine Aircraft Group -11
(2) Commanding General, 1st Marine Aircraft Wing
(3) Commanding General, Fleet Marine Force, Pacific

Subj: Commissioning of Enlisted personnel Demonstrating Exceptional Leadership Potential; case of Gunnery Sergeant John W. Curry,
1370305/6214/6219/6216 USMC

Ref: MCO 1421. 7B

Encl: (1) SF 88 and SF 89 (report of physical)
(2) Special Fitness Report on GySgt Curry

1. Gunnery Sergeant John W. Curry, 1370305/6214 USMC, is recommended with enthusiasm for commissioning under the provisions of reference (a), as having positively demonstrated exceptional leadership potential.

2. The following facts are pertinent in this case and have been verified by official records:

a. Date of birth: 2Jun34.

b. GCT: 122.

c. Final Top Secret Clearance based on an NAC completed on 27 May 1964.

3. He is physically qualified for commissioning as evidenced by reference (1).

4. I have observed Gunnery Sergeant CURRY'S performance from 16 October 1967 until the present and he has consistently demonstrated exceptional leadership potential. He has a deep understanding of people and guides their performance masterfully. He quickly recognizes the tolerance levels of those assigned to his charge and realizes that to ask too much is as to demand too little. He leads by precept an example an requires that his subordinates attain a degree of perfection based on their individual capabilities. Realizing that men need to be tested, he does not lower his expected standards to the norm but through endless training; and encouragement develops his subordinates to assume positions of responsibility. During this Combat tour he has been faced with an extreme shortage of experienced Staff Non-Commissioned Officers to assist in the maintenance of the highly complex A6A Weapons System. Realizing the lack of experience of his subordinates he instituted a dynamic training program to not only qualify his personnel as technicians but to instill in them a sense of responsibility and a realization that self discipline and application of sound management fundamentals will overcome many deficiencies in personnel assets. He continually strives for self-improvement and demands the same from those under his supervision. His positive and tenacious approach to seemingly insurmountable problems have been inspirational to his men. Gunnery Sergeant CURRY possesses a virtually unlimited growth potential and would be a credit to the Officer Corps. His other outstanding straits of character and professionalism are contained in enclosure (2).
5. Gunnery Sergeant CURRY will be recommended for a Navy Commendation Medal as an end-of-tour award for his significant contribution to the maintenance effort of this command.

(Signed)

J. R. Penny

No one knows what happened to the original recommendation for a Navy Commendation Medal in 1968. In 1986, I located my ex-maintenance officer, Major (now Colonel retired) John D. Carlton and he resubmitted the request in 1986.

In May 1987, I received the following from the Secretary of the Navy:

THE SECRETARY OF THE NAVY

Washington

The Secretary of the Navy takes pleasure in presenting the NAVY COMMENDATION MEDAL to

CAPTAIN JOHN W. CURRY

UNITED STATES MARINE CORPS

for service as set forth in the following

CITATION:

For heroic achievement while serving as Avionics Chief, Marine All Weather Attack Squadron 242, Marine Aircraft Group 11, 1st Marine Aircraft Wing, Fleet Marine Force, Pacific from July 1967 to July 1968 in support of combat operations against insurgent Vietcong forces in the Republic of Vietnam. Captain (then Gunnery Sergeant) Curry established and trained an effective team of personnel that set new standards for A6A Aircraft as "Full Mission Capable." Working under extreme environmental conditions and with a shortage of trained personnel, he instilled a sense of pride and professionalism that produced remarkable results. His positive and tenacious approach to seemingly insurmountable problems was an inspiration to all who observed him and contributed significantly to the accomplishment of his unit's mission. Captain Curry's initiative, courageous actions, and selfless devotion to duty reflected great credit upon himself and were in keeping with the highest traditions of the Marine Corps and the United States Naval Service.

The Combat Distinguishing Device is authorized.

(Signed)

John Lehman

Secretary of the Navy

During my career I was awarded the following medals and ribbons:

1. Navy Commendation Medal (with "Combat V").
2. Combat Action Ribbon (For being shot at during 1968 TET).
3. Presidential Unit Citation.
4. Naval Unit Commendation.
5. Marine Corps Good Conduct Medal (with silver star for five additional awards).
6. Naval Occupational Award (Marine Corps) with Europe Clasp.
7. National Defense Service Medal (with * for second award).
8. Armed Forces Expeditionary Service Medal.
9. Vietnam Campaign Service Medal (with **** for four campaigns).
10. Vietnamese Cross of Gallantry (with palm and device).
11. Vietnam Service Medal (with date device).

Bibliography

The following books were referenced in this work or read to establish proof to a previous source.

1. *The Complete Book of Emigrants, 1607 - 1660; 1661 - 1669;* by Peter Wilson Colham. Published by Genealogical Publishing Company Inc., 1001 North Calvert Street, Baltimore, Md 21202.

2. *The North Carolina Historical and Genealogical Register, Volume 1, Numbers 1 to 4, Volume 2, Numbers 1 to 4, Volume 3, Numbers 1 to 3,* by J. R. B. Hathaway, Editor and Financial Agent, Edenton, N. C. 1900 to 1903. Republished by Genealogical Publishing Co., Inc.

3. *Some Georgia County Records, Volumes 1 and 2,* by The Reverend Silas Emmett Lucas, Jr. Published by Southern Historical Press, Inc., P. O. Box 1267, Greenville, Sc 29602.

4. *Roster of South Carolina Patriots in the American Revolution,* by Bobby Gilmer Moss. Published by Genealogical Publishing Company, Inc.

5. *Cavaliers and PIoneers, Abstracts of Virginia Land Patents and Grants, Volume One, 1623 - 1666 and Volume Three, 1695 - 1732,* abstracted by Nell Marion Nugent. Volume One published by The Genealogical Publishing Company, Inc and Volume Three published by Virginia State Library, Richmond, Virginia.

6. *Records of Clarke County, Georgia 1801 - 1892,* complied by Robert Scott Davis, published by Southern Historical Press, Inc.

7. *Georgia Revolutionary War Soldiers' Graves,* (two volumes), complied by H. Ross Arnold, Jr and H. Clifton Burnham, published by The Iberian Publishing Company, 548 Cedar Creek Drive, Athens, Ga 30605 - 3408.

8. *Spartanburg County/District, South Carolina, Deed Abstracts Book A - T (1785 - 1827)(1752 - 1827),* by Albert Bruce Pruitt. Published by Southern Historical Press, Inc.

9. *Marriages of Some Virginia Residents, 1607 - 1800, Volume I, Surnames A - H, Volume II, Surnames I - Z,* by Dorothy Ford Wulfeck. Published by Genealogical Publishing Company, Inc.

10. *Marriages and Deaths, 1820 to 1830,* by Mary Bondurant Warren with Sarah Fleming White. Printed by Heritage Papers, Danielsville, GA 30633.

11. *Early Virginia Families Along the James River, Volume III,* James City, County - Surry County. Complied by Louise Pledge Heath Foley. Published by Genealogical Publishing Company, Inc.

12. *History of Perquimans County, North Carolina,* by Mrs. Watson Winslow. Published by Genealogical Publishing Company, Inc.

13. *Tidewater Virginia Families,* by Virginia Lee Hutcheson Davis. Published by Genealogical Publishing Company, Inc.

14. *Cemetaries of Clay County, Alabama,* published by Clay County Historical Society, P. O. Box 998, Ashland, Alabama 36251.

15. *North Carolina Wills: A Testator Index, 1665 - 1900,* by Thorton W. Mitchell. Published by Genealogical Publishing Company, Inc.